RECORDS

OF

PLYMOUTH COLONY.

COURT ORDERS.

VOL. II.

1641—1651.

Records
of the
Colony
of
New Plymouth
in
New England

ORIGINALLY PRINTED BY ORDER OF THE LEGISLATURE OF THE
COMMONWEALTH OF MASSACHUSETTS

Edited by

Nathaniel B. Shurtleff, M.D.

MEMBER OF THE MASSACHUSETTS HISTORICAL SOCIETY, FELLOW OF THE AMERICAN ACADEMY OF ARTS
AND SCIENCES, MEMBER OF THE AMERICAN ANTIQUARIAN SOCIETY, FELLOW
OF THE SOCIETY OF ANTIQUARIES OF LONDON, ETC.

Court Orders
Volume II: 1641–1651

HERITAGE BOOKS
2013

HERITAGE BOOKS
AN IMPRINT OF HERITAGE BOOKS, INC.

Books, CDs, and more—Worldwide

For our listing of thousands of titles see our website
at
www.HeritageBooks.com

A Facsimile Reprint
Published 2013 by
HERITAGE BOOKS, INC.
Publishing Division
100 Railroad Ave. #104
Westminster, Maryland 21157

Originally published
Boston:
From the Press of William White,
Printer to the Commonwealth
1855

— Publisher's Notice —
In reprints such as this, it is often not possible to remove blemishes from the original. We feel the contents of this book warrant its reissue despite these blemishes and hope you will agree and read it with pleasure.

International Standard Book Numbers
Paperbound: 978-0-7884-0840-3
Clothbound: 978-0-7884-6981-7

REMARKS.

THE original manuscript from which the following pages are copied comprises the portion of the acts of the General Court and the Court of Assistants of the Colony of New Plymouth, generally known and designated as the second volume of Court Orders, and includes the records of about ten years, commencing with the proceedings held on the first day of December, 1640, and closing with those of the seventh of October, 1651. The first entry more appropriately belongs to the first volume, being recorded out of place in respect to strict chronological order.

A considerable part of the volume is written only on one side of the paper, which will account for the omission in many instances of the usual marginal entry denoting the pages of the original. The chirography is chiefly by Nathaniel Souther and Nathaniel Morton, the well known secretaries of the colony; a few pages, however, are in an unknown hand.

Dispersed throughout the original volume are very imperfect indexes, which have been rejected in printing, and others very carefully prepared have been substituted in their place.

The general remarks which are printed as an introduction to the first volume apply equally well to this, as the same plan has been adhered to in conducting it through the press.

N. B. S.

DECEMBER, 1855.

MARKS AND CONTRACTIONS.

A Dash ‾ (or straight line) over a letter indicates the omission of the letter following the one marked.

A Curved Line ~ indicates the omission of one or more letters next to the one marked.

A Superior Letter indicates the omission of contiguous letters, either preceding or following it.

A Caret ˄ indicates an omission in the original record.

A Cross × indicates a lost or unintelligible word.

All doubtful words supplied by the editor are included between brackets, [ ].

Some redundancies in the original record are printed in Italics.

Some interlineations, that occur in the original record, are put between parallels, ‖ ‖.

Some words and paragraphs, which have been cancelled in the original record, are put between ‡ ‡.

Several characters have special significations, namely:—

@, — annum, anno.
ā, — an, am, — curiā, curiam.
ã, — mātrate, magistrate.
b̄, — ber, — numb̄, number; Rob̄t, Robert.
c̄, — ci, ti, — accōon, action.
c̃ŏ, — tio, — jurisdiccōōn, jurisdiction.
ĉ, — cre, cer, — acs, acres.
d, — dd, delivered.
ẽ, — Trẽr, Treasurer.
ē, — committē, committee.
g̃, — g̃n̄al, general; Georg̃, George.
h, — chr, charter.
ī, — begīg, beginīg, beginning.
ł, — łre, letter.
m̄, — mm, mn, — com̄ittee, committee.
m̃, — recom̃dacŏn, recommendation.
m̊, — mer, — form̊ly, formerly.
m̂, — month.
ñ, — nn, — Peñ, Penn; año, anno.
ň, — Dn̄i, Domini.
ñ, — ner, — mann̄, manner.
ō, — on, — mentiō, mention.

ŏ, — mō, month.
p̄, — par, por, — p̄t, part; p̄tion, portion.
p, — per, — pson, person.
p̧, — pro, — pporcōn, proportion.
p̃, — pre, — p̃sent, present.
q, — qstion, question.
q̃p̃, — esq̃p̃, esquire.
r̄, — Apr̄, April.
s̄, — s̃, session; s̄d, said.
ṣ, — ser, — ṣvants, servants.
ť, — ter, — neuť, neuter.
ṯ, — capṯ, captain.
ū, — uer, — seflal, seueral.
ū, — aboū, aboue, above.
v̂, — ver, — sev̂al, several.
w̃, — w̃n, when.
yᵉ, the; yᵐ, them; yⁿ, then; yʳ, their; yˢ, this; yᵗ, that.
ʒ, — us, — vilibʒ, vilibus.
Ɛ, — es, et, — statutƐ, statutes.
&, &c̄, &cᵃ, — et cætera.
viz̧, — videlicet, namely.
./ — full point.

CONTENTS OF VOLUME II.

PAGE

COURT ORDERS, 1641—1651, ... 3

GENERAL INDEX, ... 179

PLYMOUTH COURT ORDERS.

1641—1651.

PLYMOUTH RECORDS.

THE RECORDS OF THE COLONY OF NEW PLYMOUTH IN NEW ENGLAND.

[The second volume of the Plymouth Court Orders commences here, with the record of the proceedings of the General Court held on the first of December, 1640, and ends with that of the meeting held on the seventh of October, 1651, containing the acts of the General Court, grants of land, and other entries of a miscellaneous character. The first 141 pages are in the handwriting of Mr. Secretary Souther; pages 143 to 158 inclusive are in an unknown hand, and the remainder of the volume is in the well-known chirography of Mr. Nathaniel Morton, Secretary of the colony. The imperfect indexes of the original volume are incorporated in the general index, prepared for the printed volume.]

ACTS AND PASSAGES OF COURT AND GRANTS OF LAND FROM THE YEAR 1641 UNTIL THE YEAR 1651.

NEW PLYM. BRADFORD, GOU^R.

*.*At the Gen^{r}all Court of our Sou^{r}aigne Lord, Charles, by the Grace of God King of England, Scotland, France, & Ireland, Defendor of the Fayth, &c., held at Plym afores^d, the first of Decemb^r, in the xvjth Yeare of his said Maties now Raigne, of England, &c.*

1640.
1 December.
[*1.]

BEFORE Willm Bradford, gent, Goũ,   Willm Collyer,
    Thom̃ Prence,   Tymothy Hatherley, and
    Capt Miles Standish,   John Jenney,
       Gent, Assistant℄ of the said goũment.

Walter Woodward,
Edmond Eddingden,
Thom̃ Ensigne,
Edmond Freeman, Junr, } pposed to be made freeman the next Court.
Willm Nicholson,
James Cade,
Willm Parker,

3

1640.

1 December.
BRADFORD, Goŭ.

P'sentmentⓈ. Thomas Atkins and John Wood p'sented for delifting but fiuescore herings to the hundred, whereas they should haue delifted sixscore and twelue, are censured by the Court to make restitucōn to the psons so wronged, and so are discharged of their p'sentment.

John Dammon for takeing tobaccoe contrary to the act of the Court, xij^d.

Walter Knight for the like, xij^d.

Marke Mendlowe discharged of his p'sentment in regard it appeared to be donn of necessytie meerely — drawing eele pottⓈ on the LordⓈ day.

Sympkins fined 40^s. Remited to him Decemb^r 16, bec. she neither had shoes nor was in health to come.

Mr Nicholas Sympkins is discharged of his p'sentment for attempting to lye with an Indian weoman, but is enjoyned to bring Jonathan Hatch to the next Court to receiue punishment for slandering him; and for not bringing his Indian mayde servant to the court, contrary to the Goŭnors comaund, is fined xl^s.

Kenelm Win. fine remitted him.

Kenelme Winslowe, being elected surveyor of the heigh wayes for the towne of Plymͫ, and neglecting the same, is fyned x^s.

[*2.]

*Whereas the trade is not now followed by any man, and there may be some smale thinges some tymes had of the Indians in the plantacōns wthin the goŭment, and that an auncient act doth restraine all psons, wthout the consent of such as haue the trade, to trade or traffic with the Indians or natiues, it is thought meete by the Court, that if any inhabitants wthin the gou^{r}nt shall trade wth the natiues in any of the plantacōns wthin the patent, for corne, beades, veneson, or some tymes for a beaver skine, hee shall not be reputed nor taken to be a transgressor of the said acte.

Also, concerneing the trade, it is thought meete, that if any man be disposed to vndertake the same for some yeares, they shall bring in their names before the next Court of AssistantⓈ, that if the Gouen^r do approue of them, and the condicōns on wch they will vndertake the same, they may be approued of, or els the Gou^t to vndertake the same, wth such ptners as he shall like of for the mannageing of it, in such wise for the summer season as he shall thinke best for the space of one yeare.

Their names, 244.

Whereas by the act of the Geñall Court held the third day of March, 1639, it was agreed vpon that the purchasers, or old comers, shall make choyce of two or three plantacōns for themselues & their heires by this December Court, — now the said purchasers, or old comers, do signifie vnto the Court that accordingly they haue made choyce of these three places, vizⓈ: First, from the bounds of Yarmouth, three miles to the eastward of Naemskeckett, and from sea to sea crosse the neck of land. The second place, of a place called

Acconquesse, al^s Acokcus, wch lyeth in the bottome of the bay, adjoyneing to the west side of Poynt Perrill, and two miles to the westerne side of the said riuer, to another place, called Acqussent Riuer, wch entreth at the westerne end of Nickatay, and two miles to the eastward thereof, and to extend eight miles vp into the countrey. The third place, from Sowamset Riuer to Patuckquett Riuer, wth Causumpsit Neck, wch is the cheefe habitac̄ōn of the Indians, & reserued for them to dwell vpon, extending into the land eight miles through the whole breadth thereof, the which choyce beinge made as aforesaid, and allowed in the Court, Mr Willm Bradford, for himself and his associat͠e, doth tenter a surrender to the body of freemen of all the rest of the lands wthin the patent͠e, (wch are not graunted to plantac̄ōns in genãll, or psons in p̄ticuler.) And the said Willm Bradford is ready further to confirme the same, on the p̄te and behalf of himself & his associat͠e, to the body of the freemen, when he shalbe required.

1640.
1 December.
BRADFORD, Got^{ju}.

*Presentment͠e. [*3.]

John Barnes, for exaction in takeing rye at foure shillings p bushell, and selling it againe for fiue, wthout adventure or long forbeareance in one and the same place. Witnes, Capt Standish.

Trauersed; found not guilty.

Thomas Atkins & John Wood discharged.

Richard Knowles, for denying passage of cattell in the heigh way. Witnes, Ed Banges.

Thomas Coachman, Nicholas Snow, & Josias Cooke, for not mending the heigh wayes at the Second Brooke, Smylt Riuer, New Bridge, and other places.

Discharged, vpon condic̄ōn that they shall repaire the heigh wayes this yeare.

John Jordaine, for takeing stuff to line a dublet throughout, & yet lyned not the skirts, & restored not the rest. Witnes, Jonathan Brewster, Raph Chapman.

Acquit, but to pay for a yard of stuffe to Raph Chapman, as he payd Jonathan Brewster for yt.

Jonathan Brewster, for neglecting the ferry. Witnes, John Lewis, John Bryant, Thom̄ Pinchin, & his wyfe.

1640-1. *At a Court of Assistantℓ, held the fift Day of January, in the xvjth Yeare of his Maties now Raigne, of England, &c.

5 January.
NEW PLYM.
BRADFORD, Goū.
[*4.]

BEFORE Willm Bradford, genī, Goū,   Wm Collyer,
Thom̃ Prence,   Tymothy Hatherley, &
Capī Miles Standish,   John Jenney.
Genī, Assistantℓ, &c.

THE differencℓ betwixt Georḡ Bower & Georḡ Bonum, by the consent of both p̄ties, are referred to foure arbitrat^{rs}, viz$\S$, John Winslow and Willm Paddy on George Bowers p̄t, and Manasseth Kempton and James Hurst on Georḡ Bonums p̄t; and if they cannot agree, then the said foure arbitrators to choose a fift man vnto them, to make a fynall end thereof.

Thomas Robertℓ, of Duxborrow, is ordered by the Court that hee shall lodge no more wth Georḡ Morrey, a diseased pson, and betwixt this and the next Court of Assistantℓ p̄uide himself of lodging; and then make report to the Court how it may be p̄bable he may liue wthout being chargeable.

It is ordered by the Court, that Willm Hiller shall pay vnto John Holmes, the messenger, liij^s iiij^d in corne, for his man wages.

It is ordered by the Court, that Francis Billington & Christian, his wyfe, shall giue Jonathan Brewster & Loue Brewster possession of her thirds the lands bought of them; & then Jonathan Brewster to pay him in corne the remaynder, which is xxxviij^s vj^d.

The differenc̃ betwixt Mr Jonathan Brewster & John Ford, for the crop of corne at Ferry, vpon the North Riuer, is referred, by consent of ˙p̄ties, to be arbitrated and ended by Leiftennant Wm Holmes and Samuell Fuller; and if they cannot end it, then they to choose a third man, and what end they shall make, they, s̃d p̄ties, to stand to it.

6 January.

Jañ 5th, 1640. Memorand̃: that John Cooke, for good considerac̃on, hath, wth & by the consent of Phillip Dauis, assigned & set ouer the residue of the terme of yeares wch the said Phillip Dauis is to serue the said John Cooke, vnto Henry Sampson, to be serued out wth the said Henry Sampson, the said Henry Sampson paying the said Phillip Dauis thirteene bushells of Indian corne in thend of the said terme. His indenture beares date the xxth of Aprill, 1638, & is to serue for eleauen yeares & two months from the first day of his arriuall in New England. Taken before Capī Standish.

Richard Bushop hyred to dwell wth Nathaniell Sowther for vij^{li} p añ, and came the xxth of January.

COURT ORDERS.

*At a Court of Assistants held at Plymouth aforesaid, the first Day of Februar., in the xvjth Yeare of his Maties now Raigne, of England, &c.

1640-1.

1 February.
NEW PLYM.
BRADFORD,
Gou.
[*5.]

BEFORE Wiltm Bradford, gent, Goū, Wiltm Collyer, &
Thom̄ Prence, John Jenney,
Capt Miles Standish,
Gent, Assistants, &c.

A JURY was impannelled and sworne to lay forth certaine heigh wayes now in differrence, and to set forth the bounds and land markes betwixt John Shawe, Kenelme Winslowe, and Mr John Atwood, at Playne Dealeinge, and the heigh wayes from the towne of Plymouth to Wellingsley, and through Georḡ Bowers ground, and a heigh way for John Dunhame and Wiltam Pontus, from their meddows at the waterside, and a heighway for Nathaniell Sowther, from his field to the towne.

The Names of the Jury.

Mr John Done,		John Cooke,	
Edward Banges,		Josuah Pratt,	
Wiltm Paddy,	sworne.	Josias Cooke,	sworne.
Thom̄ Willett,		Richard Sparrow,	
Francis Cooke,		George Watson,	
Thom̄ Cushman,		John Jenkine,	

It is ordered by the Court, that the twenty acres of land wch Thom̄ Clarke bought of Raph Wallen shalbe layd forth at the lower end of the two lotts of 40 acres that he hath at the Eele Riuer, and that Edward Banges, Nicholas Snowe, & Josuah Pratt shall also lay forth Sarah Mortons lott there, and after they are layd forth, the bounds to be entred in the booke of records, that there may be no more controūsy about them.

---

*At a Court of Assistants held the first Day of March, 1640, in the xvjth Yeare of his Maties now Raigne, of England, &c.

1 March.
[*7.]

BEFORE Wiltm Bradford, gent, Goū, Miles Standish, &
Thom̄ Prence, John Jenney,
Wiltm Collyer,
Gent, Assistants, &c.

1640-1.
1 March.
BRADFORD,
Gov.

IT is ordered and graunted by the Court, that the bounds of Duxborrow towneship shall begin where Plymouth bounds do end, namely, at the brooke falling into Black Water, and so along Mattachusetts Payth to the North Riuer; the said payth to be the westerne bounds thereof, (excepting & reserueing all those landℓ graunted wthin the said limmitℓ to p̱ticuler p̱sons in Plymouth, Greens Harbour, and Scituate, whose cattell may likewise depasture vpon the said comons wth them.

2 March.
NEW PLYM.
[*8.]

*At a Gen^rall Court of our Sou͡aigne Lord the Kinge, held at Plym̃, afores^d, the second Day of March, in the xvjth Yeare of his said Maties now Raigne, of England, &c.

BEFORE Willm Bradford, gent, Gou,   Tymothy Hatherley,
Thom̃ Prence,   John Jenney,
Wm Collyer,   John Browne, and
Miles Standish,   Edmond Freeman,
Gent, Assistantℓ, &c.

WILL̃M PARKER & Walter Woodward were admitted freemen, & sworne, &c.

Mr Richard Blindman,
Mr Heugh Prychard,
Mr Obadiah Brewen,
John Sadler,
Heugh Cauken,
Walter Tibbott,
} were p̱pounded to be made free the next Court.

Mr William Bradford is elected Gou͡n^r.

Mr Thom̃ Prence,
Mr Willm Collyer,
Mr Miles Standish,
Mr Edward Winslow,
Mr John Browne,
Mr Tymothy Hatherly,
Mr Edmond Freeman,
} are elected Assistantℓ.

Mr Francis Doughty, of Taunton, for selling a pound of gunpowder to the natiues, (contrary to the actℓ & orders of the Court,) wch was confessed by himself, is fyned xxx^s.

COURT ORDERS.

Constables elected.		Surveyors of heigh wayes.	1640-1.
Plymouth,	Josias Cooke,	The same that were the last yeare, bec̃ they neglected.	2 March. BRADFORD, Gov.
Duxborrow,	‡Job Cole,‡ Constant Southwᵈ,	Joseph Bidle & Samͫ Nash.	
Scituate,	Samuell Fuller,	Thomͫ Chambers & John Williams.	
Sandwich,	Nathaniell Willis,	Edward Dillingham & Robte Botefish.	
Taunton,	Willm Parker.		
Barnestable,	Henry Rowley.		
Yarmouth,	Edward Sturgess.	Willm Clark & Emanuell White.	

Rexame, Josias Winslow, who was now also sworne to execute the office of constable there vntill June come twelue months.

Edward Hall, servant to Francis Doughty, for sweareing pfanely, is censured to be set in the stocks, wᶜʰ was accordingly donn.

The Court appoynt{ Mʳ Edward Winslow & Nathaniell Sowther to draw vp a conveyance, or surrender, for the land{ wᵗʰin the patent{ vngranted, for Mʳ Bradford to surrender into the hand{ of the whole body of freemen.

*The Court hath granted a competent porc̃on of vpland & hey ground to yt, sufficient for a plantac̃on at Mattapoyst, to Mʳ Charles Chauncey, Mʳ John Atwood, & Thomas Cushman, and to be bounded by by such as the Court shall especially assigne therevnto, wᶜʰ were nominated to be Mʳ Thomas Prence and Captaine Miles Standish ; puided alwayes, that such of the purchasers as shall take vp their lands there shall not haue it elswhere also. [*9.]

It is concluded and agreed betwixt Captaine Miles Standish, Mʳ John Alden, Jonathan Brewster, & Willm Basset, and Mʳ Edward Winslowe, the xxviijᵗʰ day of December, 1640, that from a great rock that is flatt on the topp, called Parting Rock, shalbe the p̃sent bounds betweene Greenes Harbour & Duxborrow, and shall rang̃ from thence norwest, to the South Riuer, & on the contrary south east to the payth betweene Scituate & Duxborrow, and from thence, the payth to deuide them, to the bridg̃ ouer Greens Harbour Fresh.

Willm Chase, of Yarmouth, plant̃, oweth the King . . . xxˡⁱ. Released.

The condic̃on, that he shall psonally appeare at the next Genͫall Court of oʳ soͫaigne lord the R., to answere such matters as shalbe objected against him, & abide the further order of the Court, & not depte the same wᵗʰout lycence ; that then, &c.

Robte Dennis, of Yarmouth, plant̃, acknowledg̃, &c, . . . xˡⁱ. Released.

The condic̃on, that the said Robte shall frame & pferr, or cause to be framed & pferred one bill of indictment against Edward Morrell, at the next

1640-1.
2 March.
BRADFORD,
Gou.

Geñall Court, &c, for the stealeing of certaine corne out of an house in Yarmouth aforesd, & giue euedence there vnto ; that then, &c.

It is also agreed and concluded vpon by the Court, that the twenty pound℔ for this yeares benefit of the trade comeinge to the colonies, shalbe giuen to the Gouern^r.

It is also concluded and agreed vpon by the whole Court, that Nathaniell Sowther, the clark of the Court, shalbe & is authorized, in the name of the whole Court & body of freemen to receiued & take the surrender of the residue of the land℔ vngranted, (wch Mr Bradford is to surrender into their hands,) wch are wthin the patent℔.

[*10.]

*Whereas diuers and sondry treaties haue beene in the publike & Geñall Court℔ of New Plymouth, his ma^{tie}, our dread soūaigne, Charles, by the grace of God King of England, Scotland, France, and Ireland, &c, concerning the pper right and title of the lands wthin the bounds and limmitt℔ of his said ma^{ties} łres patent℔, graunted by the right hon^{ble} his ma^{ties} counsell for New England, ratifyed by their coñon seale, and signed by the hand of the Right Honble Earle of Warwick, then president of the said counsell, to William Bradford, his heires, associat℔, and assignes, beareing date, &c ; and whereas the said Wilłm Bradford and diuers others, the first instrument℔ of God in the begiñinge of this greate work of plantacōn, together wth such as the alorderinge hand of God, in his puidence, soone added vnto them, haue beene at very greate charges to pcure the said lands, ꝑviledges, & freedomes, from all entanglements, as may appeare by diuers and sundry deeds, enlargements of graunt℔, purchases, payments of debts, &c, by reason whereof the title to the day of this p^rnt, remayneth in the said Wilłm, his heires, associat℔, and assignes, — now, for the better setling of the state of the said land℔ aforesaid, the said Wilłm Bradford and those first instrument℔ termed and called in sondry orders vpon publike record, the purchasers, or old comers, witnes two in especiall, thone beareing date the third of March, 1639, thother in Decemb^r ye first, 1640, wherevnto these p^rnt℔ haue speciall relacōn & agreement, and whereby they are distinguished from other℔ the freemen and inhabitant℔ of the said corporation, — be it knowne vnto all men, therefore, by these p^rnt℔, that the said Wilłm Bradford, for himself, his heires, together wth the said purchasers, do onely reserue vnto themselues, their heires and assignes, those three tract℔ of land℔ menēoned in the said resolucōn, order, & agreement, beareing date the first day of December, 1640, viz§, first, from the bounds of Yarmouth, three miles to the eastward of Naemskockett, and from sea to sea, crosse the said neck of land ; the second, of a place called Acconquesse, al^s Acockcus, wch lyeth in the bottome of the bay,

COURT ORDERS. 11

adjoyneing to the west side of Poynt Perrill, and two miles to the westerne 1 6 4 0-1.
side of the said riuer, to another place, called Acqussent Riuer, wch entreth at
the westerne end of Nickatay, and two miles to the eastward thereof, and to   2 March.
extend eight miles vp into the countrey; the third place from Sowamsett   BRADFORD,
Riuer to Patucquett Riuer, wth Causumpsit Neck, wch is the cheef habitacõn   Goū.
of the Indians, and reserued for them to dwell vpon, extending into the land
eight miles through the whole breadth thereof, together wth such other smale
p̃cells of landę as they or any of them are psonally possessed of or interested
in by vertue of any former titles or grauntę whatsoeuer. And the said Willm
Bradford doth, by the free and full consent, approbacõn, and agreement of the
said old planters or purchasers, together wth the likeing, approbacõn, & accep-
tacõn of the other part of the said corporacõn, surrender into the handę of the
whole Court, consistinge of the freemen of this corporacõn of New Plymouth,
all that ther right & title, power, authorytie, p^{r}viledges, immunities, & freedomes
granted in the said łres patentę by the said right hon^{ble} counsell for New England, reseruing his & their psonall right of freemen, together wth the said old
planters aforesaid, except the said lands before excepted, declareing the freemen
of this present corporacõn, together wth all such as shalbe legally admitted
into the same, his associatę. And the said Willm Bradford, for him, his heires
and assignes, doe further hereby p̃mise and graunt to doe & pforme *whatsoeuer [*11.]
further thinge or thinges, act or acts, wch in him lyeth, which shalbe needfull
and expedient for the better confirmeing & establishinge the said p̃misses as
by counsell learned in the lawes shalbe reasonably aduised and deuised, when
he shalbe therevnto required. In witnes whereof, the said Willm Bradford
hath in publike Court surrendred the said łres patentę actually into the handę
and power of the said Court, bynding himself, his heires, execut^{rs}, adminis-
trat^{rs}, and assignes, to deliā vp whatsoeuer specialties are in his handę that do
or may concerne the same.

Memorand: that the said surrender was made by the said Willm Bradford, in publick Court, to Nathaniell Sowther, especially authorized by the
whole Court to receiue the same, together wth the said łres patentę, in the name
and for the use of the whole body of freemen.

It is ordered by the Court, that Mr Willm Bradford shall haue the keepeing of the said łres patentę, wch were afterwards delifled vnto him by the said
Nathaniell Sowther in the publike Court.

Pr͠esentm^{nts} by the Grand Inquest.

We p̃sent Georḡ Bowers, for defamacõn of the { Capt̃ Standish,
gouīment.   { Mr Collier,
                                                 { Mr Done.

12 PLYMOUTH COLONY RECORDS.

1640-1.
2 March.
BRADFORD,
Gou.
June 1st, 1641, discharged.

'We p̃sent the aforesaid Georg̃ Bowers, for a defamacon against Mr John Browne, Assistant, the wch defamacon doth or may appeare by łres vnder his owne handł.

We p̃sent Georg̃ Pidcock, that whereas there was delifled to him one yard or ellne of canvasse, the said Georg̃ detayned or vnjustly wthheld from the owner some part thereof, the wch first he denyed, & after acknowledged. Witnes, Thom̃ Goodman.

We p̃sent John Bryant & Daniell Pryor, of Barnestable, for drinking tobacco vpon the heigh way. Witnes, Henr̃ Bourne.

We p̃sent Edward Hall, of Taunton, for swearoing. Censured.

We p̃sent ⁁ , the sonne of widdow Hoble, for swearing. Witnes, Wiłtm Evans, John Golope.

We p̃sent John Barnes, for selling black & browne threed at fiue shillings foure pence p li. Witnes, Mr Prence. Trauersed ; found not guilty.

1641.
5 April.
NEW PLYM.
[*12.]

*At a Court of Assistantł held at Plym̃ aforesaid, the fift Day of Aprill, in the xvijth Yeare of his Mats now Raigne, of England, &c.

BEFORE Wiłtm Bradford, genł, Goū,   Capł Miles Standish, &
Thomas Prence,   John Jenney,
Wiłtm Collyer,
Genł, Assistantł, &c.

WHEREAS Georg̃ Lewes attached certaine corne of Thomas Robertł in the handł of Captaine Standish, and neither came nor any one for him to psecute his suite, was nonsuited, & the corne released.

Whereas seūall p̃cells of landł are graunted to diuers psons in Duxborrow, lying betwixt Stoney Brook, in Duxborrow, & Greenł Harbour & thereaboutł, and John Washborne should haue 40 acrees thereaboutł ; also the Court doth order that when those p̃cells are layd forth to the seūall psons abouesaid, that then the said John Washbourne shall haue the said 40 acrees, if it be there to be had.

Whereas it appeareth to the Court, by the testymony of John Rowse, that John Irish and Henry Wallis did make a couenant in the life tyme of the said Henry, that the longer liuer of them should haue eich others fiue acrees of landℓ lyinge by the Stony Brooke, in Duxborrow, the Court doth therefore order, that the said John Irish, the survivour of them, shall haue the said fiue acres of land wch were the said Henry Wallis, deceased.

1641.
5 April.
BRADFORD, Go^u.

The fift of Aprill, 1641. Memorand: that whereas John Barnes hath sould his house and landℓ wch he lately bought of Marke Mendloue, at the Eele Riuer, vnto Will̴m Baker, now, the said Will̴m Baker hath relinquished the said bargaine vnto the said John Barnes; and the said John Barnes hath set, & to farme lett, vnto the said Wm Baker, the said house and landℓ, wth thapp^{r}tencℓ therevnto belonging; to haue & to hold the said house & land from the day of the date hereof vnto the last day of October now next ensuing; the said Will̴m Baker yeilding & paying therefore vnto the said John Barnes, his execut^r & assignes, the sum of fifty shillings in money, or corne as the price goes, when itℓ merchantable, the said corne to be delifted at John Barnes house in Plym̃; and the said Will̴m is to leaue the house tennan$a$ble, and the fence vnbroken, at thend of the said terme; and the said John Barnes is to haue the rye now sowne vpon some p̃te of the said landℓ.

*The xxiijth Aprill, 1641. Memorand: that it is agreed vpon betwixt M^{ris} Bridgitt Fuller, widdow, and Nehemiah Smyth, concerning certaine sheepe wch the said Nehemiah hath of the said Bridgittℓ to keepe to the halfes, vpon the condic̃õns following: Inprimis, the said Bridgitt hath delifted four ewe sheepe to the said Nehemiah, wch hee is to keepe vntill the xxiiijth of June, 1643, and then the encrease is to be deuided, and the said M^{ris} Fuller to haue one half, and the said Nehemiah thother half thereof; and the wooll to be yearely diuided, and thõne half sent to M^{ris} Fuller yearely, to Plym̃, or where shee shall dwell, and likewise the stock at thend of the termes. It^m: It is agreed vpon betwixt the said p̃ties, that the said Nehemiah, after the said xxiiijth June, 1643, shall haue the said foure ewes againe, wth her half of thencrease, for the terme of six yeares longer, saue that there shalbe a diuision of thencrease at thend of the first three yeares, and thother diuision to be made at thend of the said terme of six yeares; always prouided, that the said Bridgitt shall haue thone half of the woll sent her yearely to Plym̃, or where she shall dwell, and thone halfe of the money for such weathers as shalbe sould out of thencrease during the said terme.

23 April.
[*13.]

1641.

3 May.
NEW PLYM.
BRADFORD, Goū.
[*14.]

*At a Court of Assistantℓ held the third Day of May, in the xvijth Yeare of his Maties now Raigne, of England, &c.

BEFORE Wiłłm Bradford, genť, Goū,   Capť Miles Standish,
          Thom̄ Prence,   Tymothy Hatherley, &
          Wiłłm Collyer,   John Jenney,
                  Genť, Assistantℓ, &č.

IT is ordered that Mr Raph Smyth and Edmond Tilson shall pay John Finney, for Henry Cramptons vse, for keepeing of theire goates, that wch due unto him, viz𝔰, Mr Smyth, ix^s; and Edmond Tilson that wch is due to him, all reckonings being deducted.

Released.

Thom̄ Chambers, of Scittuate, planter, acknowledgeth to owe the King . . . . } xl^{li}.

John Twisden, of the same, planter, &č, ... xl^{li}.

The condičon, that if the said Thomas Chambers doe psonally appeare at the next Geñall Court of o^r sođaigne lord the King, to be holden at Plym̄, to answere to all such matters as shalbe objected against him on his s̄d ma^{ts} behalf, and not dep̄t the Court wthout lycence; that then, &č.

Released.
Mr Hatherly pmised to pay the fees, 4^s.

John Twisden, of Scituate, planť, acknowledgeth to owe the King, &č, ... } xl^{li}.

Thom̄ Chambers, of the same, planť, &č, ... xl^{li}.

The condičon, that if the said John Twisden do psonally appeare at the next Geñall Court of o^r said sođaigne lord the King, to be holden at Plym̄, to answere to all such matters as on his said ma^{ties} behalf shalbe objected agst him, & not dep̄t the same wthout lycence; that then, &č.

Released.

Georḡ Willerd, of Scittuate, planter, acknowledḡ to the king,   xl^{li}.

Thomas Chambers, of the same, planť, &č, ... xx^{li}.

Dolor Dauis, } of the same, planť, &č, ... xx^{li}.
John Twisden, }

The condičon that the said Georḡ Willerd shall appeare at the next Geñall Court of o^r said sođaigne lord the King, and abide the further order of the Court, & not dep̄t the same wthout lycence, and in the meane tyme to be of the good behauio^r towardℓ o^r sođaigne lord the King & all his leigh people; that then, &č.

For Thom̄ Williams.

To enquire of Wiłłm Brackenberry, of Charles Towne or elsewhere, for any goods that are sent out of England for Mr Thomas Tart, of Scituate, and that Thom̄ Williams may haue them for the payment of his

COURT ORDERS. 15

wines porc̃õn, because he gaue an acquittance for yt vppon p̱mise that the said Mr Tart would p̱cure her porc̃õn to be payd; the sum is xxiiij^{li} or there about(.

1641.
3 May.
BRADFORD, Goũ.

*At the Geñall Court of o^r Sou^{r}aigne Lord the Kinge, held at Plym̃ afores^d, the first Day of June, in the xvijth Yeare of his said Maties now Raigne, of England, &c.

1 June.
NEW PLYM.
[*15.]

BEFORE Willm Bradford, gent, Goũ,
Edward Winslow,
Thom̃ Prence,
Willm Collyer,

Miles Standish,
Timothy Hatherly,
John Browne, and
Edmond Freeman, gent,

Assistant(of the said goũ^{nt}.

MR WILLM BRADFORD was sworne Goũn^r for this ensuing yeare.

Mr Edward Winslow,
Mr Thom̃ Prence,
Mr Willm Collyer,
Mr Miles Standish,
Mr Timothy Hatherley,
Mr John Browne,
Mr Edmond Freeman,
} sworne Assistant(of this goũ^{nt} for this ensuing yeare.

Edmond Eddenden, of Scittuate, admitted freeman & sworne.
Willm Newland, Joseph Holly, & Willm Nicholson tooke the oath of fidelity, &c̃.

Constables.

Plym̃, ... Josiah Cooke sworne.
Duxborr̃, ... Constant Southwood sworne.
Scittuat, ... Samuell Fuller sworne.
Sandwich, ... Nathaniell Willis sworne.
Taunton, ... Willm Parker sworne.
Barnestable, ... Henry Rowley sworne.
Yarmouth, ... Edward Sturges sworne.
Rexhame, ... Josias Winslow, form̃ly sworne.

1641.

1 June.
BRADFORD, Goũ.

The Grand Enquest.

John Dunhame,
John Cooke,
Josuah Pratt,
Gyles Rickett,
Gabriell Fallowell,
Samuell Nash,
Henry Sampson,
Richard Sillis,
} sworne.

George Kenfiick,
Wiłłm Newland,
Joseph Holly,
Henry Andrewes,
Wiłłm Nicholson,
Samuell Hinckley,
Samuell Jackson,
Kenelme Winslowe,
} sworne, { ‡except Kenelm Winslow & Giles Rickett.‡

*Comittees of the seũall Tounes.

Plym̃, ... {
Mr John Jenney,
Mr John Atwood,
Mr John Howland,
Mr Wiłłm Paddy.

Duxborrow, . . . {
Mr John Alden,
Jonathan Brewster.

Scittuate, ... {
Edmond Eddenden,
Humfrey Turner.
} Edward Foster,

Sandwich, ... {
Richard Burne,
George Allen.

Taunton, ... {
Capt Wm Poole,
John Stronge.

Barnestable, ... {
Mr Thom̃ Dimmack,
Anthony Annable.

Yarmouth, ... {
Mr John Crow,
Richard Hore.

Rexhame, ... {
Mr Wiłłm Thomas,
Mr Thom̃ Bourne.

Concerneing the differrence betwixt Richard Lambert & Gowen White, it is by mutuall assent referred to be ended by Thomas Rawlins and Richard Sillis on Lambertẽ, and John Stockbridḡ and John Hollot on the said Whitẽ p̃te ; & if they cannot decide it, then these foure to choose fifth man ; and what end they shall conclude, the p̃ties to abide yt.

It is agreed by the Court, that James Skiffe shall haue the lands due to him layd forth or assigned him in some new plantac̃on.

Wiłłm Honywell is to haue the landẽ due to him for his service layd forth or assigned him at Joanes Riuer, or some other convenyent place.

Francis Baker, a coop, is admitted to dwell at Yarmouth, but not to haue the land{ that are assigned form̄ly to others w{th}out their consent.

The names of those that are ꝑpounded this Court to be admitted freemen the next Court : —

Josuah Barnes & W{m} Nicholson, of Yarmouth ; Samuell Jackson, Thomas Hatch, Henry Ewell, Abraham Blush, & W{m} Betts, of Barnestable ; John Parker & John Bushop, of Taunton ; W{m} Newland.

The towne of Taunton is graunted the xxx{s}, the fine of M{r} Francis Doughty, vpon condic̃õn that the townesmen of Taunton shall make all the swamps betwixt Plym̄ & Taunton passable for man & horse.

*Georḡ Willerd, of Scittuate, planter, for his contemptuous wordes, proued vpon oath, in saying that they were fooles, & knaues, and gulls that payd the rate, or word{ to that effect, and other ꝑphane & vngodly speeches against the churches, likewise prooued by difũs oathes, — viz{, in saying that the churches here & in the Bay held forth a deuelish practise in that they did not baptise children, & other words to that effect; and also, being demaunded his answere why he did so say, did very contumeliously aske the assistant{, or some of them in p̃ticuler, why they did not take the oath of supremacy before they entred vpon their plac{s} yesterday, — was therefore to be bound to his good behaũ.

Georḡ Willerd, of Scittuate, planter, oweth the King, &c̃, . xl{li}.
Thomas Chambers, of the same, plant{, ... xx{li}.
John Twisden, of the same, plant{, ... xx{li}.

To be levyed of euery one of their good{, cattells, &c̃, if he fayle in the condic̃õn followinge : —

The condic̃õn of, &c̃ : That if the said Georḡ Willerd shall appeare at the next Geñall Court of our said soũaigne lord the Kinge, to answere to all such matters as on his ma{ties} behalf shalbe objected against him conc̃ning his contumelious speeches, &c̃, and abide the further order of the Court, & not dep̃t the same w{th}out lycenc̃ ; and in the meane tyme to be of the good behaũ toward{ our said soũaigne lord the King & all his leigh people ; that then, &c̃.

Whereas there is an act against the selling of sheepe out of the collonies, and that Nehemiah Smyth, haueing some sheepe, is dep̃ting the collonies, and would carry them away w{th} him, contrary to the said act, the Court doth order that the said Nehemiah Smyth shall bringe his sheepe to the towne of Plymouth the next second day at night, or the morning following, and shall sell them to any pson or psons that is disposed to buy them, viz{, his ewes at fourty shillings a peece, and the lambes at twenty shillings a peece, to bee payd

1641.
1 June.
Bradford,
Goũ.

[*17.]

Released.

1641.
1 June.
BRADFORD,
Goū.

in money or such comodities as the said Nehemiah shall like ; of and for the rest that are not bought, he to be pmitted to carry them wth him whither he goes to dwell.

It is ordered, that Jonathan Brewster shall pcure the horsboate of the North Riuer, to be brought out of the bay thither by the first of July next ; & if afterwards men goe oū at Mr Vassells ferry, & not there, then the said Jonathan Brewsters servant℮ to be discharged from their attendance at the said ferry, (further then they please,) and not engaged to answer for any damnage for neglect thereof.

That the Court of Assistant℮ be held at Plyṁ euery first Teusday in the month, saue when the Geñall Courts, and then to be kept the day before.

[*18.]

*Edward Morrell, late of Yarmouth, labor, indicted for stealeing certaine corne for Robert Dennis there, is found guilty, but is runn away.

Georḡ Bowers, for his defamacōn of the goūment, wch notwthstanding his trauers, was found agst him, is fyned v^{li}.

Georḡ Bowers is p̄sented for a neusance in setting his fence toward℮ the Goose Poynt so neare the banke side that there is not roome for a cart to passe by.

L^res of administracōn are graunted vnto Katherne Hurst, the relict of Wm Hurst, late of Sandwich, deceas^d.

L^res of administracōn are graunted to ˄ Briggs, of Sandwich, the widdow of John Briggs, lately deceased.

Richard Burne vndertook & promised to make good & pay al such daṁ as might happen if Thomas Applegate should by bringing the suite about againe recouer any thinge against Wm Newland, who this Court hath recoūed agst the said Applegate viij^{li} daṁ, and the charges of the suite.

Georḡ Allen, of Sandwich, became p̄tey to the action that Edward Dotey p̄ferrs agst Willm Alney, of Sandwich.

The rates of the seūall townes for the payment of the clark, & 30 bushells of corne for the messenger : —

	li	s	d		li	s	d
Plymouth, . . .	05	00	00	Taunton, . . .	02	10	00
Duxborrow, . .	03	10	00	Barnestable, . .	02	10	00
Scituate, . . .	04	00	00	Yarmouth, . . .	02	10	00
Sandwich, . . .	03	00	00	Rexhame, . . .	02	00	00
					25	00	00

[*19.]
See their names in the book before this new bound, p. 105.

*Whereas those seauen first freemen, men of Taunton, that haue vndergone great trauell and charges about the attending of the Court℮, laying out of land℮,

COURT ORDERS.   19

and other occations for the toune, it is thought meete by the goûment that 1641.
therefore they haue a pporcõn of land in some convenyent place lying together
assigned them, so that it exceede not the quantyty of fourty acrees apeece, be- 1 June.
sides thother pporcõns of land{ in other plac{ as other of the inhabit{ of the said BRADFORD,
towne of Taunton haue, when the said land{ shall come to be deuided hereafter. Goû.

It is ordered and enacted by the Court, that Mr Edward Winslow, Cap͠t
Miles Standish, Mr John Browne, & Mr Edmond Freeman, foure of the
Assistant{·, or any two or three of them, shall goe to Barnestable & Yarmouth,
and set the bound{ of the said townes, and to heare and determine all causes
and compl͠nts (of the inhabits of Barnestable, Yarmouth, and Sandwich comeing before them) according to justice & equitie ; and what they shall doe in
the p̃misses to be as authenticall & effectuall (being committed to record by
the clark) as if the same had beene donn in the publicke Court.

‡The bound{ of Yarmouth Towneship. The bound{ of Yarmouth on
the easterly side are to a certaine brooke called by the Indians Shuckquan,
but by the English Bound Brooke, and all that neck of land northward called
by the Indians Acquind, a̓s Acquiat, wth all the land{ and marsh medow
wch lye on the westerly side of the said brooke to the towneward{ vnto the
mouth of the said brooke, and at the parte oñ the said Bound Brook where it
falls into Statuckquett Riuer, or into the sea, and at the path ouer the said
Bound{ Brooke from a marked tree, then to run vpon a straight line south &
by east to the South Sea, if it exceede not the leng̃h of eight miles, excepting
and reseruing vnto Massatampaine   ^   ^   .‡

*Francis Baker & Isabell Twineing, of Yarmouth, marryed the xvij^th day 17 June.
of June, 1641.   [*20.]

---

*At a Court held at Yarmouth the xvij^th Day of June, in the xvij^th 17 June.
Yeare of the Raigne of o^r Sou̓aigne Lord, Charles, by the   NEW PLYM.
Grace of God of England, Scotl^d, Franc, & Ireland Kinge, &c.   [*21.]

BEFORE Edward Winslow,   Miles Standish, and
Edmond Freeman, gentlem^n,

three of the Assistant{ of the goûn^t aforesaid, by vertue of the order of the
Geñall Court of the first of June last past, whereby the said Edward Winslow,
Miles Standish, Edmond Freeman, and John Browne, or any two or three of
them, were authorized to set the bound{ of Yarmouth and Barnestable, and to
heare & determine all causes & controñsies amongst the inhabits of Yarmouth, Barnestable, & Sandwich, wch shall come before them, &c.

1641.
17 June.
BRADFORD,
Gov.

THE differrenc[s] betwixt Nicholas Sympkins & Will[m] Chase, by consent of both p[ar]ties, are refered to the arbitriment of M[r] Mayo & M[r] Thom̃ Dimmack, and haue entred into an assumpsit of v[li] to eich other to abide their award; & its to be ended w[th]in a month next comeing.

A warrant grahted to distraine xij[s] vpon Emanuel White for keepeing cowes, and vpon M[r] Sympkins xvj[s], and M[r] Howes 16[s], if M[ris] Fuller will not pay the s̃d 16[s] for Howes.

It is ordered by the Court, that M[r] Andrew Hellot shall pay Massatumpaine one fadome of bead[s] w[th]in two moones, besides the nett he alleadgeth the s̃d Massatumpaine soold him, for the deare that M[r] Hellotts sonn bought of him about two yeares since.

It is ordered by the Court, that Walter Deuile shall pay two shillings to Massatumpaine for mending of the hole in his kettle, w[ch] the s̃d Deuile shott w[th] his gunn; its to be payd w[th]in one moone next ensuinge.

It is ordered by the Court, that Nicholas Symkins shall saue harmlesse the corne of Emanuell White, Thom̃ Falland, Roger and the rest that haue planted corne w[th]in that fence w[ch] they pay for the makeing of.

[*22.]
*Whereas there was complaint made by Will[m] Chase, that Nicholas Symkins had so set his fence that he hath taken in some smale p[ar]te of the land[s] of the s̃d W[m] Chase, w[ch] vpon view appeared to be so,—it is now ordered and concluded by the Court, that notw[th]standing the fence shall stand as now it is sett, and that M[r] Anthony Thacher, for peace sake, will allow the said W[m] Chase as much land out of his owne land[s] of those land[s] w[ch] lye next to the said Chases land[s], and the land so taken in by Nicholas Symkins as afores̃d shalbe his owne. And the said Nicholas Symkins is to allow the said Chase a little p[ar]cell of marsh meddow, lying next to the said Chase, from the end of his fence by a straight line to a crecke easterly, p[ro]uided that the said Will[m] Chase do fence the same in by March next ensuinge.

It is also ordered and concluded, that the inhabitant[s] of the towne of Yarmouth shall p[re]sently meete together, and make a rate for the defraying of all the publike charges w[ch] haue beene layd forth by any p̃ticuler pson or psons for the good of the whole, saue that in the com̃ittees charges wher Will[m] Chase, Thom̃ Howe, & Josuah Barnes were sent as com̃ittees for the towne, these are to be exempted out of those rates, vizt: M[r] Mathews, Will[m] Palmer, Thomas Payne, Anthony Thacher, Thom̃ Falland, Emanuell White, & Thom̃ Starr; but in all other rat[s] and charges to be rated p̃portionably w[th] the rest of the inhabit[an]ts; and that, by vertue of this order, it shalbe lawfull for the constable to distraine all such psons as shall refuse to pay the sums they are rated vnto.

It is ordered by the Court, that the meddow appoynted to M[r] Hellots farme shalbe p̃sently layd forth by the com̃ittees according to his graunt.

COURT ORDERS.

It is ordered also by the Court, that the seũall pporc̃õns of land allotted vnto the inhabits shall p̃sently be layd forth by the com̃ittees to the seũall psons to whom they are so graunted.

It is ordered by the Court, that Willm Lumpkine & Hugh Tilly shall pay to Gabriell Wheildon xv^s for his third p̃te of the skiffe or boate they were p̃tners in, & his damnag̃ sustayned in the want thereof to fetch fish to fish his corne wthall, and the boat or skiffe to be theires.

It is ordered by the Court, that Mr Thom̃ Starr shall haue two acrees of land in some convenyent place assigned him, for one acre of his land giuen to the towne to gett clay vpon.

It is ordered and concluded vpon, by the joynt consent of all the inhabitants of Yarmouth, that Captaine Standish shalbe joyned to the com̃ittes of the said towne of Yarmouth for the disposeing of landꝭ there, and that not any lands hereafter be graunted or layd forth wthout his consent, and that all landꝭ hereafter to be layd forth shalbe assigned to euery pson by lott, except those wch are already graunted & assigned in p̃ticuler, whereof sale & exchaung̃ haue beene made.

1641.
17 June.
BRADFORD,
Goũ. *1*

*The Boundꝭ of Yarmouth.

[*23.]

The bounds of Yarmouth on the easterly side are from the towne to a certaine brooke called by the Indians Shuckquam, but by the English Boundbrooke, and all that neck of land northward called by the Indians Atquiod, al^s, Aquiatt, wth all the vplandꝭ and marsh meddow wch lye on the westerly side of the said brooke, to the townewardꝭ vnto the mouth of the said brooke; and from a marked tree at the payth oũ the said Bound Brooke by a straight line south and by east to the south sea, so it extend not in lengh aboue eight miles, excepting and reserueing vnto Massatanpaine, the sachem, the landꝭ from Nobscussetpann westerly, from a marked tree there vnto another marked tree at a swamp extending westerly, and from thence to another marked trey northerly by a straight line to the sea, and from the northerly end of the said Nobscusset pan to the sea by a line from the westerly side of the said pan.

The bounds betwixt Yarmouth & Barnestable are as followeth, vizꝫ : that the river of Stoney Coue shalbe the bounds from the sea as farr as it runeth to the landwards, and from thence from the vpward p̃te thereof to begin at the easterly side of the lott of Andrew Hellot, at a knowne marked tree, by the heigh way leading betwixt Barnestable and Yarmouth aforesaid, and from the easterly side of the vpward p̃t of the said lot to runn vpon the south southwest poynt of the compasse to the south sea, pvided alwayes that the meddow land that was allotted and appoynted to the said Mr Hellotts farme be still reserued vnto the said farme, according to the form̃ intent & graunt thereof; excepting & reserueing vnto Nepaiton & Twacommacus, & their

1641.

17 June.
BRADFORD,
Goū.

heires and assignes, if they shall dwell vpon yt, all that ƥcell of playne land bordering to the seawardℓ from a pond to a tree by the wood side, marked by Mʳ Winslow, Capt Standish, & Mʳ Freeman, and from thence easterly by the wood side to another marked tree, & from thence northerly to the sea, ƥuided that if the said Nepaiton shall at any tyme sell the same, he shall sell it to the inhabits of Barnestable before any other.

The Agreement betwixt Nepaiton & Twacommacus & their Heires and the Inhabitants of Barnestable.

In consideraōōn besides what the said Nepaiton hath had already of the said inhabits of Barnestable, that they shall build the said Nepaiton one dwelling house, wᵗʰ a chamber flored wᵗʰ bordℓ, wᵗʰ a chimney and an ouen therein, the said Nepaiton hath giuen and graunted vnto the said inhabits of Barnestable all the rest of his landℓ lying about Barnestable aforesaid, wᶜʰ were his & his owne ƥper inheritance, excepting & reserueing vnto the said Nepaiton and Twacommacus & their heires & assignes foreuer, if they shall dwell vpon it, all that ƥcell of playne lands bordering vpon the sea, from a pond to a tree by the wood side marked by Mʳ Winslow, Capt Standish, and

[*24.]

Mʳ Freeman, & from thence easterly *by the wood side to another marked tree, and from thence northerly to the sea; prouided alwayes, that if the said Nepaiton shall at any time sell the said landℓ, he shall sell them to the inhabits of Barnestable before any other, and shall from tyme to tyme giue leaue for a draught to come through his ground when they shall desire it; and lastly, that they shall haue liberty to gett wood for fenceing a fyer out of the woods there, and enjoy and reap the corne this yeare wᶜʰ they haue set out of the foresaid boundℓ, and in winter to liue where he pleaseth.

---

6 July.
NEW PLYM.
[*25.]

*At a Court of Assistantℓ held at Plym̄ aforesᵈ, the vjᵗʰ Day of July, in the xvijᵗʰ Yeare of his Maᵗˢ now Raigne of England, &c.

BEFORE Wᵐ Bradford, gent, Goū,   Wᵐ Collyer, &
        Edward Winslow,   Capt Miles Standish,
        Thom̄ Prence,
                Gentℓ, Assistantℓ, &c.

AN action was tryed betwixt Leiftennant Holmes & James Luxford. Mʳ Parker, of Weymouth, had a view of the patent and that clause in writing wᶜʰ concerned the boundℓ from Narragansetts Bay to the vtmost p̄ts & limmits of the countrey called Pockanockett, in regard the Bay men would haue had Sicquncke from us.   **1641.**

James Luxford agreed to lett the attachment rest vpon the sowe attached at Mr Aldens suite vntill he be satisfyed, the said Luxford runing the adventure.   6 July BRADFORD, Gou.

At a townes meeting for the towne of Plym̄, held the xvj^th August, in the xvij^th yeare of the now raigne of o^r soūaigne lord, Charles, King of England, &c, it was ordered and agreed as followeth, viz̄ : —   16 August.

That the second day of the weeke after the Geñall Court, the ma^trats and com̄ittees shall meete to graunt land(, and then to appoynt a certaine tyme when to meete againe.

That a p̄cell of land lying betweene the Eele River swamps shalbe reserued to the towne of Plymouth, for the inhabit̄s to sowe hempe and flax vpon, p̄uided that Wm Paddy haue other land(graunted him in lue thereof, bec̄ the said land(were form̄ly graunted to him.

*Thomas Southerne and Elizabeth Reynor marryed the first of September, 1641.   1 September. [*26.]

Robert Finney & Phebe Ripley marryed the first of Septem̄b̄r, 1641.

Mr Wm Hanbury & Hannah Sowther marryed the xxviij^th Septem̄b̄r, 1641.   28 September.

Henry Sirkman & Bridgitt Fuller marryed the xxx^th Septem̄b̄r, 1641.   30 September.

It is agreed that the prison be erected, & that Capt̄ Standish and Jonathan Brewster shall see it laden into the leighter on Duxborrow side, & the Court to see them payd for their charge about yt; that Mr Atwood & Mr Paddy shall vndertake the receipt thereof on this side, & that Mr Paddy will lay forth 5^li or 6^li aboute it, p̄vided the Court take order he shalbe payd againe in due tyme, and not put him to gather it himself.

At the Gen^rall Court of o^r Sou^raigne Lord the Kinge, held at Plym̄ aforesaid, the vij^th of Septemb^r, in the xvij^th Yeare of the Raigne of o^r said Sou^raigne Lord, Charles, King of England, &c.   7 September. NEW PLYM. [*27.]

BEFORE Willm Bradford, gent̄, Gou,   Willm Collyer,
Edward Winslow,   Capt̄ Miles Standish, &
Thom̄ Prence,   Tymothy Hatherly,
Assistant(, &c.

MR MARMADUKE MATHEWES, Thomas Fallard, Richard Hore, Willm Newland, John Parker, Giles Rickett admitted freemen this Court, & sworne.

1641.
7 September.
BRADFORD,
Go^r.

Samuell Hicks,
John Smaley,
John Dunhame, Ju^r,
Willm Fallowell,
Edmond Tilson,

Thomas Lambert,
John Rogers,
Oliuer Purchas,

p̱pounded to be made free the next Court.

All differrenc̱ now depending betwixt Thomas Chettenden & X̱pofer Winter are, by consent of both p̱ties, referred to be ended by Thomas Raulins and Edward Foster ; and the said p̱ties haue entred into assumpsitt to eich other of 40^{li} to abide their end & order.

The dep^ric̄ōn of Willm Holmes taken by and affirmed in the open Court : This depo^{nt} sayth, Willm Hatch used these wordes, or the like effect, vizt, that the warranṯ sent from the gouern^r were nothing but a stincking com̄issary warranṯ or attachmenṯ, and that the warranṯ sent in that kynd are no better than com̄issary court warranṯ ; and that the warrant sent to the constable to warne him, the s̄d Hatch, to appeare at the Court of o^r soūaigne lord the Kinge was but a com̄issary warrant, and

The messenger, being deposed conc̄rning the words that Willm Hatch used, sayth that

[*28.]   *Willm Hatch, of Scittuate, com̄itted to the goale for want of sureties for his good behaū.

It is ordered by the Court, that Mr Edmond Freeman, one of the Assistanṯ, shall, at the next Court holden towarḏ Yarmouth & Barnestable, inflict such punishment upon Mr Crowes mayde servant, for pilfering goods in his house, as according to her fault shalbe just & equall.

Mr John Done, Mr Willm Paddy, & Nathaniell Sowther, are appoynted by the Court to view James Luxforḏ bookes, and to certify the Court what they find therein.

George Allen & Mr Edward Dillingham are nominated, by consent of both p̱ties, to apprize the swyne Willm Newland hath in execuc̄ōn of Thom̄ Applegaṯ, and what the want in value of eight pounds & charges the said Applegate is to giue his bill to the said Newland for payment thereof.

James Coles fyne of fiue pounds, vpon due considerac̄ōn had thereof, is by the Court remitted the said Cole, allowing the dyett of John Mynard during the tyme he was erecting the prison.

It is ordered by the Court, that John Mynard shall haue iij^{li} more allowed him, besides his dyett, for his worke donn about the prison ouer & aboue the *the* bargaine.

Gowen White, of Scittuate, for his assault vpon Willm Holmes, is fyned by the Court fiue shillings.

Wilłm Hatch, of Scittuate, planter, acknowledgeth to owe o^r soūraigne lord the Kinge, &c̄, ... } xl^{li}.

John Combe, of Plym̄, gent̄, ... xx^{li}.

Thom̄ Cushman, of the same, p̄ant̄, ... xx^{li}.

1641.
7 September.
BRADFORD,
Goū.

The condic̄ōn, that if thaboue bounden Wilłm Hatch shall p̄sonally appeare at the next Geñall Court of o^r s̄d soūaigne lord the Kinge, &c̄, to be holden at Plym̄, &c̄, and in the meane tyme to be of the good behaū toward[o^r said soūaigne lord the King and all his legh people, and abide the further order of the Court, & not dep̄te the same wthout lycence; that then, &c̄.

Released.

*At a townes meeting by the inhabitants of Plym̄, holden the xvjth of September, 1641, xvij° Caroli, &c̄, for grant of lands wthin the said towneship of Plymouth, according to the order of the Court, by Mr Wilłm Bradford, Mr Thomas Prince, and the then com̄ittees, viz{, Mr John Atwood, Mr John Jenney, & Mr Wilłm Paddy.

16 September.
[*29.]

The lands lying at Caughtacanteist Hill, betwixt Josias Cooks feild and Mr John Howland[land, towards the brooke, is graunted to Mr John Reynor, the teacher.

It is ordered, that the lands beyond the Second Brook, lying at the head of Mr Bradford[land there, and the lands there about[, shall not bee graunted forth to any man except to a pastor or a teacher.

It is also ordered, that the lands remaineing in Alkermans feild, & not belonging to p̄ticuler p̄sons, shalbe reserued to be graunted to a pastor.

Richard Sparrow is graunted the meddow ground at the Wood Iland, wch was M^{ris} Fullers, containeing about two acrees.

Andrew Ring is granted an enlargement at the west ende of his garden, to be viewed and set forth for him by Mr Bradford, Mr Jenney, & Mr Paddy, or any two of them.

Edward Banges is graunted a p̄cell of fourscore acrees of vpland about Warrens Wells, to be viewed and layd forth for him by Mr Jenney, Manasseth Kempton, & Josuah Pratt.

Thomas Cushman is graunted a p̄cell ∧ upland remayneing about Turners feild, and two acrees nere the new feild betwixt Mrs Fullers and the brooke, in lue of two acrees lying by Georḡ Watsons & John Barnes.

Wilłm Paddy, John Finney, Rob̄te Finney, are graunted six acrees apeece of vpland abutting vpon the brooke that comes from the Fresh Lake, p̄uided thē leaue convenyent passage for cattell by the brooke side, and Mr Paddy to haue more then six acrees, if it be there to be had.

1641.

16 September.
BRADFORD, Gou.

[*30.]

Thurstone Clarke is graunted tenn acres of vpland at the head of Edward Doteys lott toward Mount Hill Payth.

*John Groomes is graunted twelue acrees of vpland at the head of Blackbrooke, to be layd forth next after John Winslowes enlargment, and Josuah Pratts xij acres are layd forth ; and all to be viewed and layd forth by Mr Wm Paddy, Nathll Sowther, & Josuah Pratt.

Francis Billington is graunted an enlargement where he desireth, if, vpon the view of Mr Prence, Mr Atwood, & Wm Paddy, it shalbe there found to be had.

Wiltm Fallowell, John Wood, are graunted six acrees a peece of vpland, at the Loute Pond.

Steeven Wood, Henry Wood, are graunted eight acrees apeece of vpland, at Loute Pond.

John Dunhame, the yeonger, is graunted twenty acres of vpland about the north easterly side of Josias Cook Haystack Pond, and the odd hobs of meddowing he desireth thereabouts.

John Dunhame, the elder, is graunted threescore acres of vpland lying at the Swann Holt on the north side thereof, and eight acrees of meddow to yt there.

Samuell Eddy is graunted six acrees of vpland lying on the northwest side of Fresh Lake, about the fishing place, and thirty acrees of vpland at the Narrogansett Hill, and foure acrees of meddow, or els half the meddow ground there to yt.

Edward Doteys pcell of vpland at Lakenham is graunted to be made vp fourty acres.

Mr John Atwood is graunted one hundred acrees of vpland to his meddow at Lakenhame, and to abut vpon the said meddow as neere as may bee.

Mrs Bridgitt Fuller is graunted one hundred acrees vpland to her meddow at Lakenhame, and to abutt vpon her meddow there, as nere as it can convenyently be layd forth.

Mr Wiltm Paddy is graunted 100 acrees of vpland at the North Meddow by Jones River vpon view to be layd forth.

& Nathaniell Sowther is to haue the next land.

Mr Thomas Prence is graunted an enlargement at the head of his lott at Joanes Riuer, to be layd forth vpon view.

[*31.]

*Mr John Jenney is graunted as much more vpland as will make his farme at Lakenhame two hundred acres, and when that is used, then to haue more added to yt, in lue of some land he hath yeilded vp at the towne to Gabriell Fallowell.

James Cole is graunted fifty acres of vpland at Lakenhame Meddow, and some meddow to be layd to yt vpon view.

COURT ORDERS. 27

Josuah Pratt is graunted a garden place about the house he hath bought of Thomas Savory, at Squerrell, and Mr Jenney & Mr Paddy to lay it forth.

Nathaniell Sowther is graunted a little p̱cell ⁁ vpland, taken in wth his meddow at the watering place, and also a garden place at Wellingsly, to be viewed by Mr Paddy.

1641.
16 September.
BRADFORD, Goū.

*At a Court of Assistantꝭ held the second of Novemb^r, in the xvij^th Yeare of his s^d Ma^ts now Raigne, of England, &c.

2 November.
[*32.]

BEFORE Wilłm Bradford, genṯ, Goū, Thomas Prence, and
  Edward Winslow,   Wm Collyer,
   Genṯ, Assistantꝭ, &c̃.

LRES of administrac̃on are graunted to Mrs Elizabeth Kemp, to administer vpon all the goods, cattells, and debtꝭ wch Wilłm Kempe, her late husband, dyed possessed of, or were due & apptaineing vnto him at the tyme of his decease, p̱uided shee exhibite vpon oath a true inventory thereof wth all convenyent speed, or when shee shalbe therevnto required by the Court.

*At the Geñall Court of o^r Sou̅aigne Lord the King, held at Plym̃ aforesaid, the vij^th Day of Decemb^r, in the xvij^th Yeare of the Raigne of o^r Sou̅aigne Lord, Charles, by the Grace of God King, of England, Scotland, France, & Ireland Defend^r of the Fayth, &c.

7 December.
NEW PLYM.
[*33.]

BEFORE Wilłm Bradford, genṯ, Goū, Miles Standish,
  Edward Winslow,   Tymothy Hatherley, and
  Thom̃ Prence,   Edmond Freeman,
  Wilłm Collyer,
    Assisṯ, &c̃.

WHEREAS compl^nt is made by Francis Linceford, that Thomas Bray detayneth certaine goods from the said Francis, it is ordered by the Court, that Mr Anthony Thacher, Mr Nicholas Sympkins, and Richard Hore, or any two of them, shall see that the said Bray shall deliuer all the rest of the goods of the said Lincefordꝭ wch are in his hands, except one white rugg, one bed and boulster, sword, musket, & bandilires, foure iron wedges, one

1641.

7 December.
BRADFORD,
Goũ.

Released.

hoggshead, one tubb, one kettle, & two iron ringes, wch were made ouer to the said Bray, vpon condiĉõn that he should pay iiij^li to seũall psons, wch the said Linceford was endebted vnto when he went from Yarmouth to go to the West Indies.

Willm Kersley, of Barnestable, plant, acknowledgeth to owe the Kinge, &c̃, ... } xx^li.

Henry Rowley, of the same, pl^t, ... x^li.

Anthony Annable, of the same, pl^t, ... x^li.

The condiĉõn, &c̃, that the said Willm Kersley shall psonally appeare at the next Geñall Court of o^r said soũaigne lord the King, to be holden for this goũment, to answere to all such matters as shalbe (on his said ma^ts behalf) objected against him for vncleane carriages toward(̃ men that he hath lyen w^thall, and abide the further order of the Court, and not dep̃t the same w^thout lycence ; that then, &c̃.

It is ordered by the Court, that there shalbe no wood felled or cutt downe vpon the heads of the lotts of the heires of John Adams at Playne Dealeing, vntill that the towne haue taken order that there shalbe some land layd forth in quañty as shalbe thought meete to make vp their measure in lengh wch is wanting in breadth.

An attachment of a calf, (in the hand(̃ of Roɓte Boatefish, of Sandwich,) of the goods of Willm Almey, was made this Court to answere the jury vj^s vj^d, and iij^s to the clarke for the charges of a suite he left vnpayd when hee lefte the towne of Sandwich.

[*34.]

*Forasmuch as Thomas Bray, of Yarmouth, a single pson, and Anne, the wyfe of Francis Linceford, haue cõmitted the act of adultery and vncleanesse, and haue diuers tymes layne in one bed together ·in the absence of her husband, wch hath beene confessed by both p̃ties in the publike Court, the Court doth censure them as followeth : That they be both seuerely whipt immediately at the publik post, & that they shall weare (whilst they remayne in the goũment) two letters, viz(̃, an AD, for Adulterers, dãly, vpon the outeside of their vppermost garment, in a most emenent place thereof; and if they shalbe found at any tyme in any towne or place w^thin the gouerment w^thout them so worne vpon their vppermost garment as aforesd, that then the constable of the towne or place shall take them, or either of them, omitting so to weare the said two letters, and shall forthw^th whip them for their negligence, and shall cause them to be iõmediately put on againe, and so worne by them and either of them ; and also that they shalbe both whipt at Yarmouth, publikely, where the offence was cõmitted, in such fitt season as shalbe thought meete by Mr Edmond Freeman & such others as are authorized for the keepeing of the Courts in these p̃tes.

COURT ORDERS.

A warrant to be directed to Edward Holman, John Whetston, of Scittuate, Willm Lumpkine, and Josuah Barnes, of Yarmouth, to answere at the next Genall Court for goods they tooke, wch were found by shipwrecke. That if any man be disposed to take the trade for a yeare, or some yeares, that they bring in their names to the next Court of Assistants in February next, and that the Goũnor, Mr Winslow, Mr Collyer, Mr Prence, Mr Wm Thomas, Mr John Howland, Mr John Atwood, Mr John Jenney, & Jonathan Brewster shall treate wth them about yt that will then adventure any thing therein, and that those that haue the trade shall take their corne that makes their biskett w^thin this collony, and that the skins had by the trade shalbe vented for the collonys use.

1641.
7 December.
BRADFORD,
Goũ.

*At a townes meeting, held the last day of Decembr, in the xvij^th yeare of his ma^ts now raigne, of England, &c, before Wm Bradford, gent, Goũ, Thomas Prence, gent, John Atwood, John Jenney, John Howland, and Willm Paddy, comittees authorized to graunt lands to the inhabits of the towne of Plymouth.

31 December.
[*35.]

Willm Hoskine is graunted vj or viij acrees of vpland at the head of James Hurst land, or neare his land, and a garden place by the brooke side, or by his house, to be viewed and layd forth for him by the Goũ, Mr Prence, and Josuah Pratt.

Steeven Wood and Henry Wood are graunted eich of them a garden place in the neighbourhood at Wellingsly, ag^st Francis Goulders fence, puided that it be not pjudicious either to the heigh wayes in geñall, nor any man in pticuler, & Mr Paddy to see them layd forth.

Willm Pontus is graunted two acrees of vpland to his half acre of meddow in the woods beyond his house about Agawem Payth.

‡John Groomes is graunted eight acrees of vpland at the Lout Pond, to be layd forth for him by Josuah Pratt, puided that he relinquish his form graunt at the Smylt Brooke.‡

Vacat.

Richard Sparrow is graunted a pcell of vpland.

Gyles Rickett is graunted a pcell of vpland, about two acrees, lying on the south & east side of his feild.

Mr John Combe is graunted a pporcõn of land at the head of his ground where he now dwelleth, in consideracõn of a lott of land he had there formly graunted wch he hath now yeilded vp.

John Cooke is graunted a porcõn of land lying neere Georg Clarkes, if it be there to be had, after Mr Prence, Mr Howland, & Mr Jenney, & Joshua Pratt haue viewed it.

1641.
31 December.
BRADFORD,
Goū.

John Smaley, Anthony Snow, are graunted fiue acrees a peece of meddow in Cole Brooke Meddow.

John Dunhame is graunted a p̄cell of meddow at Swanholt, and some vpland to yt, at the discretion of those that shalbe appoynted to view yt.

Mr John Holmes is graunted fourty acrees of vpland at Narrogansett Hill, lying betwixt the heighway and Derbys pondℓ.

Robte Paddock is graunted foure acrees of vpland where hee desired about Kenelmes dingle.

1641-2.
4 January.
NEW PLYM.
[*37.]

At a Court of Assistantℓ held the fourth Day of January, in the xvijth Yeare of his Ma^{ts} now Raigne, of Engl^d, &c.

BEFORE Willm Bradford, genℓ, Goū,   Thomas Prince, &
      Edward Winslow,   Willm Collyer,
              Genℓ, Assistantℓ, &c.

CONCERNING the differencℓ betwixt Edward Dotey and Thurstone Clarke, it is ordered by the Court, that the said Thurstone Clarke shall pay unto the said Edward Dotey xij bushells & j peck of Indian corne, and xij^s in money, or iiij bushells of Indian and xj^s for charges that the said Edward layd forth for the said Thurstone; and this to be payd before the next Court, or els to haue execuc̄on.

Thomas Byrd, servant to Mr James Cudworth, of Barnestable, for runinge away from his s̄d master, and breaking a house or two in Barnestable, and taking some apparell and victualls, is censured to be once whipt at Plym̄, and once whipt at Barnestable, before the next Court of Assistantℓ; and when his s̄d master comes, then order to be taken for payment of his fees; and at the next Court of Assistantℓ following, the said Byrd remayneing in the messengers handℓ, vpon ℓres from Mr Freeman that the said Thomas Byrds father had agreed wth the said Mr Cudworth for the tyme he was to serue the said Cudworth, the said Thomas Byrd was released, paying the messenger his fees; and for thother p̄t of his censure, wch should haue beene executed vpon him at Barnestable, in regard of the coldenesse of the p̄sent season, it is to be inflicted vpon him at Scituate, whither he goes to dwell, when it shalbe a convenyent season.

Mr John Jenney is graunted an attachment for the money in Clarkes handℓ, due to Edward Dotey. 31^s 6^d condem̄ for Mr Jenney.

COURT ORDERS. 31

John Whetston confesseth that he had (of the good$ taken vp in the bottome of the bay about Satuckquet) a paire of drawers, a wascoat, & a shirt.
Edward Holman had canvas to make a mayne saile, a pair drawer, a wascote, & a shirt.
Mr Wm Lumkin a paire of breeches and a wascoate.
Joshua Barnes a suite of cloth.
John Didcutt a cloath coate.

1641-2.
4 January.
BRADFORD,
Go$.

For wch he hath made satisfac͠con at March Court, 1641, is thereof discharged.

*At a townesmeeting held at the Go$^s house the xxiiij^th day of Januar̃, in the xvij^th yeare of his ma^ts now raigne, of England, &c̃.

[*39.]

It is ordered and agreed vpon that the inhabit̃ on eich side of the towne, viz$, the Eele Riuer & Joanes Riuer, shall for eich side bring six muskett, w^th shott, pouder, and the towne of Plym̃ other six euery Lord$ day, to the meeting, wth their sword$ & furniture to euery peece, ready for seruice if need require.

Mr John Atwood,
Mr John Done,
Mr Wm Paddy,
John Cooke, Junr,
} elected com̃ittees for the towne.

The Contributors for building of a Bark of 40 or 50 Tunn, estimated at the Charge of 200^li.

Willm Paddy,	. .	j eight part.	Mr Willm Bradford,	j xvj^th part.
Mr Willm Hanbury,		j eight part.	Mr John Jenney, . .	j xvj^th part.
John Barnes, . . .		j eight part.	Mr John Atwood, .	j xvj^th part.
			Samuell Hicks, . .	j xvj^th part.
			Georḡ Bower, . . .	j xvj^th part.
			John Cook & his fath^r,	j xvj^th part.
			Samuell Jenney, . .	j xvj^th part.
			Thomas Willet, . .	j xvj^th part.
			Mr Hopkins, . . .	j xvj^th part.
			Edward Bangs, . .	j xvj^th part.

Appoynted to vndertake the pcureing her to be built, are Mr Thom̃ Prence, Mr Wm Paddy, Mr Thom̃ Willett, & John Barnes.

It is agreed vpon that Mr Willm Paddy shall haue liberty to set vp a stage for makeing fish at Sagaquash, and shall haue the use of the vpland

1641-2.
4 January.
BRADFORD, Goũ.

there so long as he, or any for him, shall mayntaine the said stage there, puided they keepe no swyne there nor at Clarkꝭ Iland; but vpon notice of harme donn by them, they shalbe taken away.

Mr John Jenney & M^r Wiłłm Paddy are to be added to those that are to dispose of the pcores stock, (formły nominated) instead of Mr Hopkins, and to haue liberty to alter or chaunge them or some of them for such cattell as may be most usefull for the help of the poore.

That the Assistantꝭ within the towne, and the comittees, shall graunt landꝭ this yeare.

M^r Wiłłm Paddy, Mr Atwood, Nathan^l Sowther, Mr John Jenney, John Dunham, thelder, Thomas Willett, John Barnes, & Josuah Pratt shall view the landꝭ on both sides the towne, that convenyent heighwayes & passages for cattell into the woods being reserued & set forth, such landꝭ as shall remayne, & may be spared, may be graunted to such as stand in need.

1 February.
NEW PLYM.
[*41.]

*At a Court of Assistantꝭ held the first Day of February, in the xvijth Yeare of his Ma^{ts} now Raigne, of England, &c.

BEFORE Wm Bradford, genŧ, Goũ,   Wiłłm Collyer, &
        Edward Winslow,   Miles Standish,
        Thoɱ Prince,
                Genŧ, Assistantꝭ, &c.

CONCERNING ye deffẽnces betwixt Mr John Jenney & Edward Dotey, the accountꝭ were, —

	li s d		li s d
Mr Jenney demanded	03 : 10 : 00	Ed Dotey payd	01 : 02 : 06
			00 : 04 : 00
			00 : 02 : 00
			00 : 10 : 00
			01 : 18 : 06

The Court ordered, that vpon attachment of the moneyes in Thurstons Clarkes handꝭ, Mr John Jenney reĉ them; he should pay the said Edward Dotey fiue bushells & a half of Indian m̃chantable corne, & iij^d for so much remayned due to the s̃d Dotey vpon the account.

COURT ORDERS.

The Court ordereth, that Georg Clarke shall pay foure bushells of Indian corne vnto Edward Dotey, vpon the differenc[now depending betwixt them.

1641-2.
1 February.
BRADFORD, Goū.

Whereas Edward Dotey hath two cowes and a yeong steere of Thomas Symons to keepe for tyme, and that by reason the said Edward Dotey doth not put his cattell to a keep in the sumer tyme, & that they use to break into mens corne, and may thereby be endangered either to be spoyld wth corne, or come to some other harme, whereby the said Symons may be endamnaged, the Court doth order, that the said Edward Dotey shall take order that his cattell be safely kept by a keep, or els, if any damnage befall the said Thomas Symons by default thereof, that the said Edward Dotey shall make good the same to the said Thomas Symons.

---

*At the Gen^{r}all Court of o^r Sou^{r}aigne Lord the King, holden at Plym afores^d, the first Day of March, in the xvijth Yeare of the now Raigne of o^r said Sou^{r}aigne Lord, Charles, by the Grace of God King of England, Scotland, France, & Ireland, Defendor of the Fayth, &c.

1 March.
NEW PLYM.
[*43.]

BEFORE Wiłłm Bradford, gent, Goū,   Miles Standish,
Edward Winslow,   Tymothy Hatherley, and
Thomas Prence,   Edmond Freeman,
Wiłłm Collyer,
Gent, and Assistant[, &č.

SAMUELL HICKS, John Dunham, Junr, Edmond Tilson, John Smaley, & John Rogers admitted freemen and sworne.

M^r Wiłłm Bradford elected Goūnor.

Mr Edward Winslow,
Mr Thom̄ Prence,
M^r Wiłłm Collyer,
Mr Tymothy Hatherley,   } elected Assistant[.
Mr Wm Thomas,
Mr Edmond Freeman,
Mr John Browne,

VOL. II.   5

1641-2.
1 March.
BRADFORD,
Goῦ.

Emanuell White, of Yarmouth,
Mr Thomas Allen, of Barnestable,
James Hamlen, of the same,
Arthur Howland, of Marshfeild,
} ꝑpounded to be freemen.

Constables & Surveyors of the Heigh Wayes.

Plymouth, . . {
  Giles Rickett, constable & survey^r,
  Mr Wm Hanbury,
  Francis Cooke,
  } for Joanes Riuer,
  James Cole & the constable for the towne,
  & Thomas Clark, for the Eele Riuer.
}
Duxborrow, . . Edmond Hawes.
Scituate, . . . Josias Checkett.
Sandwich, . . Michaell Turner.
Taunton, . . . Wm Parker.
Barnestable, . . Thomas Lathrope.
Yarmouth, . {
  Emanuel White,
  Wm Parker,
  Gabriell Wheilden,
} surveyors.
Marshfeild, . . Francis West.

Mr John Atwood elected Treasurer for this ensuing yeare.
That the clark shall haue xx^li p añ, as formῆly payd by the Treasurer, &c̄.

[*44.]   *Grand Jurymen.

Plymñ, . . . {
  John Winslow,
  John Dunham, Señ,
  Edward Banges, &
  Richard Church.
}
Duxborrow, . . Mr Thomas Besbeech, John Willis.
Scituate, . . . Thomas Raulins, Thom̄ Ensigne.
Sandwich,   ^
Taunton,   ^
Barnestable, . . Henry Bourne, Henry Euell.
Yarmouth, . . . James Mathews.
Marshfeild, . . ‡Kenelme Winslow,‡ Francis West.

Concerning the differenc℄ betwixt the townes of Duxborrow & Marshfeild, about the bound℄ of Marshfeild, the com̄ittees of Duxborrow are to acquaint their townesmen wth yt, and that Duxborrow elect some man or men

COURT ORDERS.   35

to conferr wth Marshfeild men about their bound{, that so they may know the bound{ of their towne of Marshfeild.

1641-2.
1 March.
BRADFORD, Go^u.

All difference{ betwixt Mr Nicholas Symkins & Walter Devile are by mutuall consent and order of the Court referred to be decided and ended by Mr Edward Dillingham & Mr Thomas Dimmack ; and if they cannot end them, then they two to choose a third man vnto them, and so to make an end ; but if any losses fall vpon the said Symkins goods in other mens hand{, to make report thereof to the Court. And if any need be of witness^s, to proue any thing on either p̄t, they may be sworne before Mr Freeman, that a finall end may be made betwixt them.

Edward Holmans demaund{ for his paynes about a chest of goods found at Mannamoyit, —

	li	s	d
For fetching the chest to Yarmouth,	00	05	00
For charges of an Indian at boatside,	00	06	00
For fetching the chest after to Barnes,	00	05	00
For a hatchet giuen to the Indn,	00	01	06
For drying the goods at the boateside,	00	12	00
For bringing the chest to Plym̄,	00	08	00
	01	17	06

besides xvj^s allowed Mr Lumpkins for washing & drying of the goods, wch was payd out of the goods.

Mr William Paddy and Thomas Willet are appoynted by the Court to value these goods, and to exhibite an inventory of them to the Court. And the Court doth allow the said Edward Holman xx^s for his paynes and demaund{ about them.

Memorand: that the said Edward Holman did account wth the Gourn^r and Assistant{ for the said goods, according to an inventory thereof exhibited, and is thereof discharged according to the said inventory.

*Lydia Hatch, for suffering Edward Michell to attempt to abuse her body by vncleanesse, & did not discouer it, & lying in the same bed wth her brother Jonathan, is censured to be publickly whipt ; was accordingly donn.

[*45.]

Edward Michell, for his lude & sodomiticall practices tending to sodomye wth Edward Preston, and other lude carryages wth Lydia Hatch, is censured to be p̄sently whipt at Plymouth, at the publike place, and once more at Barnestable, in oonvenyent tyme, in the p̄sence of Mr Freeman and the com̄ittees of the said towne.

Edward Preston, for his lude practises tending to sodomye wth Edward Michell, and pressing John Keene thereunto, (if he would haue yeilded,) is

PLYMOUTH COLONY RECORDS.

1 6 4 1-2.
1 March.
BRADFORD,
Gov.

also censured to be forthwth whipt at Plym̄, and once more at Barnestable, (when Edward Michell is whipt,) in the p̃sence of Mr Freeman & the com̄ittees of the same towne.

John Keene, because he resisted the temptac̃õn, & vsed meanes to discouer it, is appoynted to stand by whilst Michell and Preston are whipt, though in some thing he was faulty.

Jonathan Hatch was taken as a vagrant, & for his misdemeanors was censured to be whipt, & sent from constable to constable to Leiftennant Dauenport at Salem.

Forasmuch as the inhabit^s of Barnestable complayne that they are streitned betwixt two plantac̃õns, and desire enlargement into the depth of the land southerly, they are graunted to view the same and make report thereof at the next Court, that they may haue the lands wch. they desire, when they are again viewed by speciall appoyntment; p̃uided they be not p̃judiciall to thother two plantac̃õns, or fitt to be a plantac̃õn itself.

Mr Thomas Star, of Yarmouth, Heugh Tilley, of the same, Joshuah Barnes, of the same, Wm Nicholson, of the same, are complayned of to be scoffers & jeerers at religion, &c̃, and making disorders in their towne meetings, &c̃; are to be sent for to answere the next Court, &c̃.

Tristram Hull, of Yarmouth, for vnclean practises.

17 March.
[*46.]

*The xvijth day of March, 1641, Alexander Williams, servant to Mr Willm Thomas, of Marshfeild, was exãnd for ruñing away from his said m^r foure seuall tymes, and long absenting himself from his service; could not say any thing for himself wherefore he should not be punished; was therefore censured to be whipt at the publike place, wch was accordingly donn.

1 March.
Com̄itted to prison & clothed, & 5 to Capt. Standish.
Tyme giuen to do yt within vi weeks vpon penalty of 5^{li}.
Discharged.
Discharged.

Remitted the same Court.

Presentment℟, March 1st, 1641, by the Grand Jury.

Wee p̃sent Webb Adey for his licentious and disorderly manner of liueing.

Wee p̃sent the towne of Duxborrow for not haueing a pound or penn for cattell.

Wee p̃sent the towne of Plymouth for the same default.

Wee p̃sent Mr Edmond Freeman, of Sandwich, for lending a gun to an Indian.

Wee p̃sent John Wing, of Sandwich for lending a gun to an Indian.

Wee p̃sent Nicholas Symkins, of Yarmouth, for lending a pistoll to an Indian.

Wee p̃sent Thomas Tupper, of Sandwich, for misdemeanor in lãcivious & vncleane carriages towards Linceford℟ wyfe, late of Yarmouth.

COURT ORDERS. 37

We p̃sent Linceford⁀ wyfe for the same miscarriage. 1641-2.

We p̃sent Mr Gray, of Yarmouth, for sweareing. Com̃itted to prison. 1 March.

We p̃sent John Caseley, of Barnestable, & Alis, his wyfe, for fornicac̃on, in vnlawfull companying before their marriage. John to be whipt, & Alis to be set in the stocks.

BRADFORD, Goũ.

Man to be whipt, the weoman stocks during the whiping.

A quere. The plantac̃on of Puidence haueing in it many honest & peaceable people, wch groane vnder the want of goũment and the ryotts and disorders falling out therevpon, the place being reputed wthin the goũment of Plym̃, least worse thinges may fall out to the further and greater trouble of the colony, or honest people there, being ouerpressed by vyolent and turbulent psons should submit or subject the place to another goũment, we desire that a seasonable considerac̃on may be had thereof, for p̃vention of future mischeefs, if the place be wthin this gouerment, as it is geñally reputed.

**At a Court of Assistant⁀ held the fift of Aprill, in the xviijth Yeare of the now Raigne of our Soũaigne Lord, Charles, King of England, &c.* 1642. 5 April. [*47.]

BEFORE Willm Bradford, genĩ, Goũ,   Willm Collyer,
Edward Winslow,   Capĩ Miles Standish,
Thomas Prence,
    Assistant, &c̃.

Mris ELIZABETH KEMP exhibited, vpon her oath, an inventory of all her husbands good⁀, debt⁀, and cattell⁀, this Court.

The Court, vpon heareing the differrenc̃ betwixt Thomas Clarke & Mathew Fuller about a share, ordereth that the said Fuller shall deliũ the said Clarke the said share, because it appeareth by seũall testymonies that it is Clarks share; and the said Fuller to haue a warr̃nt to require Phillip Dellanoy to testyfye that he deliũed the said Fullers share, sent by him to Goodman Hill in the Bay, that the said Fuller may recouer the said share of him.

It is ordered, that Mr Jenney shall allow Raph Goarome ten bushells of Indian corne, at ijs & vjd, and the rest at iijs, & rye for xxs, for Tristram Clark, & that Tristrame is discharged for the two pigges.

Whereas Raph Goarume demaund⁀ of Mr John Comb a debt of three pound⁀ foure shillings and six pence, wch the said Combe acknowledgeth due, the said Gorame is content to deliuer foure or fiue bushells of wheate to the

1642.

5 April.
BRADFORD, Gou.

said Mʳ Combe, to sowe his ground wᵗʰ all this spring, so that hee may haue his said debt of 3ˡⁱ 4ˢ 6ᵈ payd him out of the crops, & so much wheat then againe also as now he lendꝭ. And the Court doth order, by both their consentꝭ, that the said crop shall remayne securitie to the said Gorame for his said debt vntill it be payd, wᵗʰ the wheat he now lends, and the rest or ouerpluꝭ to be the said Mʳ Combs.

Memorand : that Mʳ John Combe, for & in consideracōn of the sum of xijˡⁱ, and fourty shillings more in corne, payd him by Mʳ Wᵐ Thomas, hath, wᵗʰ and by the consent of Willm Launder, assigned & set ouer all the residue of his terme of yeares wᶜʰ he is to serue the said Mʳ Comb to be serued forth wᵗʰ the said Mʳ Willm Thomas ; and that the said Mʳ Thomas shall pay the said Launder six poundꝭ of the tenn menc̄ōned in his indenture, at thĕnd of his terme, in good cloaths, corne, or goates, according to his said indenture.

Jonathan Hatch, by the consent of the Court, is appoynted to dwell wᵗʰ Mʳ Steephen Hopkins, & the said Mʳ Hopkins to haue a speciall care of him.

18 April.
[*48.]

*Memorand, the xviijᵗʰ day of Aprill, 1642 : that Francis Billington and Christian, his wyfe, haue put Elizabeth, their daughter, apprentis to John Barnes and Mary, his wyfe, to dwell wᵗʰ them and to do their service vntill shee shall accomplish the age of twenty yeares, (shee being now seaven yeares of age the xᵗʰ of July next,) the said John Barnes & Mary, his wyfe, finding her meate, drink, & cloathes during the said terme.

Relesed.

John Stockbridg de Scituate, wheelwr̄t, ... xxˡⁱ.
Wᵐ Holmes, ... xˡⁱ.
₽ bona portu & comprend, &c.

---

3 May.
NEW PLYM.
[*49.]

*At a Court of Assistantꝭ held at Plym̃ afores ᵈ, the third of May, in the xviijᵗʰ Yeare of his Maᵗⁱᵉˢ now Raigne, of England, &c.

BEFORE Willm Bradford, gent̃, Goũ,   Willm Collyer,
Thomas Prence,   Miles Standish, &
Edward Winslow,   Edmond Freeman,
Gent̃, Assistantꝭ, &c.

CONCERNING the differrencᵉ betwixt Mʳ John Jenney, Samuell Stertevaunt, & Joseph Ramsden, about their corne in p̃tñshipp, the Court doth order, wᵗʰ consent of all p̃ties, that the fiue bushells and halfe of corne, wᶜʰ Mʳ Jenney should pay to the said Dotey for Thurston Clark, and also eight bushell wch the said Joseph Ramsden should pay the said Edward Dotey, shalbe payd to the said John Jenney, by the said Joseph, wch said fiue bushells & half and the said viij bushells do make vp the thirteene bushells & half wch Edward Dotey was to pay the said Samuell for his p̃t of the said cropp, and so the said Edward Dotey to be freed from any further incumbrance therein.

1642.
3 May.
BRADFORD, Goũ.

Mr Wilłm Collyer, Captaine Standish, & Jonathan Brewster are ordered by the Court to set the auncient bound⸨ right betwixt the lands of Mr Thomas Beesbeach and John Washbourne, and to require the help and knowledg̃ of any that can giue them information about the same.

In the suite com̃enced agst James Luxford for 5^{li} debt & 11^s 6^d charges, —

	li	s	d
Mr Prenc̃ hath had of Luxford in swyne, ...	03	00	00
of Mr Wilłam Hanbury, for Luxford,	00	19	04
of John Chaundlers debt, . . .	01	12	02
	05	11	06

There remaynes due to Luxford more by John Chaundler 16^s 11^d, wch Edward Dotey is to haue.

The said Mr Prence & Edward Dotey are to receiue the s̃d sums of John Chaundlor, vpon condic̃õn that if John Chaundlor can proue there is errour in this account betwixt him & Luxford, then the said Mr Prenc̃ & the said Dotey to repay so much againe to the said Chaundlor as shall manefestly appeare to be vnduly or vnjustly accounted.

---

*At the Gen^{r}all Court of o^r Sou^{r}aigne Lord, Charles, by the Grace of God King of England, Scotland, France, & Ireland, Defendor of the Fayth, &c., held at Plym̃, the vijth of June, in the xviijth Yeare of his said Ma^{ts} now Raigne, of England, &c.

7 June.
NEW PLYM.
[*51.]

BEFORE Wm Bradford, gent̃, Goũ,   Tymothy Hatherly,
Edward Winslow,   John Browne,
Thom̃ Prence,   Wilłm Thomas, &
Wilłm Collyor,   Edmond Freeman,
Gent̃, Assistant⸨, &c̃.

1642.

7 June.
BRADFORD,
Goũ.

M͞ʀ WILLIAM BRADFORD sworne Goũ for this ensuing yeare.

Mʳ Edward Winslow,
Mʳ Thomas Prence,
Mʳ Willm Collyer,
Mʳ Tymothy Hatherley, } sworne Assistantꝭ for this ensuing yeare.
Mʳ John Browne,
Mʳ Wᵐ Thomas,
Mʳ Edmond Freeman,

The Comittees of the seũall Townes.

Plymouth, . . . { Mʳ John Atwood, Mʳ John Done, Mʳ Wᵐ Paddy, John Cooke.

Duxborrow, . . . { Mʳ John Alden, Jonathan Brewster.

Scituate, ... { Edmond Eddenden, } Humfrey Turner. Georg̃ Kennerick.

Sandwich, . . . { Richard Bourne, } Thom̃ Burges, Willm Newland, } Georg̃ Allen.

Taunton, ... { John Strong, John Parker.

Barnestable, . . . { Mʳ James Cudworth, Mʳ Thom̃ Dimmack, Anthony Annable.

Yarmouth, . . . { Mʳ John Crowe, Richard Hore.

Marshfeild, . . . { Mʳ Thom̃ Bourne, Kenelme Winslowe.

Mʳ John Feake, of Sandwich, & Emanuel White, of Yarmouth, admitted freemen this Court, & sworne.

[*52.]

*Constables.

Surveyors.

Plymouth, Giles Rickett, sworne. . { Mʳ Wᵐ Hanbury, Francꝭ Cooke, James Cole, & Thomas Clarke.

Duxborrow, Edmond Hawes, sworne.
Scittuate, Josias Checkett, sworne.
Sandwich, Michaell Turner, sworne.
Taunton, Willm Parker.
Barnestable, Thomas Lathrope, sworne.

COURT ORDERS.

1642.
7 June.
BRADFORD, Gov.

Yarmouth, Emanuel White, sworne. Surveyors. { Wᵐ Palm̄, & Gabriell Wheilden.

Marshfeild, Francis West, sworne.

The Grand Inquest.

John Dunhame, Señ,
John Winslowe,
Richard Church,
John Willis,
Richard Sparrow,
Thomas Rawline,
Thomas Ensigne,
Edward Case,
Humfrey Turner,
Mʳ Henry Feake,
} sworne. {
John Winge,
Walter Deane,
Henry Ewell,
James Mathews,
Josias Winslowe,
Samuell Nash,
Mʳ Anthony Thacher,
Henry Bourne,
Steuen Tracy,
Xp̄ofer Waddesworth.

Thomas Starr, of Yarmouth, chirurḡ, acknowledgth to owe yᵉ King, ... } xlˡⁱ. *Released.*

Heugh Tilly, of the same, planter, ... xlˡⁱ.

The condiçōn, that the said Thomas Starr shalbe appeare at the next Genʳall Court of our soūaigne lord the Kinge, to be held at Plym̄, and answere to all such matters as on his said Maᵗˢ behalf shalbe objected agˢᵗ him, & in the meane season be of the good behaū towardꝭ oʳ soūaigne lord the King and all his leigh people, and not dep̄t the Court wᵗʰout lycence, and forbeare comeing to the townes meetings during the pleasure of the Court, that then, &c̄.

Willm Nicholson, of Yarmouth, plant̄, oweth the King, &c̄, xlˡⁱ. *Released.*

Robte Dennis, of the same, carpenter, ... xlˡⁱ.

The same condiçōn as aboue, &c̄, p̄ bona port̄.

Josuah Barnes, of Yarmouth, plant̄, oweth the King, . . . xlˡⁱ. *Released.*

Mʳ Thomas Howes, of the same, planter, &c̄, ... xlˡⁱ.

The same condiçōn as abousd, &c̄, p̄ bona port̄.

*It is ordered by the Court, that there be convenyent gates made vpon all heigh wayes passable for cart & horse in all such places where they are needfull; and that Georḡ Pollerd shall make two competent gates vpon Robte Mendames land, and pay himself out of the rents for the said two gates. [*53.]

It is ordered, that the towne of Duxborrow shall giue John Rowe satisfacc̄ōn by land or otherwise for the water ouerflowing his house and ground.

1 6 4 2.

7 June.
BRADFORD,
Goū.

It is ordered, that Mr Tymothy Hatherly shall haue power to administer a constables oath to Henry Merriott, of Scittuate, to serue the office of a constable wthin that ward of Scittuate; but this to be no p̃sident for any other in like kynd.

Duxborrow hath six weeks to make a pound in, or els̃ to pay 5^{li}.

Mr Gray committed to prison for sweareing.

Mr Hatherley, Mr Freeman, and Captaine Standish are requested to view the land(wch Barnestable men desire, & to sett it forth for them, so that they doe not entrench vpon either plantac̃ōns, or be a place fitt to be a plantac̃ōn of itself, and to see that there be a convenyent farme & meddowing to it reserued for publike vse.

5^s.

Mr Thomas Beesbeach, for dep̃ting the Court wthout lycence, being warned to serue on the grand inquest, is fined v^s.

40^s payd to
Mr Holmes.

Joseph Halloway, for breakeing the Kings peace, in strikeing Peter Handbury, for wch he is indicted, is fyned xl^s.

Web Adey committed to prison vpon the p̃sentment against him.

John Casley, of Barnestable, & Alis, his wyfe, for fornicac̃ōn before marriage, is censured, the said John to be whipt, and Alis, his wyfe, to sit in the stocks whilst her husband is in whipping; wch was accordingly executed.

[*54.]

*The p̃posic̃ōn of the Inhabitant(of Marshfeild about their Bounds.

That the bounds of Marshfeild, from Greens Harbour Fresh, be from thence to the trey called Pooles, p̃uided it come not vpon any part of Mr Thomas p̃ticuler lands, and from Pooles by a line to the water side, takeing onely the lands of John Rowse. That the westerly bounds of Marshfeild, form̃ly set by Captaine Standish, Mr Alden, Jonathan Brewster, Willm Bassett, & Mr Edward Winslow, shalbe from a great rock flatt on the topp, norwest to the south riuer, & from thence to the leiftennant(ground by a straight line, prouided that Mr Starr, Job Cole, Daniell Cole, Willm Bassett, John Mynard, &c̃, shall not by Marshfeild men be rated or assessed to any publike charges vntill they or any of them there come to inhabite and do close wth Marshfeild men.

This being the desire & p̃posic̃ōn of Marshfeild men, the Court doth order that Mr Thomas Prence, Mr Brewster, Mr Paddy, and John Cooke to treate wth Duxborrow men about their desire & p̃posic̃ōn, and to sett their bounds betwixt them; and what they shall doe therein all parties to rest fully satisfyed therewth.

The towne of Yarmouth p̃sented for want of a pound.

Mr Thomas Burne had judgment agst John Chaundler for seauen shillings and six pence.

COURT ORDERS. 43

*At a Court of Assistant£ held the second Day of August, in the xviij[th] Yeare of his said Ma[ts] now Raigne, of England, &c.

BEFORE Wilłm Bradford, genť, Goů,   John Browne,
Thomas Prence,   Wilłm Thomas, &
Wilłm Collyer,   Edmond Freeman,
Tymothy Hatherley,
        Genť, Assistant£, &ĉ.

2 August.
NEW PLYM.
BRADFORD,
Goů.
[*55.]

THERE was a request made by some, to sit down at Sickuncke, of Hinghame. Theire names are these : John Porter, Thomas Lorine, Steephen Payne, Nicholas Baker.

It is ordered, that warrňt be sent to fetch John Hasell, that liues at Sickuncke, to answere his contempt£ at the Genłall Court; w[ch] was made & signed by all the Assistant£ p̃sent.

Ephraim Tinckhame is to haue xxv acrees of land£, due for his service by indenture. Affirmed by M[r] Hatherley & John Winslowe, the indenture being lost.

Execuc̃on graunted John Joyce ag[st] Walter Deuell.

The differrenc£ betwixt Roƀte Caruer & Wilłm Hiller, about the payment of the corne, the Court doth order that the corne shalbe valued by two men chosen by either p̃t; & if they cannot agree, then they two to choose a third man to apprise yt as corne will then passe when it is payable.

A warrant graunted ag[st] Walter Deuell, at Captaine Standish suite, to giue him securitie to pforme his worke he is payd for already.

Francis Sprague, of Duxborrow, inholder, doth acknowledg̃ to owe the Kinge, &ĉ, ... } c[li].   Respited to the next Court.

Jonathan Brewster, of the same, plant̃, ... l[li].   Respited to the next Court.

The condic̃on, that if the said Francis Sprague do psonally appeare at the next Genłall Court of our sofiaigne lord the King, to answere to all such matters as shalbe objected against him for selling a fouleing peece to an Indian, and abide the further order of the Court, and not dep̃te the same w[th]out lycence; that then, &ĉ.

Released
June 3[d], 1647.

1642.
7 September.
NEW PLYM.
BRADFORD, Goũ.
[*61.]

*At a Gen'all Court of o' Sou'aigne Lord, Charles, by the Grace of God of England, Scotland, France, and Ireland King, Defend' of the Fayth, &c, held at Plymñ afores'd, the vij'th Septemb'r, in the xviij'th Yeare of his said Ma'ts now Raigne.

BEFORE Willm Bradford, gent, Goũ, John Browne,
  Thom Prence, Edmond Freeman, &
  Willm Collyer, Willm Thomas,
  Tymothy Hatherly,
    Gent, Assistants, &c.

THE differrenc betwixt M'r Willm Hanbury and Abraham Perse, about the luging and killing M'r Hanburies swine, are by mutuall consent referred to be ordered and ended betwixt them, and all things concerning the same, by M'r Willm Paddy and John Howland for the sd M'r Hanbury, and Stephen Tracy and John Cooke the yeong'r for the sd Pearse; and if they cannot agree, then the foure to choose a fift man, and so to end the same.

In the controũsie betwixt Samuell Hinckley and M'r Joseph Hull, about the lands the said Hinckley bought of the said Hull in Barnestable, it is ordered, by the consent of both pties and by the towne of Barnestable, being referred to the bench, that the said M'r Hull, according to his owne pffer, shall abate fourty shillings of that the said Samuell Hinckley should haue payd him for the said land, and that the towne of Barnestable shall returne thone halfe of the lands they tooke away from the said Samuell Hinckley to him againe, and so a fynall end to be of all suits & controũsies about the same.

Thomas Graunger, late servant to Loue Brewster, of Duxborrow, was this Court indicted for buggery w'th a mare, a cowe, two goats, diuers sheepe, two calues, and a turkey, and was found guilty, and receiued sentence of death by hanging vntill he was dead.

John Hasell, of Seacuncke, acknowledgeth himself to owe the } xl'li.
 King . . . .
Kenelme Winslowe, of Marshfeild, plant, ... xx'li.
Released. Edward Dotey, of Plymñ, plant, ... xx'li.

The condic̃on, that if the said John Hasell shall psonally appeare at the next Court of o'r soũaigne lord the King, to be holden at Plymñ in Nouember next, and answere to all such matters as in his said ma'ts name shalbe objected against him, and abide the further order of the Court, and not dept the same w'thout lycence; that then, &c.

COURT ORDERS.

John Stockbridg̃, of Scittuate, wheelewright, for his contemptuous speeches against the goũment, proued by oath against him, is fyned v^{li}. Remitted the sum of xl^s.

*Elisha Beesbeach, of Scittuate, planter, acknowledgeth to the King, &c̃, ... } xx^{li}.

The condic̃õn, &c̃, that if the said Elisha Beesbeach do psonally appeare at the next Court of o^r soũaigne lord the King, to be held at Plym̃ the first Tewsday in Nouember next, to answere to all such matters as on his said ma^{ties} behalf shalbe objected against him concerning a libell made agst Mr Charles Chauncey, and abide the further order of the Court, and not dep̃t the same wthout licence; that then, &c̃.

It is ordered by the Court, that the rates of the townes in this goũment for publike charges, for payment of the officers, shalbe made this yeare as they were the last yeare, and to be brought in to the milners of eich plantac̃õn by the first of Decemb^r next, and to be taken as corne is sold at Plym̃.

Mr Willm Hanbury, Thomas Southwood, John Burne, Robte Waterman, and Mathew Fuller ppounded to be freemen the next Court. James Mathewes, John Tisdall.

1642.
7 September.
BRADFORD,
Goũ.
[*62.]
Released.

At a Gen^{r}all Court of our Sou^{r}aigne Lord the King, held at Plym̃ the xxvijth of Septemb^r, in the xviijth Yeare of his said Ma^{ts} now Raigne, of England, &c.

27 September.
NEW PLYM.
[*63.]

BEFOR Willm Bradford, genṫ, Goũ,	Tymothy Hatherley,
Edward Winslow,	Willm Thomas, &
Thom̃ Prence,	Edward Freeman,

Genṫ, Assistantṫ, &c̃; & Mr Browne was there the first day.

THIS Court was occationed by the Indians to puide forces against them for an offensiue & defensiue warr; and though all the inhits were warned, yet they appeared by their seũall deputies, as they had liberty to doe.

For Plymouth, ... {
Mr John Atwood,
Mr John Jenney,
Mr Wm Paddy,
Mr John Done,
John Cooke,
Manasseth Kempton,
John Dunhame.

1642.

27 September.
BRADFORD,
Goū.

For Duxborrow, ...
- Capt Miles Standish,
- Mr John Alden,
- Johathan Brewster,
- Mr Comfort Starr,
- Mr Wm Wetherrell,
- Willm Basset,
- Christopher Waddesworth,
- Georg̃ Soule.

For Scittuate, ...
- Mr Willm Vassell,
- Willm Hatch,
- Thom̃ Rauline.

For Sandwich, ...
- Mr Edward Dillingham,
- Richard Chadwell.

For Taunton, ...
- Capt Willm Poole,
- Henry Andrewes.

For Barnestable, ...
- Anthony Annable,
- John Cooper.

For Yarmouth, ... Willm Palmer.

For Marshfeild, ...
- Mr Nathaniell Thomas,
- Kenelme Winslowe.

The Court, being mett together, & haueing intelligence of a gen̄all conspiracy intended by the natiues to cutt of all the English in this land, tooke the same into serious consideracõn, and duly waying such informacõns wch they haue receiued, together wth the circumstanc℮ concurring there wthall, do adjudge it absolutely needfull & requisite to make speedy p̄paracõn throughout the gouerment for a defensiue and offensiue warr against them, as if they were p̄sently to be sent forth.

2. It is agreed and concluded, that Mr Edward Winslow, Mr Tymothy Hatherley, & Captaine Miles Standish shalbe sent into the Bay to, & haue power to agitate and conclude wth them for a p̄sent combinacõn wth them in he p̄sent warrs, and to treate wth them about a further combinacõn or league, but not to conclud that wthout consent of the Court here.

Their com̃ission is as followeth : —

Mr Edward Winslow, Mr Tymothy Hatherley, and Captaine Miles Standish are deputed and authorized by the Gen̄all Court, this day, to treate and conclude wth such com̃issioners as the Goūnor & Court of Massachusett℮ shall appoynt for that purpose, vpon such heads & p̄posicõns as the Lord shall direct them for our combineing together mutually in a defensiue and

COURT ORDERS. 47

offensiue warr for our p̱sent defence against the intended surprisall of the
natiues; and also to treate & conferr wth them about a further combinaĉŏn &
league to be concluded betwixt vs for future tymes, & to certyfy this Court of
the head(l thereof, that vpon our approbaĉŏn of the same they may be confirmed by a Gen̈all Court.

1642.
27 September.
BRADFORD,
Go⁰.

*It is also agreed & concluded, that Captaine Miles Standish shall goe
captaine to lead those forces that shalbe sent forth; and that Mr Thomas
Prence shall go wth him, to be his counsell and advise in the warrs, &ĉ; and
that Wil̃m Palmer shalbe leiftennant, and Peregrine White the auncient
bearrer.

[*64.]

It is agreed vpon & concluded, that the charges for & about y^e souldiers
wch are to be sent forth shalbe payd by euery towneship according to their
rates to the publike charges, viz$^{\beta}$: —

	li	s	d			
Plym̃,	05	05	00	Barnestable,	02 : 10 : 00
Duxbor̃,	03	10	00	Yarmŏ,	02 : 10 : 00
Scittuat,	04	00	00	Taunton,	02 : 10 : 00
Sandwood,	03	00	00	Marshfeild,	02 : 00 : 00

And so according to this pporĉŏn, for a greater or lesser sum.

The Counsell of Warr.

The Gouern^r,
Mr Edward Winslow,
Mr Thom̃ Prence,
Mr Wm Collyer,
Mr Tymothy Hatherley,
Mr John Browne,

Mr Wm Thomas,
Mr Edm̃ Freeman,
Mr Wm Vassell,
Capt̃ Standish,
Mr Thom̃ Dimmack,
Mr Anthoñ Thacher.

If any of these be absent when they should come together, the townes
where such dwell are to send other sufficient men in their stead.

Whereas the towneshipps wthin the goũment are maruelously vnprouided
of leade and powder to secure our p̱sent dangers, and that to supply the extreame wants thereof, and to p̱cure pōder and lead, no course can be found out
but by sale of some moose skins and other skins out of the gouerment, w^{ch}
those that hold the trade are p̱hibited to doe by a certaine clause in their graunt,
the Court, takeing the same into serious consideraĉŏn, and fynding the danger
to be so great, and euery mans life in such hassard, the Court doth, vpon due
caution, order, that no advantage shalbe taken against the said p̱tners of the
trade for the p̱cureing of leade and pōder for p̱sent supply by sale of moose

1642.
27 September.
BRADFORD,
Gov.

skins or other skins out of the goũment. And the Court doth further order, that the p̃tners shall forthw^th do the same to p̄cure these wants supplyed, p̄uided that the townes bring in corne for them, to be delifted vpon the receipt of the pŏd^r & lead, and that when pŏd^r & lead is p̄cured, those townes shalbe first p̄uided that are in greatest wantɫ.

17 October.
[*65.]

*At a townes meeting, held the xvij^th of Octob^r, 1642, held before Mr Willm Bradford, Mr Thomas Prence, Mr John Jenney, Mr Willm Paddy, John Winslowe, & John Cooke, Junr, appoynted to graunt lands this day for the towne of Plymouth.

Andrew Ringe is graunted foure acrees of vpland at the vpper end of his, and adjoyneing to it, wth as much convenyency as may be.

Nathaniell Sowther, Mr Willm Hanbury, Richard Sparrow, and Samuell Hicks are graunted foure acrees a peece of vpland lying at the head of Mr Hicks feild, p̄uided that Mr Hanbury and Samuell Hicks do keepe their residency in the towne, or els̃ to be voyd.

Mr John Groome is graunted foure acrees there also, if it be there to be had, when thother are layd forth.

John Heyward is graunted a garden place next Andrew Ringe, and tenn acrees of vpland at the Fresh Lake by the fishing poynt.

Mr John Groome is graunted the garden place next to his vpon condiĉõn. that he build a dwelling house vpon it, or els̃, if another do it before, then they to haue it; but for the p̃sent cropp Richard Knowles to haue it, except John Groome compound wth him for it.

Mathew Fuller is graunted tenn acres of vpland, by Thurston Clarks.

James Cole is graunted an enlargement at the head of his lott, to be set forth vpon view.

Mr Prence, Mr Paddy, Mr Done, Mr Jenney, & Josuah Pratt are appoynted to lay forth all the landɫ aboue graunted.

Ephraim Tinckhame is graunted tenn acrees of vpland by Thurston Clarkɫ, and to be layd forth by those aboue named, and the rest of his landɫ to be layd forth in some other place.

James Hurst, John Winslow, & Joshua Pratt appoynted to lay forth Mr Groomes landɫ, and those graunted at Thurston Clarks lott.

Gyles Rickett is graunted six acrees of meddow and fifty acrees of vpland beyond Mountɫ Hill Playne, the place where he desireth.

[*66.]

*Whereas fourescore acrees of vpland are form̃ly graunted to Edward Banges at Warrens Wells, he now desireing to haue some landɫ neere his house, it is graunted that he shall looke out a p̃cell of landɫ, wch vpon view

COURT ORDERS.

shalbe layd forth for him, and to be deducted out of the 80 acrees he should haue at Warrens Wells.

1642.

These seuall psons following are graunted these seuall pporcons of meddow at the North Meddow by Joanes Riuer, of that wch remaynes : —

17 October.
BRADFORD, Goũ.

For the church fiue acrees next to wch is layd forth.

Mr Thomas Prence,
Mr Wm Hanbury,
John Cooke, Junr,
Mr John Howland,
Francis Cooke,
} to eich of them six acrees a peece, if it be there to be had.

Thomas Southwood,
Thomas Cushman,
Nathaniell Morton,
John Shawe,
John Winslow,
} to eich of them foure acrees a peece, if it be there to be had.

And that they appoynt a convenyent tyme to lay it forth, and agree amongst themselues, wth Josuah to do it.

**At a Court of Assistant*℮ held at Plym̃ afores^d, the first Day of Novemb^r, in the xviij^th Yeare of the now Raigne of o^r Sou^r-aigne Lord, Charles, by the Grace of God King of England, &c.*

1 November.
NEW PLYM.
[*67.]

BEFORE Wm Bradford, gent̃, Goũ,   Willm Collyer,
         Edward Winslow,   John Browne, &
         Thomas Prence,   Edmond Freeman,
               Gentlemẽ, Assistant℮, &c̃.

JOHN HASSELL affirmeth that Vssamequine chose out x fathome of beads at Mr Williams, and put them in a baskett, and affirmed that he was fully satisfyed therew^th for his land℮ at Seacunck, but he stood vpon it that he would haue a coat more, & left the bead℮ wth Mr Williams, & willed him to keepe them vntill Mr Hubberd came vp.

He affirmed the bound℮ were to Redstone Hill, viij miles into the land, & to Annawamscoate, vij miles downe the water.

1642.
1 November.
BRADFORD,
Goū.

John Hassell doth acknowledḡ himself to owe the King, to be levyed of his landℯ, goodℯ, & cattels, &ͨ, if he fayle in the condiͨōn following, &ͨ, ... } xx^li.

The condiͨōn, that if the said John Hassell shall either take the oath of allegiance to the King, & fidelitie to the goṽment, betwixt this and March Court next, or elṣ remoue his dwelling from Seacunck ; that then, &ͨ.

1642-3.
3 January.
NEW PLYM.
[*69.]

*At a Court of Assistantℯ holden at Plymͥ, the third Day of Januar., in the xviij^th Yeare of his Ma^ts now Raigne, of England, &c.

BEFORE Willͬm Bradford, genͭ, Goū,   Thomas Prence, &
         Edward Winslow,   Willͬm Collyer,
              Genͭ, Assisͭ, &ͨ.

THE controûsy betwixt Mrs Bridgitt Fuller & Josias Winslow about a boare resteth for want of better euedence.

In the differrence betwixt Mr Comfort Starr & Thomas Clark, for tenn shillings remayneing of xx^li x^s for a cowe, the Court doth order that the said Thomas Clark shall pay the said Comfort Starr the said x^s.

Thomas Clark doth enter his trauerse to the judgment at the next Geñall Court.

Execuͨōn is graunted to Richard Church, ag^st Mathew Fuller for xx^s damͫ, and the charges of the suite.

Execuͨōn is graunted to John Shawe ag^st John Barnes, for Richard Derby, &ͨ.

Whereas Richard Willis is endebted vnto Richard Derby the sum of fourty shillings for a bedd, the which bed not being seene by the said Willis, but taken vpon the said Derbys word, and it now appeareing, by the oath of Willͬm Nelson, that the said bed was not answerable to that goodness the said Derby affirmed it to be of, nor of such waight by sixteene pounds as he affirmed also it was, and that the tick of the said bed was full of patches, for wch the said Willis was to haue payd three pounds fiue shillings, whereof xxv^s is payd, — now, the Court doth order that twenty shillings more shalbe payd in full satisfacͨōn for it, & no more.

Lͬres of administraͨōn are graunted to Mr Tymothy Hatherly & Edward

COURT ORDERS.

Eddenden, of the goods & chattells of Thomas Granger, of Scituate, in the behalf of his wyfe & children, and to pay debts, as farr as it will goe, & to puide for her & her children.
Mr Holmes account on thother side.

1642-3.
3 January.
BRADFORD, Gofi.

*Mr John Holmes, the Messengers Account this Court. [*70.]

	li	s	d
Remayneing for the first yeares wages,	1	06	08
For the second yeare,	0	10	00
For the third yeare,	1	05	02
For his goinge to Taunton,	1	00	00
For going to Sandwich,	0	10	00
For whipping 3 malefactors, &c̃,	1	02	06
For two bushells of corne to the prison,	0	06	00
For going to Scittuate,	0	10	00
For a latch for the prison doore,	0	00	06
For x weeks dyett for Granger,	1	00	00
For executing Granger and viij beast𝓔,	2	10	00
Summ total,	10	00	08
P^d hereof by the company out of the trade of Kenebeck,	01	03	00
P^d to him by Mr Hanbury,	01	00	00

---

*At a ‡Generall‡ Court of Assistant𝓔 holden the vjth of March, in the xviijth Yeare of the now Raigne of o^r Sou'aigne Lord, Charls, King of England, &c.

6 March.
NEW PLYM.
[*71.]

BEFORE Willm Bradford, gentl̃e, Gofi,   Thomas Prence, &
Edward Winslow,   Willm Collyer,
Gent̃, Assist̃, &c̃.

IT is ordered by the Court, that Willm Spooner shall pay for the debt of Mr Combe, his master, vnto Mr Wm Hanbury, the sum of x^s, wch was attached in Mr Prenc𝓔 hand, wch Mr Prence did acquit to Mr Combe ; but the debt remayneing due to Mr Hanbury as aforcẽd, the said Spooner shall pay it to Mr Hanbury by a bushell of wheate, & a bushell & a half of barley.

It is also ordered by the Court, that Mr John Holmes shall haue the saw

1642-3.
6 March.
BRADFORD, Goũ.

he bought of Walter Deuell from Daniell Cole, paying him iiij^s remayning due for it.

It is ordered, that Edward Dotey shall pay fiue bushells of Indian to Mr Hanbury, & Mr Hanbury to pay three bushells of wheat to John Jordaine, & what more it shall want of xiiij^s vij^d.

---

7 March.
NEW PLYM.
[*73.]

At the Gen^{r}all Court of our Sou^{r}aigne Lord, Charles, by the Grace of God King of England, Scotland, Franc, & Ireland, Defendor of the Fayth, &c., holden at Plym̃ afores^d, the vijth of March, in the xviijth Yeare of his Ma^{ts} now Raigne, &c.

BEFORE Willm Bradford, gent̃, Goũ,   Tymothy Hatherly,
Edward Winslow,   John Browne,
Thomas Prence,   Edmond Freeman, &
Willm Collyer,   Wm Thomas,
Gent̃, Assistantẽ, &c̃.

MR WILL̃M BRADFORD elected Gouernor.

Mr Edward Winslow,
Mr Thomas Prence,
Mr Willm Collyer,
Mr Tymothy Hatherley,   } elected Assistantẽ.
Mr John Browne,
Mr Edmond Freeman,
Mr Willm Thomas,

Mr Willm Hanbury, Thomas Southwood, James Mathews, Robte Waterman, & John Tisdall admitted freemen this Court, & are sworne.

Robte Carver, of Marshfeild, John Russell, Edward Sturges, Richard Prichard, Willm Holloway, Georg̃ Hall, Richard Williams, & Willm Haiston ppounded to take vp their freedome the next Court.

Vpon the peticõn of John Washburne, it is ordered by the Court, that Mr Edward Winslow, Captaine Miles Standish, Mr John Alden, & Jonathan Brewster shall view the bounds betwixt Mr Thomas Besbeech & the said John Washbourne, and wth the help of Mr Willm Vassells instrument, according to their best informacõn & judgment, set the bounds of their lands betwixt them; and what bounds they shall sett shall so remayne ppetually, wthout any alteracõn.

*It is ordered, that a warrant shalbe directed to the constable of Yarmouth, to app̄hend Mr Joseph Hull, (if he do either exercise the ministery amongst them or administer the seales,) to bring him before the next majestrate, to fynd sufficient sureties for his app̄arance the next Geñall Court, to answere his doings, (beiñ an excom̄unicant.

1642-3.
7 March.
BRADFORD, Gov.
[*74.]

Constables for eich Towne, & Surveyrs of the Wayes.

Plymouth, . .
- John Finney, constab̄,
- John Dunham, Richard Sparrow, ⎫
- Franc̄ Cooke, & Richard Church, ⎬ grand jury.
- John Barnes, Thom̄ Southwood, ⎫
- for the towne,
- Thom̄ Clark for the Eele Riuer, & ⎬ surveyors.
- John Shaw for Jones Riuer, ⎭

Duxborrow, . .
- Thom̄ Bonney, constable.
- Loue Brewster & Georḡ Soule, grand jury men.

Scittuate, . . .
- John Stockbridḡ & Rob̄te Steedson, constā.
- Humfrey Turner & Thom̄ King, grand jury men.
- Thomas Rauline & Henry Merrict, surveyors.

Sandwich, . . .
- Georḡ Knott, constab̄,
- James Skiffe & Richard Chadwell, grand jury m̄.

Taunton, . . .
- Willm Parker, const̄,
- Edward Case, grand jury man.

Barnestable, . .
- James Hamlen, const̄,
- Isaack Wells, Abraham Blush, grand jur̄.

Yarmouth, . .
- Emanuell White, const̄,
- Willm Lumpkin, grand jur̄,
- Gyles Hopkins, Andrew Hellot, Juñ, surveyrs.

Marshfeild, . .
- John Russell, constā,
- Rob̄te Waterman, Rob̄te Caruer, grand jur̄.

Mr Edward Winslow & Mr Willm Collyer are elected by the Court to go to treate wth Massachusett Bay, &c̄, about ye combynac̄ōn.

Joseph Rogers is graunted the p̄cell of meddowing containeing 4 or 5 acrees lying aboue Massachusett Path, about two miles from Mr Bradfords farme.

Lr̄es of administrac̄ōn are graunted to Joane Swyft, of Sandwich, to administer vpon her husband estate, and to pay the debts as farr as the estate will amount vnto, by equall p̄porc̄ōns, and is bound to the Gou & Assistant to do it, & Daniell Wing wth her.

1642-3.

7 March.
BRADFORD,
Gov.
[*75.]

Raph Chapman is graunted a p̄cell of land lying at Namassacuset, to that he hath bought of Peeter Collymer there.

*Nathaniell Sowther is graunted a farme land of 200 acrees of vpland, wth competent meddowing to it, in some convenyent place, so that it do not much p̄judice a plantacon.

Mr Wil̄m Bradford is granted liberty to seek forth a place for to place his children vpon, and when the Court doth know it, to be confirmed to him.

Resolued White is graunted all that marsh and meddow land that lyeth w^thin the coue wch is at the west end of the land(̨ of Mr Wil̄m Vassell, called the West New Land, by the North Riuer; that is to say, from a marked tree that is on thother side of the coue, ouer against the said West Newland, wch tree standeth vpon the northermost poynt of the vpland there, vpwards to the head of the coue, so farr as there is any marsh or meddow, and so on both sides of the creeke wch runneth vp the coue, excepting all that marsh & meddow that was formerly graunted to the said Wil̄m Vassell.

It is ordered by the Court, that the bounds of Scittuate towneship, on the westerly side of the said towne, shalbe vp the Indian Head Riuer to the pond wch is the head of the said riuer, and from thence to Accord Pond, and from thence to the sea by the lyne that is the bound betwixt Massachusetts & Plymouth.

It is concluded vpon by the Court, that the northerly bound(̨ of Marshfeild shalbe from the rock that is flatt on the topp to the North Riuer by a norwest lyne from Greens Harbour Fresh to the tree called Pooles, & to take in Edward Bumpass land(̨. Puided that Duxborrow haue enlargement beyond Massachusetts Payth when they haue view̄d it.

[*76.]

*It is ordered by the Court, that Mr Wil̄m Vassell shalbe allowed to take for setting ouer the North Riuer man & beasts as much as is to be payd at the old ferry place on the North Riuer.

John Barker, of the North Riuer, is fyned for his misdemean^r v^s.

Rob̄te Barker, of the same, for his misdemean^r, is fynd x^s.

Ephraim Kempton, of Scituate, Seni^r, for his misdemean^r in vncleane speeches & carriages, is censured as followeth, viz(̨: for his miscarriage in words to Mr Hatherley, a ma^trate, is fyned xx^s.

And for his other laciuious speeches & misbehau, to sit in the stocks during such tyme as shalbe thought meete by the Court, wch was ymmediately donn vpon him.

11 March.

The xj^th March, 1642. Memorand: that Joane Swyft, administratrix of Wm Swyft, deceased, hath payd to John Barnes v^li iij^s & iiij^d vpon the administra̅c̅o̅n of her husband(̵ estate, yt amounting to pay eich of his creditors vj^s viij^d in the pound, so that there is more due vnto him vpon this payment x^s, his debt being xvij^{li} vj^s viij^d, and hath delifted vnto her her husband(̵ bills & writings for that money, ꝑuided that if there doe arise any more due vnto him, others being payd according to the like ꝑporc̅o̅n, tha'. he haue his ꝑporc̅o̅n as it will come to. 1642-3. 11 March. BRADFORD, Goꝟ.

---

*At a Court of Assistant(̵ holden ˄ Plym̃ aforesaid, the second of May, in the xixth Yeare of the now Raigne of o^r Sou'aigne Lord, Charles, by the Grace of God King of England, &c. 1643. 2 May. NEW PLYM. [*77.]

BEFORE Willm Bradford, genṯ, Goûn^r,   Wm Collyer,
         Edward Winslow,   John Browne, and
         Thomas Prence,   Willm Thomas,
               Gentlemẽ, Assistant(̵, &c̃.

IN the case betwixt Willm Newland, compl^{nt}, agst Mr Wm Thomas, deffen^t, for a debt of iiij^{li} x^s, wch he vndertooke to pay for the towne of Marshfeild, and whereas the Court is informed that Mr Thomas ꝑferreth the payment thereof in a cowe to Thomas Shillingsworth, for the said Wm Newlands use, the Court doth order, that Mr John Alden and John Winslowe shall indifferrently prize the said cowe accordingly as shee will passe betwixt man and man, and if the cowe shall come to more, that Thomas Shillingsworth shall satisfye Mr Thomas for yt, as the said arbitrators shall in equitie judḡ fitt, if the said Mr Thomas & the said Thom̃ Shillingsworth do not agree themselues.

It is ordered by the Court, first, conc̃neing Edward Manton, of Seacunck, whereas he challengeth his house lott vpon the neck at Seacunck to be xij acrees, as he sayth, the rest of the lots were at the first diuision, were, that if it be so, that then he haue his xij acrees accordingly there; but if it were but six acrees to a house lott, then he to haue no more, or els̃ valuable considerac̃o̅n for his labours, according to Mr Winslowes agreement wth him, whether it be six or twelue, and a lott els̃where; and for Roɓte Morris, that hee haue the six acrees his house stands vpon, and six acrees els̃where in some convenyent place, for the six acrees he hath cleared on Watchymoquett side, and to haue as much donn vpon it as is vpon that on Watcheymoquett side, and for other lands that they shall haue an equall ꝑporc̃o̅n wth the rest there

56   PLYMOUTH COLONY RECORDS.

1643.   when the diuision of lands are there made; and the Courte requesteth M{r}
2 May.   Browne to see the same pformed on their behalfe according to the same rule
BRADFORD, that the diuision is made by.
Gou.

---

6 June.   *At a Gen{r}all Court holden at Plymouth, aforesaid, the vj{th} of June,
NEW PLYM.   in the xix{th} Yeare of the Raigne of o{r} Sou{r}aigne Lord, Charles,
[*79.]   by the Grace of God King of England, Scotland, Franc, &
          Ireland, Defend{r} of the Fayth, &c.

BEFORE Willm Bradford, gent, Gou,   Willm Collyer,
        Edward Winslow,   Tymothy Hatherley, &
        Thomas Prence,   Willm Thomas,
               Gentlemē, Assistantƺ, &d.

M{R} WILLIAM BRADFORD, Gou, sworne.

M{r} Edward Winslow,   M{r} Tymothy Hatherley, ⎫
M{r} Thom̃ Prence,   M{r} Willm Thomas,   ⎬ Assistantƺ, sworne.
M{r} W{m} Collyer,   ⎭

M{r} John Browne, ... ⎫
M{r} Edmond Freeman, ... ⎬ absent.

It is ordered and concluded by the Court, that M{r} Edward Winslow and M{r} Willm Collyer shall haue full com̃ission & authoryty, in name of the whole Court, to subscribe the articles of confederacōn (now read in the Court) w{th} the Massachusetts, Coñectacutt, and New Haven, and to subscribe the same in name of the whole, and to affix thereto the com̃on seale of the gou̅ment.

The Grand Inquest.

John Dunhame,   ⎫   Richard Chadwell,   ⎫
Gabriell Fallowell, │   Edward Case,   │
Richard Sparrow,   │   M{r} Thom̃ Gilbert,   │
Francis Cooke,   │   Isaack Wells,   │
Loue Brewster,   ⎬ sworne.   Abraham Blush,   ⎬ sworne.
Georḡ Soule,   │   Robte Waterman,   │
Humfrey Turner,   │   Job Cole,   │
Thomas Kinge,   │   Willm Lumpkine,   │
James Skiffe,   ⎭   W{m} Hoskine.   ⎭

COURT ORDERS.

M⁺ Thomas Gilbert ꝓpounded to be a freeman.

*Thomas Rauline, of Scituate, } are fyned xˢ a peece for non appar-
James Mathewes, of Yarmouth, } ance vpon the grand inquest.

1643.
6 June.
BRADFORD, Goū.

Comittees for eich Towne.   [*80.]

Plymouth,	Mʳ John Atwood, Mʳ John Done, Mʳ Willm Paddy, John Cooke, Junʳ.
Duxborrow,	Mʳ Thom̃ Besbeech, Willm Bassett.
Scittuate,	Thomas Chambers, Edmond Eddenden.
Sandwich,	Willm Newland, Mʳ Henry Feake.
Barnestable,	John Coop, Anthony Annable.
Yarmouth,	Mʳ Anthony Thacher, Mʳ Crowe, Sen.
Taunton,	Mʳ Henry Andrews, John Stronge.
Marshfeild,	Josias Winslow.

Mʳ John Howland, of Duxborrow, acknowledgeth to owe the King xx^{li}.   Released.
The condic̃on, that if John Walker, sonn in law of Arthur Howland, do psonally appeare before the Goū and Assistant(at the next Geñall Court, to be holden for this goūment, to answere to all such matters as shalbe objected against him on his s̃d ma^{ties} behalf, conc̃ning lying wth a bitch, and abide the further order of the Court, & not dep̃t the same wthout lycence; that then, &c̃.

*Whereas there is a suite depending this Court betwixt Mʳ John Jenney,   [*81.]
compl^{nt}, and Samuell Stertevaunt and Joseph Ramsden, deff^{nt}, by the consent of both p̃ties, it is referred to be decided & fully ended by the bench.

Whereas Mʳ Dauid Offley did by warrant sum̃on Thomas Payne, of Yarmouth, to appeare here to answere to a suite, and had neither entred action against him nor appoynted any to p̃secute for him, but onely to vex the said Payne, & put him to charges, the Court doth order and award the said Dauid Offley to pay the said Thomas Payne xij^{s}, according to the rate of ij^{s} p day for vj dayes.

VOL. II.   8

58   PLYMOUTH COLONY RECORDS.

1643.

6 June.
BRADFORD,
Goū.

Released.

M{r} Andrew Hellott, for the like, is awarded by the Court to pay M{r} John Alden and M{r} John Howland v{s} a peece.

Willm Halloway, of the South Riuer, plant, ... xx{li}.
W{m} Bassett, of Duxborrow, plant, ... x{li}.
Josias Winslowe, of Marshfeild, ... x{li}.

The condicon, that if the said Willm Halloway shall psonally appeare at the next Geñall Court to be holden for this goūment to answere to all such matters as on his sd ma{ties} behalf shalbe objected against him concerning eating of certaine stolne herins, and for suspicon of stealing some corne from Edward Brough, and abide the further order of the Court, and not dept the same w{th}out lycence; that then, &c.

Concerning the request of the inhab{its} of Taunton for wood and land{.}

The Court is willing to condiscend thus farr, viz{.} : that those lands w{ch} belong to Hesbone may be pcured them by all due meanes, and w{th} what convenyent speede may be; also, that the best & speedyest meanes be used to pcure them further enlargment on that side the mayne riuer to answere M{r} Hooks and M{r} Streets farmes on thother side; and whereas they desire the neck of Assonett for pastureing yeong beasts, it is also graunted by the Court, puided leaue can be pcured from Vssamequin, and all payments to be made by themselues, w{th}out any charg to the countrey; but whereas the tymber is requested below the said bounds, that we cannot graunt w{th}out great detryment to another plantacon intended belowe that.

The first Tewsday in July the ma{trats} meete, and eich towne are to send such men as they shall think fitt to joyne w{th} them to consult about a course to saueguard ourselues from surprisall by an enemie.

---

4 July.
NEW PLYM.
[*83.]

*.At a Court of Assistant{s} holden the fourth Day of July, in the xix{th} Yeare of the now Raigne of o{r} Sou{r}aigne Lord, Charles, by the Grace of God King of England, Scotland, France, & Ireland, Defendor of the Fayth, &c.

BEFORE Willm Bradford, gent, Goū,   Willm Collyer, and
        Edward Winslowe,   Willm Thomas,
        Gentlemē, Assist{s} of the said goūment, &c.

WHEREAS Joseph, the sonn of Francis Billington, according to the order of the Court, was by the towne of Plymouth placed w{th} John

COURT ORDERS. 59

Cooke the yonger, and hath since beene enveagled, and did oft depte his said masters service, the Court, vpon longe heareing of all that can be said or alleadged by his p̃ent£, doth order and appoynt that the said Joseph shalbe returned to his said master againe immediately, and shall so remaine wth him during his terme; and that if either the said Francis, or Christian, his wyfe, do recciue him, if he shall againe dept from his said master w^thout his lycence, that the said Francis, and Christian, his wyfe, shalbe sett in the stocks euery lecture day during the tyme thereof, as often as he or shee shall so receiue him, vntill the Court shall take a further course wth them; and also, that if Benjamin Eaton, now liueing wth the said Francis Billington, shall counsell, entice, or enveagle the said Joseph from his said master, that then he shall haue the same punishment wth his father and mother.

1643.
4 July.
BRADFORD,
GoÊ.

---

*At the Gen^rall Court of o^r Sou^raigne Lord the King, holden at Plym̃ the xxix^th of August, in the xix^th Yeare of the now Raigne of our Sou^raigne Lord, Charles, by the Grace of God King of England, Scotland, France, & Ireland, Defendor of the Fayth, &c.

29 August.
NEW PLYM.
[*85.]

BEFORE Willm Bradford, gent̃, GoÛ,   Tymothy Hatherley,
        Edward Winslow,   John Browne, &
        Willm Collyer,   Wm Thomas,
               Gentlemẽ, Assistant£, &ċ.

MR JOHN BROWNE, form̃ly elected an Assistant, was now sworne this Court.

The Com̃ittees of the seûall Townes.

Plym̃, ... {
  Mr John Atwood,
  Mr Willm Paddy,
  Mr John Done,
  John Cooke, Juñ.

Scittuate, ... {
  Georg̃ Kenr̃ick,
  John Williams.

Barnestable, ... {
  Henry Rowley,
  Henry Bourne.

Taunton, ... {
  Henry Andrewes,
  John Strong̃.

1643.
29 August.
BRADFORD, Gov.

Duxborrow, ... { Willm Bassett,
                    Edmond Chaundlor.

Sandwich, ... { Mr Henry Feake,
                    Willm Newland,

Yarmouth, ... { Willm Palmer,
                    Thomas Falland.

Marshfeild, ... { Kenelme Winslowe,
                     Robte Waterman.

Whereas ^ , an Indian of Barnestable, accedentally tooke a cowe of Thomas Hinckleys in a trapp, and lay so longe therein that the flesh was lost, onely the hide was saued; and yet because the Indian did so ingenuously & playnely confesse the fault, and made dilligent enquiry whose the cow was, the Court doth order the said Indian to pay the said Hinckley fifty shillings in full satisfacćōn, and do desire him to be therewth content.

Mowers that haue taken excessiue wages, viz\$, 3ˢ p diē, are to be p̄sented, if they make not restitućōn.

It is ordered, that the comissioners, viz\$, Mr Winslow & Mr Collyer, shall pcure a bushell and a half bushell, to be made by the Bay standard, that our measures made be all made according to them.

[*86.]   *Tyme is giuen to the townes of Barnestable and Yarmouth vntill the next Court to amend their heigh wayes, or els to be fyned vpon their p̄sentmentȩ.

Tyme is giuen to Mr Done and the rest of that jury to giue in their verdict for the heigh wayes to the Eele Riuer, &c, before the next Court, or els those to be fyned that refuse to come in to do yt.

Concerning the differrencȩ betwixt Mr Willm Thomas & Wm Newland, for the 4ˡⁱ 10ˢ he vndertooke to pay for the towne of Marshfeild to Richard Church and Robte Bartlett, it is ordered, by consent of both parties, that a cow of Mr Willm Thomas, now in the hands of Christopher Waddesworth, of Duxborrow, shalbe prized by John Winslow and another man, chosen by the sd Christopher, and be deliuered vnto Thomas Shillingsworth; and the said Thomas to giue a note vnder his hand to the said Mr Thomas to pay him so much more as the said cowe comes to, at or before March next; and so all differrencȩ betwixt the said Mr Thomas, Willm Newland, and Thomas Shillingsworth, to be fynally decided and ended.

The Court hath allowed & established a millitary discipline to be erected and mayntained by the townes of Plymouth, Duxborrow, & Marshfeild, and haue also heard their orders and established them, viz\$: —

COURT ORDERS.

Officers chosen by the Company & allowed by the Court.

That Miles Standish shalbe captaine for this yeare.
Nathaniell Thomas leiftennant for this yeare.
Nathaniell Sowther clark of the band or company.
Mathew Fuller, } serjeant℟.
Samuell Nash,

1643.
29 August.
BRADFORD,
Go℞.

Orders.

1. That the exercise be alwayes begunn and ended with prayer.

2. That there be one procured to preach them a sermon once a yeare, viz℟, at the elec℞on of their officers, and the first to begin in Septemb^r next.

3. That none shalbe receiued into this millitary company but such as are of honest and good report, & freemen, not servants, and shalbe well approued by the officers & the whole company, or the major part.

*4. That euery pson, after they haue recorded their names in the millitary list, shall from tyme to tyme be subject to the co$\bar{m}$aunds and orders of the officers of this millitary company in their places respectiuely. [*87.]

5. That euery delinquent shalbe punished at the discretion of the officers and the millitary company, or the major part thereof, according to the order of millitary discipline & nature of the offence.

6. That all talking, and not keepeing sylence, during the tyme of the exercise, jereing, quarrelling, fighting, dep̃ting collers wthout lycence, or dismission, &℞, or any other misdemeanor, so adjudged to be by the officers and the company, or the maj^r part thereof, to be accounted misdemeanors, to be punished as aforesaid.

7. That euery man that shalbe absent, except he be sick or some extraordinary occation or hand of God vpon him, shall pay for euery such default ij^s. And if he refuse to pay it vpon demaund, or wthin one month after, then to appeare before the company, & be distrayned for it & put out of the list.

8. That if any man shall, vpon the dayes appoynted, come wthout his armes or wth defectiue armes, shall forfaite for euery trayneing day as followeth : —

For want of a muskett or a peece approued, euery tyme, . . vj^d.
For want of a sword, ... vj^d.
For want of a rest, ... vj^d.
For want of bandelires, ... vj^d.

Six months tyme giuen to puide in.

9. That euery man that hath entred himself vpon the millitary list, and hath not sufficient armes, & doth not or will not pcure them wthin six monthes next ensuing, his name to be put out of the list.

1643.

29 August.
BRADFORD,
Gou̅.

10. That there be but xvj^{teene} pikes in the whole company, or, at the most, for the third p̃t, viz$\}$: viij for Plymouth, vj for Duxborrow, and two for Marshfeild.

11. That all that are or shalbe elected cheefe officers in this millitary company shalbe so titled and foreuer afterwards be so reputed, except he obtayne a heigher place.

12. That euery man entred into the millitary list shall pay vj^d the quarter to the vse of the company.

13. That when any of this millitary company shall dye or depart this life, the company, vpon warneing, shall come together wth their armes, and interr his corps as a souldier, and according to his place and quallytye.

[*88.]

*14. That all that shalbe admitted into this millitary company shall first take the oath of fydellyty, if they haue not taken it already, or els̃ be not admitted.

15. That all postures of pike and muskett, motions, rankes & files, &c̃, messengers, skirmishes, seiges, batteries, watches, sentinells, &c̃, bee always pformed according to true millitary discipline.

16. That all that will enter themselues vpon this company shalbe ppounded one day, receiued the next day, if they be approued.

The like liberty is graunted to the townes of Sandwich, Barnestable, and Yarmouth for the erecting of a millitary discipline amongst them, puided they be men of honest and good report and freemen.

Concerning the differrenc̃ betwixt Mr Hedg̃ and Richard Hore, of Yarmouth, for the meddow ground at Yarmouth, first giuen to the church there, the Court doth order that the said sixe acrees shall so remayne to the church according to the first graunt, and that Mr Hedg̃ may take his remedy against him or them that sould him the same, being form̃ly disposed of to the church as aforesaid.

Pposic̃õns this Court by the Com̃ittees for o^r Lawes.

That the Goũnor and Mr Prence at Plymouth, & Mr Collyer and whom he pleaseth wth him at Duxborrow, Mr Winslow & Mr Thomas at Marshfeild, do puse the lawes of this goũment, that such as are necessary may be established, such as are vnnecessary may be repealed, and such as are defectiue may be altered, and such as are wanting may be p̃pared, and penalties to be fixed to eich law as far as may be; that, vpon the approbac̃õn of them by the Court, they may be confirmed at the Geñall Court.

Woolues : a muster master spoken of.

COURT ORDERS.

At a Gen'all Court holden at Plymouth afores'd, the xth Day of October, in the xixth Yeare of the now Raigne of o^r Sou'aigne Lord, Charles, by the Grace of God King of England, &c.

1643.
10 October.
NEW PLYM.
BRADFORD, Goũ.
[*89ᵃ.]

BEFORE Willm Bradford, genṯ, Goũ,   John Browne,
Edward Winslow,   Willm Thomas, &
Thom̃ Prence,   Edmond Freeman,
Willm Collyer,

Gentlemẽ, Assistantℭ, &ĉ.

MR EDMOND FREEMAN, form̃ly elected Assistant, &ĉ, was sworne this Court.

Wm Hatch, of Scittuate, elected by the townesmen to be their leiftennant for trayneing their men, was p̃sented by their then com̃ittees to the Court, and allowed, according to the order of the Court.

Mr Thomas Dimmack was likewise allowed leiftennant for the towne of Barnestable, for the like seruice, &ĉ.

Mr Wm Palmer was likewise allowed leiftennãt for the towne of Yarmouth, for the like service, &ĉ.

The Com̃ittees of the seũall Towneshipps.

Plymouth,	{ Mr John Done, Mr Wm Paddy, John Cooke, Ju^r, John Dunhame.	Duxborrow,	{ Capṯ Miles Standish, Jonathan Brewster, M$^:$ John Alden.
Sandwich,	{ Mr Edward Dillingham, Willm Newland.	Taunton,	{ John Stronge, Richard Williams.
Barnestable,	{ Mr Thomas Dimack, Anthony Annable.	Scittuate,	{ Thomas Robinson, Thomas Raulins.
Yarmouth,	{ Mr Anthony Thacher, Willm Palmer.	Marshfeild,	{ Kenelme Winslow, Josias Winslowe.

This Court was called, vpon occation of the insurrection of the Indians agst the Dutch and English there, and haue plotted to cutt of the English, and to beginn wth the Dutch, many of whom they haue already cutt off.

It is concluded and agreed vpon by the Court, that thirty men, according to our pporõõn wth the confederates, shalbe forthwth made ready for the warr, and be sufficiently puided wth armes compleate & other puisions, and to be in continuall readynes to go forth wth the confederatℭ when they shalbe called.

1643.
10 October.
BRADFORD, Gov.
[*89ᵇ.]

*The rule wᶜʰ was thought most equall for number of psons in euery towneship was to take one of a score in euery towneship, as they are to make ready as followeth in euery towne : —

Plymouth, . . . seauen.	Taunton, . . . three.
Duxborrow, . . fiue.	Barnestable, . . three.
Scituate, . . fiue.	Yarmouth, . . two.
Sandwich, . . three.	Marshfeild, . . two.

xxxᵗⁱᵉ psons in all.

The rates of euery towneship to this charge are as followeth : —

	li s d		
Plymouth,	04 05 00	Taunton,	02 10 00
Duxborrow,	03 00 00	Barnestable,	02 10 00
Scituate,	04 10 00	Yarmouth,	02 10 00
Sandwich,	03 05 00	Marshfeild,	02 10 00

According to these pporc̃ons to the hundred pound charge.

It is ordered and agreed vpon by the Court, that the comittees of euery towneship do speedyly make their number of men ready and furnished wᵗʰ sufficient armes and puision, and send their names to the Gofñʳ & counsell of warr hereafter named wᵗʰ all convenyent speed, and a cattalogue of their armes.

The counsell of warr, elected & authorized by the Court, are, —

The Gouernor, who is also president thereof,
Mʳ Edward Winslow,
Mʳ Thomas Prence,
Mʳ Wilm̃ Collyer,
Capt Miles Standish.

It is ordered and concluded vpon by the Court, that the counsell of warr shall haue full power to order all things concerning the gefi̇all warrs for the gofĩment, especially in these p̃ticulers following, viz͠ : —

That the counsell of warr shall haue full power to yssue out warrants to presse such a number of men in euery towne as by pporc̃on the said towne is to set forth ; and also to yssue forth warrants to the said townes for armes & puision for them, and so for a greater or lesser number or pporc̃on as occation shall require, according to the number of psons and rates now agreed vpon in this Court for eich towneship.

That when complaint is made to the counsell of warr, either by the officers or souldiers, of any offences donn in the tyme of service, the said counsell of warr shall haue full power to heare, & determine, & punish such offenders.

COURT ORDERS.

*The armes wch shalbe accounted sufficient for the furnishing of a souldier are these :—

A muskett, either firelock or matchcock, so that they puide match wth all, a paire of bandeliers, or a pouch for pŏder and bulletts, a sword and a belt, a worme & scowrer, a rest & a knapsack.

1643.
10 October.
BRADFORD,
Gov.
[*89°.]

That the counsell of warr shall haue full power to choose a treasurer or treasurers for the p̃sent service, to make puision for them, and shall giue an account to the countrey of their receipt⌊ and payment⌊ when they shalbe required.

That the losse of armes wch shall happen in this expedition shalbe borne *shalbe borne* by the countrey according to their seŭall pporc̃ŏns.

That all the armes wch shalbe used in this expedition shalbe valued by the counsell of warr, and a record of them taken and to whom they are deliŭed by one therevnto appoynted.

That the com̃ittees do send a list of their souldiers names wth their armes to the counsell of warr to Plymouth on Munday the xxiij^th of this instant Octob^r, or before.

That the counsell of warr shall haue full power to make choyce of a leader that shall leade this company, and one to goe wth him for counsell.

That euery souldier shall haue xviij^s p month, & dyett & pillage.

That euery souldier shall haue a months puision sent wth him, viz⌠ : for euery souldier xxx^ł of biskett, xij^ł of pork or xx^ł of beefe, and half a bushell of peas or meale ; and that euery towne puide according to this pporc̃ŏn for so many men as they are to send forth.

That the leader of this company shall haue fourty shillings p month, and the serjeant xxx^s p month.

It is ordered by the Court, that if the townesmen of Yarmouth cannot p̃sently agree to appoynt a place for defence of themselues, their wiues, and children, in case of a suddaine assault, that then the Court doth order and appoynt Leiftennant Willm Palmer, Anthony Thacher, Nicholas Symkins, and Samuell Rider, wth the constable, to appoynt a place, and forthw^th to cause the same to be fortyfyed wth all speede.

It is bare still.

*It is ordered by the Court, that if the townesmen of Barnestable doe not p̃sently agree to appoynt a place or places for the defence of themselues, their wiues, and children, against a suddaine assault, that then ye Court doth order, that Mr Thomas Dimmack, Anthony Annable, Henry Cobb, Henry Coggen, & Barnard Lumberd, wth the constable, shall forthw^th appoynt a place or plac⌊ for their defence, and cause the same to be speedyly fortyfied for their defence.

[*90.]

1643.

6 October.
BRADFORD,
Goῦ.

9 October.
2 November.

11 November.

Henry Adford & Tomson Manson, of Scituate, marryed the vjth of Octob^r, 1643.

John Stockbridḡ and Elizabeth Sone, of Scituate, marryed the ixth Octob^r, 1643.

James Torrey & Ann Hatch, of Scittuate, marryed the second of Novemb^r, 1643.

The xjth of Novemb^r. Memorand : that Wil̃m Launder, for̃mly the servant of Mr John Combe, and sithence by his consent turned ouer to Mr Wil̃m Thomas, and sithence, also, in consideraĉõn of the sum of xj^{li}, payd by Mr Thom̃ Burne vnto the said Mr Thomas, is, by the said Launders consent, turned oũ to serue the residue of his tyme wth the said Thomas Burne, according to his indenture ; the said Thom̃ Burne fynding him meate, drinke, and apparell during the said terme, and in thend thereof to pay him, the said Launder, the sum̃e of three pounds in countrey commodities, as they will then passe from man to man.

---

7 November.
NEW PLYM.
[*91.]

*.*At a Court of Assistantℓ holden at Plym̃ afores^d, the vijth of Novemb^r, in the xixth Yeare of the now Raigne of o^r Sou̇aigne Lord, Charles, King of England, &c.*

BEFORE Wil̃m Bradford, genť, Goũ,   Wil̃m Collyer, &
        Edward Winslow,   Wm Thomas,
        Thomas Prence,
                    Genť, Assisť, &ĉ.

WHEREAS there was a suite com̃enced by John Hearker against Mr Josias Checkett for a house & landℓ in Scittuate, the wch was p̃secuted by Jonathan Brewster as attorney for the said Hearker, and Samuell Fuller, attorney for the said Checkett, it is ordered and agreed vpon, by the consent of both p̃ties, that the said Hearker shall haue house and lands againe, and that the charges wch haue beene really disbursed vpon the said lands to be payd out of the rent of the sayd lands ; and the said landℓ to be further confirmed to the said Hearker against any title the said Checkett or his assigns shall make therevnto.

John Barnes, proued to be drunken, both in the Bay and at Scituate, vpon the oathes of John Morton & Nathaniell Masterson, is fyned . . . . } v^{li}.

COURT ORDERS. 67

Whereas Mr Henry Andrewes hath exhibited a bill of compl^{nt} agst Mr John Gilbert, Sen, for a pcell of goods, viz$, a pack of linnen cloth, to the value of fourty pound£ or there about£, the said John Gilbert, being now required to answere therevnto vpon his oath, hath refused, but hath taken tyme to answere at March Court next, or els the Court to pceede against him for payment thereof.   1643. 7 November. BRADFORD, Go&#7;.

Mr John Gilbert, Sen, acknowledgeth to owe the King, . lxxx^{li}.   Released.

Upon condicōn that he shall answere at March Court next to the bill of compl^{nt} of Mr Henry Andrewes.

---

*At a Court of Assistant£ holden at Plym, aforesaid, the second of January, in the xixth Yeare of the Raigne of o^r Sov̄aigne Lord, Charles, by the Grace of God King of England, Scotland, France, and Ireland, Defendor of the Fayth, &c.   1643-4. 2 January. NEW PLYM. [*93.]

BEFORE Wm Bradford, gentlē, Goûnor,   Wilm Collyer, and
Edward Winslow,   Wilm Thomas,
Thomas Prence,

Gentlemē, Assistant£, &c.

VPON certyficate made to the Court, that Georḡ Pidcock, of Duxborrow, taylor, by reason of a cold palsy that his body is subject vnto, is vnable to beare armes to exercise wth a peece, ^ is therefore by the Court freed from such service, and not to be fyned for not trayneing hereafter, but to pay his fynes for the tyme past, because the Court was not so informed formly, prouided that the said Georḡ Pidcock pforme all other publicke services as to watch and ward wth such weapons as he can use, when hee shalbe therevnto required.

It is ordered by the Court, that Edward Dotey shall pay fiue bushells of Indian corne to Mr John Groome, for Manasseth Kemptons use, by the end of the next week, & pay the messenger his fee & charges of the Court.

The xviijth day of January, 1643. William Hoskine, of Plymouth, hath put Sarah, his daughter, to Thomas Whitney, and Winefride, his wyfe, to dwell wth them vntill shee shall accomplish the age of twenty yeares, the said Thomas, and Winyfride, his wyfe, vseing her as their child, and being vnto her as father and mother, and to instruct her in learneing and soweing in reasonable manner, fynding vnto her meate, drink, and apparell &   18 January.

1 6 4 3-4.

18 January.
BRADFORD, Goũ.

Ordered to dwell wth Mr Hatherley.
[*94.]

lodging during the said terme; and if it shall happen the said Sarah to marry before she shall haue accomplished the said age of twenty yeares, (she being six yeares of age the xvjth of September last past,) that then the sayd Thomas shall haue such satisfaction for her tyme then remayneing as shalbe adjudged reasonable & equall by two indifferrent men.

*James Till, of Scittuat, acknowledgeth to owe the Kinge, &č, xx^{li}.
Georg̃ Sutton, of the same, plaī, ... x^{li}.
Symon Sutton, of the same, planī, ... x^{li}.
⅌ bona port.

The Court judge him to haue broken his bondꝭ, because that Mr Hanbury sent the said Till to Scittuate wth two hides to Humphrey Turner to be tanned; & the said Till sold the said hides to Joseph Tilden for xij^s, one of them being neere vpon worth so much.

---

5 March.
NEW PLYM.
[*95.]

*.At the Gen^rall Court of o^r Soũaigne Lord the King, holden at Plym̃ afores^d, the fift Day of March, in the xixth Yeare of his said Ma^{ts} now Raigne, of England, &c.

BEFORE Willm Bradford, genī, Goũ,   Tymothy Hatherley,
Edward Winslow,   John Browne,
Thomas Prence,   Willm Thomas, and
Willm Collyer,   Edmond Freeman,
            Gentlemẽ, Assistantꝭ, &č.

THE comittees of the seũall towneshipps:—

Plymouth,   { Mr John Done,
                { Mr Willm Paddy,
                { Manasseth Kempton,
                { John Cooke, Juñ.

Scittuate,   { John Williams,
                { Thomas Chambers.

Taunton,   { Henry Andrewes,
                { John Strong, absent.

Yarmouth,   { Mr Anthony Thacher,
                { Willm Palmer.

Duxborrow,   { Willm Bassett,
                { Edmond Chaundlor.

Sandwich,   { Richard Burne,
                { Willm Newland.

Barnestable,   { Anthony Annable,
                { Henry Bourne.

Marshfeild,   { Josias Winslowe,
                { Robte Waterman.

COURT ORDERS. 69

These psons following were propounded to take vp their freedome the 1643-4.
next Court :—

5 March.
BRADFORD,
Goũ.

	Mʳ Nathaniell Thomas,	+Roƀte Caruer,
pᵈ	John Dingley,	+George Hall,
	+James Pitney,	Wiłłm Halloway,
	James Skiffe,	Wiłłm Hailstone,
	Thomas Shillingsworth,	Richard Williams.
	John Russell,	

John Smyth, of the Eele Rifl, planter, acknowledgeth to } xxˡⁱ.
oʳ soũaigne lord the King, to be levyed, &c̃, ...
Edward Banges, of the same, planť, ... xˡⁱ.
Edward Dotey, of Plym̃, planť, ... xˡⁱ.
Ᵽ bona porť.

Released the
5ᵗʰ June, 1644.

John Irish is to haue his xxv acrees of land, due for his service, mad̃ vp by Duxborrow men, because it is agreed vpon form̃ly that such servantẽ as are to haue landẽ by their coucnantẽ at the expiracõn of their terme are to be puided for in the townes where they liue or are receiued as inhabitantẽ; but if it cannot be there had, then to make it knowne to the Gouernʳ & Assistantẽ, that they be puided for elswhere.

Vpon heareing of the differrence betwixt Wiłłm Hatch, of Scittuate, & his servant Hercules, for the terme he should serue him, whether six or seauen yeares, the Court, haueing heard the euedencẽ on both sides, do order that the said Hercules is to serue the said Wiłłm six yeares, wᶜʰ wilbe vntill the third day of July next, & then to be free from him.

*Concerning the differrence betwixt James Skiffe & Samuell Jenney for the sayle, it is ordered by the Court, that the said Samuell Jenney shall cause the said sayle to be brought speedyly to the towne; and that Mʳ Prence, for the said Samuell Jenney, and Georḡ Watson, for the said James Skiffe, shall view and appraise the same, and to allow what damnage shalbe thought just & equall betwixt them; and that the said James Skiff shall haue the said sayle & the damnage to deliũ to Roƀte Waterman, wᵗʰ the boate hee hath sold him.

[*96.]

It is ordered by the Court, that James Till shall dwell two yeares now next ensuing wᵗʰ Mʳ Tymothy Hatherley, and shall haue six pounds p̃ anñ, and to see it bestowed vpon him for his necessary apparell, and to giue an account thereof to the Court, that if any thing thereof remayne, it may be payd to the countrey towardẽ the satisfaccõn of his bonds for breach of his good behauioʳ.

1 6 4 3-4.

5 March.
BRADFORD,
Gou.

Whereas Scittuate is psented for not exerciseing of armes according to the order of the Court, it is ordered, that they shall exercise eight tymes this yeare, according to the act of the Court, and that it shalbe in the liberty of the millitary officers of that towne to call forth such squadrons or files as hee shall think fitt to be exercised eight tymes ouer more.

It is ordered, that Mr Willm Thomas his half bushell shalbe brought to Plym, and to be the standard, and all measures to be made according to yt, vntill a standard can be pcured from the Bay.

Mr Nathaniell Thomas, of Marshfeild, is allowed to be captaine, to trayne the inhabit^s of Marshfeild in the vse of armes, when he hath taken vp his freedome.

Whereas the Court is informed that Mr North, called Captaine North, who came oū this summer, gaue out some speeches tending to sedition & mutyny, vizt, that if he had some of them there he would make garters of their gutts, and that as little a while as he had beene here he could haue a hundred men at his comaund, or words to the like effect, wth some other vnciuille carriages, the Court, calling the said Capt North before them, tooke knowledg of the acknowledgment of his offence, and wthall do require him to remooue himself out of this gofiment wthin a month or two next ensuing, when his occations may best suite for his convenyency, and in the meane season to carry himself inoffensiuely.

[*97.]

*Whereas information is giuen to the Court that there is a cowe or a heiffer in calue giuen or disposed by Mr Andrew Hellot, Sen, of Yarmouth, for the benefitt of the poore of the said towne of Yarmouth, which for the ordering thereof was referred to the Court by the said Mr Hellot, by his letter vnder his hand, bearing date the first day of March, 1643, — the Court doth therefore order that the said cowe or heiffer in calue shalbe on Mayday next deliuered to Thomas Payne, of Yarmouth, who shall haue her for three yeares next ensuing, and the milk and thone half of the increase during that tyme, and after the said three yeares are expired, the poore of Yarmouth shall haue her & thencrease, to be disposed of by the townesmen of Yarmouth from tyme to tyme to other poore persons dwelling in the said towne as they shall think fitt, and for such terme, reserueing the benefitt of the said stock for the benefitt of theire poore, and not be allienated to any other use.

The towne of Marshfeild is graunted liberty to haue two constables, one on the other side of the South Riuer.

COURT ORDERS. 71

*At the Gen'all Court of our Sou'aigne Lord the Kinge, holden at 1644.
Plymouth aforesaid, the fift Day of June, in the xxth Yeare
of his said Maties now Raigne, of England, &c.
    5 June.
    NEW PLYM.
    WINSLOWE,
BEFORE Edward Winslowe, gent, Gou,   Tymothy Hatherley,   GoÙnor.
   Willm Bradford,.   John Browne,   [*99.]
   Thom Prence,   Willm Thomas, and
   Willm Collyer,   Edmond Freeman,
      Gentlemen, Assistant(, &c.

MR EDWARD WINSLOW elected Goūnor, and sworne.
  Mr Willm Bradford,   Mr John Browne,
  Mr Thom Prence,   Mr Willm Thomas,   elected Assistant(,
  Mr Willm Collyer,   Mr Edmond Freeman,   and sworne.
  Mr Tymothy Hatherley,

Mr Buckley, Mr Nathaniell Thomas, John Dingley, James Skiffe, Thomas Shillingsworth, John Russell, Willm Halloway, William Hailston, Richard Williams, Mr John Combe, Richard Prichard [were admitted freemen.]

  John Finney, (admitted,)   Thomas Clapp,
  ‡Gowen White,‡   ‡Willm Reade,‡   ppounded to
  Richard Wright,   Francis Goulder,   take vp theire
  Daniell Cole,   Edmond Hawes, (admitted,)   freedome the
  Wm Crocker,   Thomas Hinckley,   next Court.

The Goūnor and Mr John Browne are elected commissioners for this yeare, and to treate wth the confederates of the Vnited Collonies.

Plymouth is graunted to haue two constables.

Mr Nathaniell Thomas is allowed to be the captaine for trayneing of the inhabit^s of Marshfeild in armes.

      *The Grand Inquest.   [*100.]
Willm Newland,   Joseph Tilden, exp ju^{r}sdiction for
John Finney,   misdemeanor amongst them,
Thom Southworth,   Robte Boatfish,
Richard Higgens,   Richard Prichard,
Robte Bartlett, sworne. Edmond Hawes, sworne.
Constant Southworth,   Henry Coggen,º
Willm Merick,   Thom Hinckley,
John Tisdale,   Willm Hailstone,º
Thom Robinson, sworne   Willm Brooke.
  in March Court,

1644.   The Constables of eich Towne sworne this Courte.

5 June.
WINSLOWE,
GOŮNOR.

Plymouth,	. . . .	James Cole,	John Jenkins, Señ.
Scittuate,	. . . . .	Willm Reade,	Gowen White.
Yarmouth,	. . . .	Thoṁ Howes, not sworne.	
Taunton,	. . . . .	James Wiat.	
Duxborrow,	. . . .	Thomas Bonney.	
Sandwich,	. . . .	Joseph Holly.	
Barnestable,	. . . .	Willm Crocker.	
Marshfeild,	. . . .	John Dingley.	

Comittees for eich Towne.

Plymouth,	. . . .	{ Mr ‖Wm Paddy,‖ ‡John Done,‡ ‡John Winslowe,‡ John Dunhame,	Manasseth Kempton, John Cooke.
Scittuate,	. . . . .	John Williams,	Humfrey Turner.
Yarmouth,	. . . .	{ Mr Anthony Thacher, ‡Mr Willm Palmer,	‡Job Cole.‡
Taunton,	. . . . .		
Duxborrow,	. . . .	Mr John Alden,	Jonathan Brewster.
Sandwich,	. . . .	Thoṁ Tupper,	James Skiffe.
Barnestable,	. . . .	{ Anthony Annable, ‡Henry Bourne,‡	Henry Cobb.
Marshfeild,	. . . .	Kenelme Winslow,	Robte Waterman.

The action depending betwixt Henry Coggen, pltiffe, & Robert Waterman, deffenᵗ, for a cannow, is, by consent of both parties, referred to Mr Anthony Thacher and Mr Thomas Dimmack, to be ended by them.

Thomas Hinckley & Henry Coggen tooke the oath of fidellyty.

[*101.]   *Surveyors for the Heigh Wayes in eich Towne this yeare.

Plymouth,	. . . .	{ John Barnes, Thoṁ Southworth, } for the towne, Thoṁ Clarke for the Eele Riuer, and John Shawe, Señ, for Joanes Riuer.
Duxborrow,	. . . .	John Rogers & Willm Sherman.
Scittuate,	. . . .	Henry Meritt & Thomas Raulins.
Sandwich,	. . . .	Richard Chadwell & Thomas Boardman.
Barnestable,	. . .	Mr Thoṁ Allen and Samuell Hinckley.

COURT ORDERS.

Yarmouth, ... Mr Anthony Thacher & Heugh Hillier.   1644.
Taunton, ... James Wyatt.
Marshfeild, ...   5 June.
                                                                   WINSLOWE,
                                                                   GOŮNOR.

It is ordered by the Court, that Mr John Crow, for Yarmouth, & Mr Thoṁ Dimmack, for Barnestable, shall assist Mr Edmond Freeman in keepeing the Court℮ & decideing the causes & suit℮ in Sandwich, Barnestable, and Yarmouth, not aboue

Łres of administraĉõn of all the goods and cattells of M^r Wiłłm Brewster, deceased, are graunted by the Court to Jonathan Brewster and Loue Brewster, and a true inventory thereof was exhibited to the Court vpon the oathes of the said Jonathan & Loue.

It is ordered by the Court, that Manasseth Kempton, Edward Banges, & Robte Bartlett, or any two of them, shall price the two oxen of Wiłłm Powells, recoũed by due course of law by Thomas Clarke and Clement Campion, John Barnes beinge Campions attorney, and the surplusage of the oxe wch Thoṁ Clarke recoũed to be payd to Campions use, wth thother oxe, as they are prised.

Mr Anthony Thacher is lycensed to draw wine at Yarmouth.
Henry Cobb is lycensed to draw wine at Barnestable.
Wm Parker is lycensed to draw wine at Taunton.
‡Wiłłm Newland is lycensed to draw wine at Sandwich.‡
Edmond Eddenden is lycensed to draw wine at Scittuate.

Mr Tymothy Hatherley is authorized by the Court to take the oathes of the witness^s for Edward Forsters will, and the executrix^s her oath to the inventory, and to returne them to the Court, that they may be recorded.

*Wiłłm Shertcliffe, for breaking the peace vpon John Smyth, is fyned v^s.   [*101^a.]
Samuell Jenney, for strikeing of Thoṁ Dunhame, is fyned iij^s iiij^d.
Thomas Dunhame, for challenging Samuell Jenney to fight wth him, and came to his bed side to do it, &ĉ, is fyned x^s.

Peter Hambrow, for stealeinge a shirt of John Presburies, is censured to be whipt at the post, wch was accordingly donn.

Charles Thurstone, for abuseing his m^{ris}, &ĉ, is censured to bee whipt at the post. Vppon a petiĉõn exhibited by the yeong men of Plyṁ, it was remitted vpon tryall of his good carryage vntill the next Court.

74 PLYMOUTH COLONY RECORDS.

1644.
3 July.
NEW PLYM.
WINSLOW, Goũ.

At a Court of Assistantƨ holden at Plym̃, the third of July, in the xx^{th} Yeare of the now Raigne of our Sou̔aigne Lord, King Charles, of England, &c.

BEFORE Edward Winslow, genť, Goũ,   Tymothy Hatherley,
    Willm Bradford,   John Browne, and
    Thomas Prence,   Willm Thomas,
    Willm Collyer,

Genť, Assisť, &ð.

Released.

Willm Maycumber, of Duxborrow, coop, acknowledgth to owe
   o^r soũaigne lord the Kinge . . . . $\Big\}$ x^{li}.
Kenelme Winslow, of Marshfeild, planť, ... x^{li}.
To be levy^d, &ð.

The condiĉõn, that if Willm Maycumber do appeare at the next Geñall Court of o^r said soũaigne lord the King, &ð, to answere to all such matters as on his said ma^{ts} behalf shalbe objected against him conðning wordƨ spoken against the natiues, tending to the breach of the league betwixt us, &ð, and not depť the Court wthout lycence, but abide the further order of the Court; that then, &ð.

---

20 August.
NEW PLYM.
[*101^b.]

*At a Gen̔all Court of o^r Sou̔aigne Lord the King, holden at Plym̃ aforesaid, the xx^{th} of August, in the xx^{th} Yeare of his said Ma^{ts} now Raigne, of England, &c.

BEFORE Edward Winslowe, genť, Goũ,   Tymothy Hatherly,
    Willm Bradford,   John Browne,
    Thomas Prence,   Edmond Freeman, &
    Willm Collyer,   Wm Thomas,

Gentlemen, Assistantƨ, &ð.

The Com̃ittees for the seũall Towneshipps.

Plymouth, . . . $\Big\{$ Mr Wm Paddy,   Manasseth Kempton,
                John Dunhame,   John Cooke.
Scituate, ... Humfrey Turner,   John Williams.
Taunton, ... Capť Wm Poole.
Yarmouth, . . . Mr Anthony Thacher, James Mathews, absent.

COURT ORDERS.

			1644.
Duxborrow, . . .	Mr John Alden,	Jonathan Brewster.	
Sandwich, ...	George Allen,	Thom̅ Burges.	20 August.
Barnestable, . . .	Anthony Annable,	Henry Bourne.	WINSLOW,
Marshfeild, . . .	‖Kenelme‖ ‡Josias‡ Winslow,	Robte Waterman, absent.	Gou.

Captaine Miles Standish & Mr Willm Bradford deposed to the last will & testament of Mr Steephen Hopkins, deceased. Caleb Hopkins, constituted execut^r thereof, exhibited an inventory ^ all his goods & cattells vpon his oath.

Mr Tymothy Hatherley, Richard Sillis, Edmond Eddenden deposed by order of Court to the last will & testament of Edward Foster, and a true inventory exhibeted vpon their oaths this Court.

John Finney admitted a freeman this Court, & was sworne.

Mr John Groomes, } pposed to be freemen.
Joseph Holly,   }

Willm Maycumb^r, of Duxborrow, coop, ... xl^{li},   Respited.
Samuell Nash, of the same, plant, ... xx^{li}.   Released.

The condic̅o̅n, that Willm Maycumb shalbe of the good behauio^r towardℯ our soűaigne lord the King, & all his leigh people, and appeare here at the next Geñall Court, &c ; that, &c.

*Attachmentℯ are to be sent forth to bring in the bodys of George Massy, [*102.] John Maycumber, Thomas Coggen, & Jacob Wilson, for non apparance this Court, for makeing the allarum at Taunton.

A warrant to be sent forth to bring in the bodies of Jonathan Fish and Mary, his wyfe, Nathaniell Fish, Jane, the wyfe of Mr Willm Wood, Rose, the wyfe of Joseph Holly, ^ , the wyfe of Richard Kerby, ^ , the wyfe of Michaell Turner, & Joane Swyft, widdow, to giue euedence in John Ellis & his wifes case.

Mr John Howland and John Cooke for Plymouth, Joseph Rogers and John Rogers for Duxborrow, are appoynted to lay forth the heigh way p̅sented by Mr Bradfordℯ farme into the Bay, and to be donn forthwth, and if they cannot agree, then to choose a fift man to them.

It is ordered by the Court, that Mr Done and the rest of that jury, for laying forth the heigh wayes to the Eele Riuer, shall giue in their verdict the first Tewsday in October, that they may be repaired that want mending before winter.

Robte Boatfish is lycensed to draw wyne at Sandwich ; and when he is at any tyme wthout, it shalbe lawfull for Willm Newland to sell wyne to p̅sons for their neede.

1644.

20 August.
Winslow,
Go⌈.

Mʳ John Groome & Joseph Tilden tooke the oath of fidellity this Court.

Mʳⁱˢ Jenney, vpon the p̃sentment agˢᵗ her, p̃miseth to amend the grinding at the mill, and to keepe the morters cleane, and baggs of corne from spoyleing and looseing.

Georḡ Allen, of Sandwich, is lycensed to cutt hey at the pond(beyond Sandwich Playnes, so he giue not the Indians any thinge for yt wᵗʰout approbac̃õn of the Bench.

Captaine Standish elected Treasurer.

Mʳ Anthony Thacher, Mʳ Thomas Howes, & Mʳ Wiłłm Lumpkin, of Yarmouth, or any two of them, are appoynted by the Court to lay forth the farme land graunted to Nathaˡˡ Sowther neere Billingsgate; and the Court confirmes the same vnto him.

[*103.]

*Vpon the petic̃õn of Duxborrow men, it is thought good by the Court that there be a view taken of the land(desired by them, namely, xij miles vp into the woods from Plymouth bound(at Joanes Riuer, and if it proue not p̃judiciall to the plantac̃õn to be erected at Teightaquid, nor to the meddowes of Plymouth at Winnytuckquett, it may be confirmed vnto them, prouided always that the Hering or Alewyfe Riuer at Namassachusett shalbe equally betwixt the two townes of Duxborrow and Marshfeild.

Mʳ Thomas Robinson, of Scittuate, for non app̃arance this Court, to serue vpon the grand inquest, is fyned xxˢ. Remitted the 3ᵈ of March, in regard that it appeared

10 October.

Memorand, the tenth of October, 1644: that whereas Mʳ John Doane had some tyme since xvˡⁱ, the childs porc̃õn of Mary Browne, whom he was to keepe and bring vp vntill shee should accomplish the age of seaventeene yeares, and should haue the use of the said pc̃õn vntill then — now, the said terme being expired, the said John Doane hath delified, wᵗʰ the consent of the said Mary Browne, and by order of the Court, vnto John Browne, of Duxborrow, two cowes at xiijˡⁱ, and fourty shillings in swyne and wheate, and is by the Court discharged of the said xvˡⁱ; and the said John Browne is to keepe the said two cowes and their encrease for their milk, wᵗʰ the rest of the stock as aforesd, vntill the said Mary shalbe marryed, or thought fitt to marry, wherevnto the said Mary hath consented.

4 November.

The fourth Novemb, 1644. Memorand: that James Adams doth acknowledḡ that he hath receiued fourty pound(of Mʳ Tymothy Hatherley, of Scittuate, for the vse of Mʳ James Shurley, of London, merchant, according to the said Mʳ Shurleys appoyntment, by his writing vnder his hand; and the said James Adams doth veryly beleeue that the said fourty pounds is payd for the said Mʳ Shurleys share of land lying at Scittuate, wᶜʰ the said Mʳ Hatherley bought of the said Mʳ Shurley.

*At a Court of Assistant₍ holden at Plymͫ aforesaid, the fift Day of Nouembr, in the xxth Yeare of the now Raigne of or Souraigne Lord, Charles, by the Grace of God King of England, Scotland, Franc, and Ireland, Defendor of the Fayth, &c.

1644.
5 November.
NEW PLYM.
WINSLOW, GoP.
[*105.]

BEFORE Edward Winslowe, gent, Goûnor,   Tymothy Hatherly, and
Wilłm Bradford,   Wilłm Thomas,
Thomas Prence,
Gentlemē, Assistant₍, &c̄.

JOSEPH PRYOR, now dwelling wth John Rogers, of Duxborrow, not yet fully xxjtie yeares of age, chooseth Mr Tymothy Hatherley to bee his guardian vntill he shall accomplish the age of xxjtie yeares; and whereas he had comēnced an action against Daniell Pryor & Mary, his wyfe, for a legacy of fiue pound₍, wch was bequeathed him by his father, deceased, and is now in the hand₍ of the said Daniell Pryor and Mary, his wyfe, whereof the said Joseph hath receiued twelue shillings, and thother foure pound₍ & eight shillings is put into Mr Hatherley his said guardians hand₍, to be payd the said Joseph when he shall accomplish his said age; and the said Daniell Pryor and Mary, his wyfe, are thereof discharged from payment of the said legacy hereafter, this being so ordered by the Court, wth consent of all p̄ties.

Whereas there was a suite comēnced by Arthur Howland against Robte Mendame for the sum of six pound₍, for goods wch the said Robte Mendams wyfe brought for the said Arthur Howland out of England, and did not delifl them, but sould them, and conuerted the money to her owne use, as was proued in the Court; and whereas the said Robte Mendame hath authorized Thomas Clarke, of the Eele Riuer, to sell a p̄cell of land the said Robte Mendam hath at Duxborrow, viz⅝, tenn acrees of vpland, and two acrees of meddow, the wch the said Thomas Clark had pformed for him, and made sale thereof vnto Wilłm Hiller, of Duxborrow, for one Dutch cowe, valued at six pound₍, and hath confirmed the same vnto the said Wilłm Hiller, his heires and assignes foreū, by quiet and peaceable liuery and seisin by twigg & turffe of the p̄misses, as appeareth by the oathes of Phillip Delanoy and Thomas Chillingsworth, the same being donn in their p̄sence; and that the said Arthur Howland comēnced his suite as aforesaid by attaching the said cowe; and vpon tryall the jury found the said six pound₍ due to the said pltiff Howland, and the charges of the suite. The Court hath, therefore, graunted judgnt and execućon vpon the said cowe for the said pltiff Howland, and do order and confirme

1644.

5 November.
WINSLOW,
Gov.

the said lands, viz$, the tenn acrees of vpland, & two acrees of meddow, wth their appurtenc₡, to be and remayne vnto the said Wilłm Hiller, his heires and assigns foreū, according to the said bargaine and sale made thereof vnto him by Thomas Clarke : to haue and to hold the said tenn acrees of vpland and two acrees of meddow, wth their appurtenc₡, vnto the said Wilłm Hiller, his heires and assignes foreū, and to their onely pper use and behoofe foreū, prouided it shalbe lawfull for the said Robt Mendam to bringe the suite about againe at any tyme w^{th}in a yeare and a day now next ensuing if he please.

5 November.
[*106.]

*The fift of Novemb^r, 1644. Memorand: that Thomas Bunting, dwelling wth Phineas Pratt, hath, wth and by the consent of the said Phineas, put himself as a servant to dwell wth John Cooke, Juni^r, from the fifteenth day of this instant Novemb^r, for and during the terme of eight yeares now next ensuing, and fully to be compleate and ended, the said John Cooke fynding vnto his said servant meate, drink, and apparell during the said terme, and in thend thereof double to apparell him throughout, and to pay him twelue bushells of Indian corne, the said John Cooke haueing payd the said Phineas for him one melch cowe, valued at v^{li}, and fourty shillings in money, and is to lead the said Phineas two loades of hey yearely during the terme of seauen yeares now next ensuinge.

21 November.

The xxj^{th} of Novemb^r, 1644. Whereas Mr Wilłm Hanbury hath farmed out his house and lands lying at Joanes Riuer, wch he purchased of Mr John Browne, vnto Francis Goole, and had w^{th}all letten a stock of vj drawing beast₡ and two cowes and a horse, wth plowes, yeokes, cheanes, and weane, &c ; and that the said Francis neglected his businesse, so as he was vnlikely to pay the rent, but p̄ferred to sell p̄t of the stock, and diuers other thinges wch were in differrence, and allegated on both sides before the Goū^r ; and in regard the said Francis could not giue the said Wm Hanbury securyty for his said stock, it is ordered and concluded vpon by consent of both p̄ties, that the said Francis shall yeild vp peacable possession of the said farme and cattell, and all the rest of the said goods vnto the said Wilłm Hanbury againe ; and all the articles, couenant₡, and agreements made betweene them concerneing the said p̄misses to be immediately cancelled and made voyde to all intent₡ and purposes.

James Cole vndertooke to pay xxij^s for the said Francis Goole, vnto the said Wilłm Hanbury, before the Goū & Nathll Sowther.

21 November.

The xxj^{th} Novemb^r, 1644. Memorand: that whereas Francis Billington is endebted vnto Caleb Hopkins, as executor vnto Mr Steeven Hopkins, his naturall father, deceased, the sum of three pound₡ sterł, in consideracōn that the said Caleb Hopkins shall forbeare the said Francis Billington the said three

COURT ORDERS. 79

pounds vntill the first of December come twelue months, the said Francis 1644.
Billington assigneth, mortgageth, and maketh ouer vnto the said Caleb Hopkins, for the secureing of the said debt of three pound₵, one blacke cowe now 21 November.
in the hand₵ of the said Francis, not to be sold or alliened any wayes to any WYNSLOW,
man vntill the said debt of three pound₵ be satisfyed vnto the said Caleb Hop- GoÊ.
kins, or his assignes.

  *John Gorome and Desire Howland marryed. [*107.]
  Richard Wright and Hester Cooke marryed the
  Stephen Wood and Abigall Dunhame marryed the vjth Novemb^r, 1644.   6 November.
  Ephraim Morton & Ann Coop marryed the xviijth Novemb^r, 1644.   18 November.
  Richard Bushop and Alis Clark marryed the vth Decemb^r, 1644.   5 December.
  John Churchall and Hannah Pontus marryed the xviijth Decemb^r, 1644.   18 December.
  Georg̃ Bonum and Sarah Morton marryed the xxth Decemb^r, 1644.   20 December.
  Henry Wood & Abigall Jenney, the xxviijth Aprill, 1644.   28 April.
  John Carew and Elizabeth ^ marryed the ^ June, 1644.   June.
  Willm Paybody and Elizabeth Alden marryed the xxvth Decemb^r, 1644.   26 December.
  Ephraim Kempton and ^ Rauline marryed the ^

---

*At a Court of Assistant₵ holden at Plym̃ afores^d, the vijth Day of 1644-5.
January, in the xxth Yeare of his said Maties now Raigne, of
England, &c. 7 January.
  NEW PLYM.
  [*109.]

  BEFORE Edward Winslow, gent̃, Goũ,   Thom̃ Prence, and
      Willm Bradford,   Willm Collyer,
          Gentlemen, Assistant₵, &c.

FRANCIS GOOLE complained agst John Shawe, Juñ, in an action of trespass, vpon the case to the dam̃ of xxj^s; the debt was prooued to be xv^s & viij^d, whereof there remaned vnpayd iij^s iiij^d, and the charges of the suite iij^s ij^d. The Court doth award the said John Shawe to pay the said pl̃ntff Goole vj^s vj^d.

Samuell Eaton deposed that his meaneing was to confirme the acre of land Mr Wm Brewster bought of his mother vnto Loue Brewster. See the great booke where it is entred one against another at large.

Whereas Mr John Done is lycensed to draw wyne in Plymouth, and that James Cole is likewise lycensed to keepe the ordinary there, wch is very

1644-5.

7 January.
WYNSLOW,
Gofl.

inconvenyent to many passengers, the Court hath, therefore, lycenced the said James Cole from this day forward to draw wyne, if he shall agree wth Mr Done to take off those wynes hee now hath in his hands. Agreement was after made betwixt them.

16 January.

January xvj^{th}, 1644. Willm Perry, of Scittuate, plant, acknowl- $\Big\}$ x^{li}.
edgeth to owe o^r soūaigne lord the King, to be levyed, &c,

Respited.
This respited vutill she is able to come.

The condicōn, &c, that if Susanna, his wyfe, shall & doe make her psonall appeareanc at the next Genāall Court of o^r said soūaigne lord the King, at Plyṁ, to answere to all such matters as on his said ma^{ts} behalf shalbe objected against her, concṙning the spoyleing & defileing of a well of water in Scittuate, and abide the order of the Court, and not dep̄t the same w^{th}out lycence, &c; that then, &c.

3 March.
[*110.]

*Anthony Annable and Ann Elcock marryed the third of March, 1644.
Thomas Boreman, of Barnestable, & Hannah Annable, marryed the third of March, 1644.

---

3 March.
NEW PLYM.
[*111.]

*At the Gen^rall Court of o^r Sou^raigne the King, holden at Plyṁ aforesaid, the third Day of March, in the xx^{th} Yeare of the now Raigne of our said Sou^raigne Lord, Charles, by the Grace of God King of England, Scotland, France, & Ireland, Defendor of the Fayth, &c.

BEFORE Edward Winslowe, gent, Goū,   Willm Collyer, and
Willm Bradford,   Willm Thomas,
Thomas Prence,
Assistantꝭ, &c.

THOMAS ROBINSON, of Scittuate, tooke the oath of fidelity, &c, this Court.

Thomas Heyward deposeth that James Torey did affirme vnto him that John Amees did come out of England for stealeing of a calf; and the said Thoṁ Heyward further enquireing of the said Torey of the said matter, the said Torey answered him that it was so coṁonly reported in the shipp that they came ouer together in; and further deposeth, that since he haueing spoken wth the said Torey about the said matter, the said Torey said that hee made no question but he could proue what he had sayd.

Edmond Hawes, of Yarmouth, admitted freeman this Court, & sworne.

COURT ORDERS. 81

It is ordered by the Court, that the goods of Georg̃ More, attached by Thomas Rickerd and John Rogers, shalbe sold to the best advantage, and the money due to them for his keepeing to be payd them as farr as it will extend; and & if there be any ouerplus, it be payd for his further mayntenance.

1644-5.
3 March.
WYNSLOW,
Gouͬnͬ.

It is ordered and enacted by the Court, that whereas by an act of the Court, made the vjth of May, 1639, Mr Richard Callicutt was either to come in pson and inhabite at Mattacheese, now called Barnestable, by June Court next following, or els̃ the graunt to be voyde, the wch hee hath altogether fayled in, and neu̍ vnto this day came there in pson to inhabite, it is therefore concluded and enacted by the Court, that all such lands in Barnestable as he hath there taken vp, or belong & appertaine vnto the said Richard Callicutt shalbe p̃sently ceased by the constable there to the colonies use; and that Captaine Standish, now Treasurer, shall sell and ymproue the moneys gotten or comeing of them to the collonies use.

Released. James Shawe,
Released. John Shawe, Ju^r,
Released. Francis Billington,
Discharged. Charles Thurston,
Discharged. Samuell Cutbert,

{ are bound one for another in x^{li} a peece for their app̃arences at the next Geñall Court, &c̃, and to abide the further order of the Court, and not dept the same wthout lycence, and in the meane tyme to be of the good behauior toward£ o^r soũaigne lord the King & all his leigh people; that then, &c̃.

James Shaw released.
John Shaw released.
Francis Billington released.
Charles Thurston discharged.
Sam. Cutberd

George Crispe,
Rob̃te Wickson,

{ x^{li} a peece for Georg̃ Crispe vpon the same condic̃on, p̃ bona port̃.

discharged.
Released.

Steeven Bryan,
Edward Dotey,

{ x^{li} a peece for the s̃d Steven Bryan vpon the same condic̃on, p̃ bona port̃.

Released.

*John Tompson,
James Hurst,

{ bound in tenn pound£ a peece vpon the same condic̃on. Default p̃sently made of this recogñ.

[*112.]
Released.

John Tompson,
Thomas Willett,

{ bound in x^{li} a peece vpon the same condic̃on, p̃ bona port̃, for John Tompson.

Released.

John Shawe, Sen.,
James Cole,

{ bound in x^{li} a peece vpon the same condic̃on, p̃ bona port̃, for John Shawe.

Released.

The Court doth graunt vnto the church of New Plymouth, or those that goe to dwell at Nossett, all that tract of land lying betweene sea and sea, from the Purchasors bounds at Naumseckett to the Hering Brooke at Billingsgate, wth the said Hering Brook and all the meddowes on both sides the said brooke, wth the great Basse Pound there, and all the meddowes and ilands lying wthin the said tract.

It is ordered by the Court, that Mr Thomas Starr shall haue p̃sently layd forth for him at Yarmouth fifty acrees of vpland, either next to Elder Howes or Mr Howes land£ at Seshewit, on wch side he will, so that it adjoyne to one

1644-5.

3 March.
Wynslow,
Goū.

of them, and six acres of meddowe lying in Nobscusset Meddowes, (late Willm Nicholsons,) and foure acrees more of meddow on the south side of the plantacōn towards the South Sea. And the Court doth further order, that if the comittees of Yarmouth do not wth all convenyent speede lay it forth, that then Mr Thacher shall do it himselfe, he paying for the laying of it forth as other men doe.

Whereas a motion is made this Court for a geñall trade wth the other gouerment{ in confederacōn wth vs, wee do thankfully acknowledg their loue and respect to vs therein; but we conceiue such a disproportion in our estates to theirs, and so many thousands required therein, the wch wee are not able to reach vnto, and wth all are very doubtfull whether it may conduce to such a geñall good and answere the ends wch are expected, we cannot concurr wth the rest of. the goūment{ to adventure an estate therein.

It is ordered, that Mr Miles Standish, Mr John Done, & John Dunhame shall take the account{ of Mr Thomas Prence for his treasurership of his receipts and payment{, and certefye the Court thereof.

[*113.]

*Informacōn was giuen vnto the Court, by Mr Browne, that John Gilbert, Juñ, of Taunton, was vehemently suspected of fellony for diuers thinges, and, obtayneing leaue to go for England, made ouer his estate in Taunton & elswhere, amounting to the sum of 40^li, or thereaboutℓ, vnto Nathaniell Sowther, for and on the behalf of the goūment of New Plymouth, for saueing this goūment harmelesse concñing such thinges as might or may be objected against him for or concerneing any matter or thing of such like nature, and for the answereing of all such matters the next Court, or els the next Geñall Court after his returne out of England, to answere in his owne pson, wch is to be in two yeares next ensuing.

1645.

3 April.

The third of Aprill, 1645.

Memorand: that Samuell Eddy hath put his sonn, John Eddy, to dwell wth Francis Goulder, and Katherne, his wyfe, vntill he shall accomplish the age of xxj^tie yeares, (being seauen yeares of age the xxv^th of December last past,) the said Francis, and Katherne, his wyfe, fynding vnto the said John, their servant, meat, drink, and apparell during the said terme, and either in the end thereof, or els at the day of the death of the said Francis, or of the said Katherne, his wyfe, whether shall last happen, to pay him fiue pounds in countrey pay; or, if it please God so to disable the said Francis, or Katherne, his wyfe, that they shall not be then able to pay so much, then to pay him so much as I shall haue left: And if it happen that both the said Francis, and Katherne, his wyfe, shall dye before thende of the said terme, that then the said John shalbe at liberty to be disposed of as his p̃ent{ shall thinke fitt;

but if either of them doe liue out the said terme, then the said John to dwell wth the longer liuer of them vntill he shall accomplish the age of xxj^tie yeares, as aforesaid.

1645.
3 April.
WYNSLOW, Goῦ.

*At the Gen'all Court holden at Plymouth, the iiij^th of June, in the xxj^th Yeare of his Ma^ts now Raigne, of England, &c.

4 June.
NEW PLYM.
BRADFORD, Goῦ.

MR W^M BRADFORD elected Goûnor, and sworne.

[*114.]

Mr Edward Winslowe,
Mr Thomas Prence,
Mr William Collyer,
Mr Myles Standish, } chosen Assistañs, and sworne.
Mr Tymothy Hatherley,
Mr John Browne,
Mr Edmond Freeman,

Mr Thomas Prence and Mr John Browne chosen comissioners for this yeare, to treate wth the comissioners of the Vnited Colonies, according to the articles of the confederacõn, at the tyme & place appoynted, &c.

It is ordered by the Court, that the Goûnor and Assistant₵ shall giue the two comissioners aboue named instruccõns about the occations they shall deale in and agitate wth them about; and that the Treasurer, Mr Alden, and Mr Paddy shall puide money and horses for the defraying of their charges & the charges of their servant₵ for that journey, &c.

The constables chosen by the seûall towneship, & p̃sented to this Court and sworne, are, viz₵: —

Plymouth, ...	Thomas Pope, Roḃte Finney.
Duxborrow, ...	John Tisdale.
Scittuate, ...	Thomas Clapp, John Allen.
Sandwich, ...	Georg̃ Bewyt.
Rehoboath, ...	Steeven Payne.
Taunton, ...	George Hall.
Yarmouth, ...	Richard Templer.
Barnestable, ...	John Bursley.
Marshfeild, ...	John Rowse, Gilbert Brooke.

Mr John Gilbert, Junior, of Taunton, was called vpon this Court; but neither hee nor any for him made answere.

1645.

4 June.
BRADFORD, Go⊎.
[*115.]

*Surveyors of the Heighwayes.

Plymouth, ... { Francis Cooke, Mr Leigh,
Robte Bartlett, and Richard Sparrow.
Duxborrow, ... John Maynard, Edmond Hunt.
Scittuate, ... John Stockbridḡ & Walter Woodward.
Sandwich, ... Thomas Burges, Anthony Wright.
Taunton, ... James Burt.
Barnestable, ... Abraham Blush, Nathaniell Bacon.
Yarmouth, ... Emanuell White, James Bursell.
Marshfeild, ... Thomas Chillingworth & Robte Barker.
Rehoboth,

The Grand Enquest.

Gabriell Fallowell,
Gyles Rickett,
John Washborne,
Henry Howland, } sworne.
Willm Brett,
(Excused.) Edmd Eddenden,
Thom̄ Ensigne,
John Dingley,

Willm Halloway,
Thomas Tupper,
Jonathan Fish,
Dolor Davis, (sick,) } sworne.
Nathaniel Bacon,
Daniell Cole,
Robte Dennis,

Daniell Cole, Thomas Hinckley, Thomas Clapp, Richard Wright, Steeven Payne, Willm Carpenter, & Georḡ Hall admitted freemen, and were sworne.

The Names of those ppounded this Court to take vp their Freedome the next Court.

Nathaniell Bacon, +
Andrew Ring, +
Dolor Davis, +
Mr Samuell Newman, +
Richard Wright,
Walter Palmore, (admitted,)
Robte Martine,
Steeven Payne, (admitted,)
Wm Carpenter, (admitted,)
Wm Cheesborrough, +
Allexander Winchester, +
Willm Smyth,
Edward Bennett,

Thomas Blisse,
Robte Tytus,
William Sabine,
Abraham Martine,
Richard Bowine,
Thomas Hitt, +
Zachary Roades,
Edward Smyth,
Peter Hunt,
Joseph Peck,
Henry Smyth,
Thomas Cooper.

COURT ORDERS.

*It was ordered by the Court, that a committee should be elected & authorised for the p̄pareing of some p̄sent lawes for redresse of some p̄sent abuses, and for p̄venting of future, wherevpon these psons following were elected and nominated, viz: Mr Wil+m Collyer, Mr John Browne, Mr John Alden, Mr Wil+m Paddy, Nathaniell Souther, Jonathan Brewster, Josias Winslow, Edward Case, Edmond Eddenden, Anthony Annable, Richard Burne, Mr Anthony Thacher, Steeven Payne, and Wil+m Carpenter.

1645.
4 June.
BRADFORD, Gof?.
[*116.]

Whereas Kenelme Winslow complayned that he had injustice, in that hee could not be heard in the suite betwixt John Mynard and himself, the Court appoynted a committee to examine and enquire thereinto, and to make report thereof to the Court as they shall fynd the same, viz: Captaine Miles Standish, Mr Wil+m Paddy, Edmond Eddenden, Edward Case, Anthony Annable, Mr Anthony Thacher, and Thomas Tupper, who, vppon due and serious examinac̄ōn thereof, do report that the sayd charge of injustice is altogether vntrue, and that the Bench and jury are free and cleare of any injustice therein, notwthstanding of whatsoeuer the said Kenelme could alleadḡ. And therefore the Court do adjudḡ him to bee committed to prison during the countreys pleasure and to be fyned x^{li}.

Kenelme Winslow was committed to prison and fyned x^{li}.

x^{li} fine.

Kenelme Winslow, by his petic̄ōn exhibited to the Court, wherein was sett forth his acknowledgment of his offence and his sorrow for the same, was released of his ymprisonment, and his fyne to stand still for one whole yeare, and vpon his good carryage then to be remitted or els̄ to be estreated.

Remitted June 4th, 1647.

Whereas, in the case betwixt Ephraim Kempton, Senior, deceased, and Ephraim Kempton, Juñ, of Scittuate, it appeared to the Court that the said Ephraim, Ju^r, and his father laboured together in p̄tnership since their comeing ouer into this countrey, and no diuision was made of what they gott, the Court doth order and appoynt Thomas Robinson and Walter Woodward to make an equall diuision of the goods now in p̄tenership betwixt them, and to deliuer thone half thereof vnto the said Ephraim, Junior, as his owne p̄per goods; and the Court doth appoynt the said Ephraim, Juñ, to exhibite a true inventory of the estate remayneing to the said Ephraim, Señ, vnto the next Court of Assistant(, that such debts as are oweing to any be payd so farr as the estate of the said Ephraim Kempton, Senr, will amount vnto, and an administrator thereof to be then appoynted by the Court.

John Ellis, of Sandwich, for abuseing himself wth his now wyfe by committing vncleanesse wth her before marryage, is censured to be whipt at publike post, and Elizabeth, his wyfe, to stand by whilst execuc̄ōn of the sentence is p̄formed; wch was accordingly donn. And the said John Ellis,

v^{li} fine.

1645.

4 June.
BRADFORD,
Goūnⁿ.

[*117.]

for his long and tedious delayes, occasioning much trouble & charge to the countrey, for that he would not confesse the truth vntill this p̃sent, is fyned vˡⁱ.

*Whereas Thomas Riddings, about a yeare since, came to Scittuate, and is dep̃ted thence, leaueing a man child about fiue yeares of age wᵗʰ Gowen White, p̃miseing him to pay him xviijᵈ p̃ weeke for his keepeing & dyetting of him, but hath hitherto payd him nothing; and the said Gowen hath since found him meate, drinke, and cloathes at his owne charge; the Court doth order and appoynt that the said child shalbe wᵗʰ the said Gowen White vntill he shall accomplish the age of twenty and foure yeares; but if his father shall come and desire to take him away before thend of the said terme, that then he shall pay the said Gowen White for the keepeing of him for such tyme as he shall haue beene wᵗʰ him; and so also if hee shalbe placed wᵗʰ another man.

Whereas Mʳ Thomas Broughton and Mʳ Willm Thomas haue mutually referred the cause depending in Court about the suite of a bond of one hundred and twenty pounds, for payment of threescore and one pound(and twelue shillings due in August, 1638, to be ended and decided by the Bench; and what end they shall make therein, they p̃mise mutually to stand vnto and abide, so that judgment and execuc̃on shall immediately yssue from this Court vpon the yssue as if it were vpon a verdict by a jury. And therevpon the Bench, vpon much deliberac̃on and serious agitac̃on, wᵗʰ a due respect vnto what both the parties had pleaded and alleadged in the pleading of the case, wee do order, determine, and decree as followeth: That the said Mʳ Willm Thomas shall pay to the said Mʳ Broughton sixtye one pounds twelue shillings principall, and for damnages sustayned twenty foure pounds eight shillings & three pence, wᶜʰ ariseth as followeth, viz(: sixteene pounds eighteene shillings & three pence, after the rates of vˡⁱ p̃ centū since the money to haue beene payd vpon exchaung̃ was heere demaunded, and for charges in trauell since the plaintiff had power to demaund and acquitt yt; seauen pounds tenn shillinges for fiue journeys, in all amounting vnto the sum̃e of fourscore and six pounds and three pence, wᶜʰ wee order and appoynt to be p̃sently payd by the said Mʳ Willm Thomas vnto the said Thomas Broughton. Judḡnt graunted for 86ˡⁱ & 3ᵈ, and the charges of the Court.

The Court doth order that Leiftennant Wᵐ Palmer shall continue in his place to exercise the townesmen of Yarmouth in armes vntill hee shalbe allowed by the Court to lay it downe; and that the towne make choyce of another constable, and p̃sent him to the Court, and that Mʳ Freeman administer the constables oath to him, &c̃.

COURT ORDERS. 87

Vpon request made to the Court by the townesmen of Plymouth, the 1645.
Court doth graunt vnto them the fiue pounds for the fine of John Hassell, of
Seacunck, due to the countrey towards their charges in searching for a delf of 4 June.
coales, whereof there is great p̱bability; and if it be found and proue benefi- Goůnͬ.
ciall, then to be repayd againe when the delf shalbe able.

*Mathew Fuller, of Plymͤ, plant̑, ⎫ [*118.]
Richard Church, carpenter, ⎭ bond in xxˡⁱ a peece. Released.

That the said Mathew Fuller shalbe of the good behavior towards oͬ
soŭaigne lord the King and all his leigh people, and appeare here againe at
the next session of this Court, and abide the further order of the Court, and
not depͭ the same wᵗʰout lycence, &c̄; that then, &c̄.

John Shawe, Señ, of Plymouth, vpon his p̱sentment, fyned . iijˡⁱ.
James Sawe, for the like, ... ijˡⁱ.
John Shawe, Juñ, for the like, ... ijˡⁱ.
Mathew Fuller, for the like, ... ijˡⁱ xˢ.
Steeven Bryan, for the like, ... xxxˢ.
John Tompson, for the like, ... xxˢ.
Francis Billington, for the like, xxˢ or corporal punishᵗ.
Samuell Cutbert, for the like, ... xxˢ.
George Crispe, for the like, ... xxˢ.
Charles Thurstone, for the like, ijˡⁱ or corporal punishᵗ;
and to stand vpon their bonds of good behaů vntill their fines be p̱d.
Francis Goole, vpon his p̱sentment, is fyned, ... ijˡⁱ.
Francis Goole, of Duxborrow, planter, ... xxˡⁱ.
John Paybody, of the same, plant̑, ... xˡⁱ.
Experience Michell, of the same, plant̑, ... xˡⁱ.

That the said Francis Goole shalbe of the good behauioͬ towards our Released pay-
soŭaigne lord the King and all his leigh people, and appeare here againe the ing his fyne &
next Geñall Court, &c̄, and abide the further order of the Court, and not depͭ fees.
the same wᵗʰout lycence; that then, &c̄.

The Court is adjörned to Tewsday come fortnight, vizß, the xxvᵗʰ of this
instant June, and from thence to the last Tewsday but one in Octobᵣ following,
and the Geñall Court to be the last Tewsday in October.

John Maycumber, of Taunton, fined vˡⁱ for abuseing the majestrat̑ₑ, in vˡⁱ.
concealeing and misinformeing the last Goŭnor & Mᵣ Browne, and diuers
other of the Assistant̑ₑ, in the case of John Gilbert, Junior, impeached for
suspic̑õn of diuers fellonies, whereby hee is at large, and diuers p̱sons are
hereby depriued of recoůing their goods againe, and the said Gilbert is gone
into England.

1645.

4 June.
BRADFORD,
Gov.

Whereas Jonathan Brewster desireth a p̃cell of land at Namassacheesett, wch Mr Collyer, Mr Alden, & Georg̃ Soule are appoynted to view and make report thereof vnto the Court; and as the Court shall approue, it so to be graunted vnto him.

[*119.]

*John Maycumber, of Taunton, carpenter, oweth the King, &c̃, xx^li.

Willm Parker, of the same, inkeep, ... x^li.

Released.

Richard Williams, of the same, plant̃, ... x^li.

The condic̃õn, that if the aboue bounden John Maycumber be of the good behauio^r towards c^r softaigne lord the King and all his leigh people, and appeare at the next Geñall Court, &c̃, & not dep̃t the same w^thout lycence, &c̃; that then, &c̃.

William Newland is allowed to trayne the townesmen of Sandwich in armes, if the townesmen shall choose him.

Mr Tymothy Hatherley is chosen to supply Mr Princes roome in the com̃ission for the United Collonies, if Mr Prence be not able, who is now sick.

11 September. Samuell Hicks and Lydia Done marryed the xj^th of Septemb^r, 1645.

20 October. John Aymes and Elizabeth Heyward marryed the xx^th of October, 1645.

Samuell Nash was p̃sented to the Court to be a leiftennãte at Duxborrow, & is allowed by the Court.

The inhabitants of the towne of Duxborrow are graunted a competent p̃porc̃õn of lands about Saughtuckquett, towards the west, for a plantac̃õn for them, and to haue it foure miles euery way from the place where they shall sett vp their center, (p̃uided it entrench not vpon Winnetuckquett, form̃ly graunted to Plymouth,) and haue nominated Captaine Miles Standish, Mr John Alden, Georg̃ Soul, Constant Southworth, Joseph Rogers, and Willm Brett to be feoffees in trust for the equall deuideing and laying forth of the said lands to their inhabitant℞.

Mr Jonathan Brewster is graunted three hundred acrees of land, to him & his heires foreuer, either in the place where hee desireth or in some other place nere, wch may be least p̃judice to the plantac̃õn graunted to Duxborrow, wch is to be layd forth for him by two men chosen by the majestrats of those six men wch shall be nominated and appoynted by Duxborrow men to order

31 October. and lay forth their land℞ about Satuckquett to p̃ticulers p̃son.

[*120.] *James Glasse & Mary Pontus marryed the 31st of Octob^r, 1645.

COURT ORDERS.

*At the Gen^rall Court of o^r Sou^raigne Lord the King, holden at Plym aforesaid, the xxviij^th of Octob^r, in the xxj^th Yeare of his said Ma^ts now Raigne, of England, &c.

1645.
28 October.
NEW PLYM.
BRADFORD, GoÜ.
[*121.]

BEFORE Willm Bradford, gent, Goũ, John Browne,
Edward Winslow, Tymothy Hatherley, and
Thomas Prence, Edmond Freeman,
Miles Standish,
Gent, Assistantꝭ, &c.

WALTER PALMER, of Rehoboth, admitted a freeman, and was sworne.

Robte Barker, of the North Riuer, made it appeare to the Court that there was due vnto him for carrying prisoners and passengers ouer the North Riuer, wch the countrey pmised to pay him iiij^s ij^d.

Thomas Heyward, of Duxborrow, is ordered by the Court to pay vnto Wannapooke, a Neipnet Indian, half a bushell of Indian corne for veneson he tooke of him.

Priscilla Browne, daughter of Peter Browne, deceased, haueing accomplished the terme shee was to dwell wth Wm Gilson, of Scittuate, who was to pay her xv^li in thend of her terme ; now the said Priscilla came into the Court, and hath chosen John Browne, her vnckle, to be her guardian, and to haue the placeing and disposeing of her vntill the Court shall judg her meete to be at her owne disposeing ; and likewise to take her porc̃on, vizt, xv^li, and to ymproue it by putting it into a breeding stock, and keepe them, and giue her half thencrease, or els to use it as his owne, and to pay her the said xv^li when the Court shall judg it meete for her to haue it at her owne disposeing.

Manasseth Kempton and Ephraim Kempton are appoynted by the Court administrat^rs of the goods and cattells of Ephraim Kempton, of Scittuate, deceased, and to pay debts oweing by the said Ephraim at his decease so farr as the estate will amount vnto. There appeared to the Court that twenty-one pounds was due vnto the said Manasseth Kempton out of the said estate, wch the Court allowed should be payd him, and to giue a just account of the rest when the Court shall require them.

Mr Richard Wright, of Rehoboth, for refuseing to come to the Court as a comittee for their towne, being by them chosen for that end, is fyned xx^s.

1645.
26 October.
BRADFORD, Gov.
[*122.]

*The Pporĉon and Names of the Souldiers in eich Towne sent forth in the late Expedition against the Narrohigganset{ & their Confederat{.

The first company, viz{, xvj^{teene}, went forth the xvth August, 1645.

Plymouth, viij men : six wth those that went out first, and two wth those y^t went out last.
{ John Tompson,
Richard Foster,
John Bundy,
Nicholas Hodges,
John Shawe,
Samuell Cutbert. } These vj were forth xvij dayes.
{ John Jenkins,
John Harman. } These two were forth xiij dayes.

Duxborrow, six men, wch went wth those that went out first. . .
{ Serjeant Sam̃ Nash,
Wil͡lm Brewster,
Wil͡lm Clarke,
John Washborne,
Nathaniell Chaundler,
Edward Hall. } These six were forth xvij dayes.

Marshfeild, foure men, wch went forth wth those that went out first. . . . . .
{ Luke Lillye,
Twyford West,
Wil͡lm Hayle,
Roger Cooke. } These foure were forth xvij dayes.

These following went forth the xxiijth of August, 1645.

Sandwich, fiue men, wch went forth wth those that went last. . .
{ Thomas Burges,
Thom^s Greenfeild,
Laurance Willis,
Thomas Johnson,
Robte Allen. } These fiue men were forth xiij dayes.

Scittuate, eight men, wch went forth wth those that went last. . .
{ John Turner,
Georg̃ Russell,
Jeremiah Burrowes,
Hercules Hill,
Edward Saunders,
Nathaniell Moate,
John Robinson,
Richard Toute. } These eight men were forth xiij dayes.

Barnestable, foure men, wch went forth wth those that went last,
{ John Foxwell,
John Russell,
Jonathan Hatch,
Francis Crocker. } These foure men were forth xiiij dayes.

COURT ORDERS.

1645.
28 October.
BRADFORD, Goū.

Yarmouth, fiue men, wch went forth wth those that went last. . . { Will̃m Northcoate, Will̃m Twyneing, Teague Joanes, Henry Wheildon, Will̃m Chase, drummer. } These fiue men were forth xiiij dayes.

These all returned the 2^d of September, being Tewsday, and were disbanded the day following, being Wensday.

*There was deliũed to eich souldier j^{lb} of p̄oder, and 3^{lb} of bullett(a peece, and j^{lb} of tobaccoe, at their going forth. [*123.]

The townes of Taunton and Rehoboth, als̃ Seacunck, were freed from sending forth any men in regard they are frontire townes, and billited the souldiers during the tyme they were forth.

The Charges of this Expedition.

	li	s	d
Inpri^s, giuen to the captaine, but not to be a president for after tymes, for himself & his man,	10	00	00
To Serjeant, now Leiftennant Nash,	02	10	00
To Plymouth for vj men 17 dayes,	05	02	00
To Duxborrow for v men 17 dayes,	04	05	00
To Marshfeild for iiij men 17 dayes,	03	08	00
To Plym̃ for two men more 13 dayes,	01	06	00
To Scittuate for eight men 13 dayes,	05	04	00
To Sandwich for fiue men 13 dayes,	03	05	00
To Barnestable foure men 14 dayes,	02	16	00
To Yarmouth fiue men 14 dayes,	03	10	00
And to the drummer, wch was one of Yarmouth, oũ & aboue, 5^s,	00	05	00
It̃, for a line to Mr Hanbury,	00	02	00
It̃, ½ dussen of kniues giuen to messengers,	00	02	06
It̃, for casting of shott,	00	05	00
It̃, for drumheads,	00	07	00
It̃, spent of the money & beads the capt̃ had,	02	05	05
It̃, worke done by Gorame,	00	04	00
It̃, James Coles bill,	14	02	00
It̃, A horsehire xj dayes,	00	11	00
It̃, 25^{li} of p̄oder taken at the barke by the captaine to bring the men hoame againe,	02	10	00
It̃, 75^{li} of hiskett the capt̃ had at the barke to vittaile his men hoamewardę, for wch is allowed j C waight,	00	16	00

41 : 11 : 00

1645.
28 October.
BRADFORD,
Gou.

It, allowed toward̃ the carriage of ꝑuisions to Secunck, wch came by sea out of the Bay, { 02 : 00 : 00   23 : 04 : 11

Tobaccoe afterward̃ allowed, 27^s 4^d, . . .   01 : 07 : 04

Sum total, ... 66 : 03 : 03
41 : 11 : 00
23 : 04 : 11
─────────
64 : 15 : 11
01 : 07 : 04
─────────
66 : 03 : 03

The barrell of p̄oder the souldiers spent & delifled to diuers of the townes was not accounted, nor 300^li of leade wch Mr Prence bought, nor the bullett̃ the souldiers had forth wch was not returned, nor what losse would be required to take the ꝑuisions againe, besid̃ the charge of euery p̃ticuler towne wth their souldiers in setting them forth, nor 5^s Mr Prenc̃ payd for casting shott, and canvas bags for to put bread & ꝑuision in.

The sale of every towne to this charḡ followeth.   Verte.

[*124.]   *The Rates of the seflall Townes to the Charges of the Warrs.

                                    li   s   d
Plymouth, ... 12 : 02 : 03
Duxborrow, ... 08 : 11 : 00
Scittuate, ... 12 : 17 : 06
Sandwich, ... 09 : 07 : 09
Taunton, ... 05 : 02 : 06
Barnestable, ... 06 : 02 : 06
Yarmouth, ... 07 : 02 : 06
Marshfeild, ... 07 : 02 : 06
                                ─────────
                                70 : 08 : 06

The Court, for speciall consideracõn, did abate xx^s to Barnestable, and 40^s to Taunton, wch is the reason they are not equall wth Yarmouth and Marshfeild, but shall not be a president for after tymes; and Rehoboth was not rated at all, both because it was a new plantacõn, and billited all the souldiers freely during all the tyme they stayed there.

The Sūmes the Townes are to pay their Souldiers, and what wilbe comeing to ye Treasurer.

                    Souldiers.   Treasurer.
                    li   s   d
Plymouth payes   .   06 : 08 : 00, & to the Treasurer   05 : 14 : 03
Duxborrow, . . .   06 : 15 : 00, & to the Treasurer   01 : 16 : 00
Scittuate, ...   05 : 04 : 00, & to the Treas̃ .   07 : 13 : 06

COURT ORDERS.

Sandwich,	. . .	03 : 05 : 00, & to the Tres	. .	06 : 02 : 06
Barnestable,	. . .	02 : 16 : 00, & to the Tres	. .	03 : 06 : 06
Yarmouth,	. . .	03 : 10 : 00, & to the Tres	. .	03 : 12 : 06
Marshfeild,	. . .	03 : 08 : 00, & to the Tres	. .	03 : 14 : 06
Taunton,	. . .	00 : 00 : 00		05 : 02 : 06

1645.
28 October.
BRADFORD, Gov.

Sum tot, 31 : 06 : 00, comeing to the Treau^r, 37 : 02 : 03
& added to it wch was remayning of the peage & 20^s, 01 : 16 : 00

$$\text{li}\quad\text{s}\quad\text{d}$$

The captaine rec̃ in peage, ... 03 : 01 : 05
More in money, ... 01 : 00 : 00

Spent thereof & layd out, ... 02 : 05 : 05

Remayneth in his hand(, ... 01 : 16 : 00

In the Treasurers hands, ... 38 : 18 : 03
Due to himself, ... 10 : 00 : 00

The remander to the countrey is . . . . 28 : 18 : 03

The Court doth order, that euery towne shall pay their owne souldiers what is due vnto them for their wages, and returne the rest to Plymouth, to the Treasurer, at Mr Paddys house, toward(the payment of other charges about the expedition, prouided that euery souldier allow by deduction of his wages what hee hath taken vp of any man to furnish him for his seruice, and like to returne their armes and bullet(againe, or els allow for them.

*The pposic̃ons to be made to the towneshipps are, that the com̃issioners agree that eich sachem keepe wthin their owne bound(. [*125.]

That the com̃issioners haue power graunted them to punish such officers & messengers as shall fayle in their duties and messages.

That the assistant(, or any of them, shall haue power to take an acknowledg^{nt} of a bargaine and sale of land(, &c̃, they ⁁ keepe a booke thereof, or cause them to be recorded wth all convenyent speed; that the wyfe hereafter shall also come in & acknowledge the sale also; but la^{ds} form̃ly sold to be firme to the buyer, notwthstanding the wyfe came not in. Confirmed.

That the colonies shall allow ij^d p day to mayntaine a prison^r for felony or misdemeanor, (if they be not able to mayntaine themselues,) and the Treasurer to pay it. Confirmed.

That the marshall haue ij^s p ^{s} for gathering of fynes, if they be not brought in by the p̃^{ties} themselues. Confirmed.

‡That for correction by whipping, the marshall shall haue v^s, in this manner to be payd by the offendor, viz(, ij^s vj^d for his ymprisonment, & ij^s vj^d his releases.‡

PLYMOUTH COLONY RECORDS.

1645.

28 October.
BRADFORD,
Gou.

Plymouth,	{ Mr John Howland,	John Dunhame, Señ,
	{ Manasseth Kempton,	John Cooke, Juñ.
Scittuate,	{ Before was Humfrey Turner & Wm Hatch;	
	{ but they had none this Court.	
Taunton,	Willm Parker,	Richard Williams.
Yarmouth,	Mr Anthony Thacher,	Edmond Hawes.
Rehoboth,	Walter Palmer.	
Duxborrow,	Mr John Alden,	George Soule.
Sandwich,	Richard Burne,	Thom Burges.
Barnestable,	Anthony Annable,	Isaack Robinson.
Marshfeild,	Mr Willm Thomas,	Mr Thom Burne.

12 November. John Turner and Mary Brewster marryed the xijth Nouemb^r, 1645.

19 November. Nathaniell Warren & Sarah Walker marryed the xixth Nouemb^r, 1645.

6 December. John Washborne & Elizabeth Mitchell marryed the vjth of Decemb^r, 1645.

26 December. John Tompson & Mary Cooke marryed the xxvjth Decemb^r, 1645.

1645-6.
2 March.
Joseph Ramsden & Rachell Eaton marryed the second day of March, 1645.

---

3 March.
NEW PLYM.
[*127.]

*_At the Gen^rall Court of o^r Sou^raigne Lord the King, holden at Plym̃, afores^d, the third Day of March, in the xxjth Yeare of the now Raigne of o^r Sou^raigne Lord, Charles, by the Grace of God King of England, Scotland, France, & Ireland, Defendor of the Fayth, &c._

BEFORE Willm Bradford, genť, Goũ,   Willm Collyer,
Edward Winslow,   Timothy Hatherley, and
Miles Standish,   Edmond Freeman,
Gentlemẽ, Assistanť, &č.

THE comittees of the seũall townes :—

Plymouth,	{ Mr Willm Paddy,	Manasseth Kempton,
	{ John Dunham, Señ,	John Cooke, Juñ.
Sandwich,	Willm Newland,	James Skiff.
Taunton,	None.	

COURT ORDERS. 95

Duxborrow,	. .	Mr John Alden,	Georg̃ Soule.	1645.
Barnestable,	. .	Henry Cobb,	Thom̃ Hinckley.	3 March.
Marshfeild,	. .	Josias Winslow,	Robte Waterman.	Bradford,
Scituate,	. . .	Humfrey Turner,	John Lewes.	Gou.
Yarmouth,	. .	Mr Anthony Thacher,	Edmond Hawes.	
Rehoboth,	. .	None.		

William Brett,
George Partrich,
John Vobes,
‡John Washborne,‡ } ppounded to take vp their freedome the next Court.
Robte Carver,
John Bourne,
John Allen,

Nathaniell Bowman is awarded to pay ij^s to Morris Truant for not psecuting his action against him.

It is ordered, that Major Gibbens shall take order to answere Mr Combes declaracõn against Morton and Mr Combs attorney to write vnto him.

Mr Allerton, vpon a motion made in the Court by Thomas Cushman, is allowed a yeares tyme for recoũing his debtℇ in this goũment, vpon bookℇ and papers.

Whereas vpon a peticõn to the Court, it appeareth that Richard Templer, the now constable of Yarmouth, in vndertakeing to pay fifty shillings for Wm Chase, to set him forth in the last expedition, and hath receiued satisfaccõn to the value of xxx^s or thereaboutℇ, it is requested by the Court, that the towne of Yarmouth would pay one third p̃t thereof, and the said Chase another third p̃t, and the countrey thother third p̃t of what remaynes, to satisfye the said fifty shillings.

Concerneing the differrence about Mr Starrs rate at Marshfeild, the Court doth not see but that it is right and equall that Mr Starr should be rated at Marshfeild pportionable to his landℇ improoued and stock there, and shall now pay his rate there vntill that Duxborrow can make it appeare that it was vnderstood that he should not be rated there vntill hee came totally wth his famyly to dwell there, and that Marshfeild condiscended therevnto.

The Court requesteth Mr Prence & Mr Freeman to heare the differrencℇ betwixt the towne of Yarmouth, Mr Lumpkine, and Mr Palmer, about the mayntenance of Willm Growse, and to order the same.

*Whereas the tyme being this Court wherein order is to be taken for letting of the trade at Kennebeck, els̃ it would endanger the losse of this yeares [*128.]

1645-6.

3 March.
Bradford, Goũ.

benefitt, by reason whereof the Court is constrayned to nominate and authorize a committee to lett forth the same to the best advantage of the gouerment, and for the tyme of ∧ yeares, to such as will giue the most for yt, haue therefore nominated and authorized the Goũnor and Assistantẽ, wth Mr John Alden, Mr Willm Thomas, Mr John Howland, Jonathan Brewster, and Josias Winslow, as a committee to lett forth the same vnto them the first Tewsday in May next.

The company for the Kennebeck trade brought in an account into the Court for the yeare 1644, wch came that yeare but to thirty poundẽ, and also an account how it was disbursed for the countreyes use, wch the Court accepted and allowed, and they are thereof discharged; and likewise towardẽ the rent for the yeare 1645 there was an account exhibited whereby there appeared to be in the store for the countreys use six barrells of pouder, three hundred waight of leade, and ∧ poundẽ of bullettẽ, and foure poundẽ nineteene shillings and six pence remayneing due to the country from them, besides thirty shillings for a case of bottells, wch was not cleared that they were spent for the countreys use; but the 300 waight of leade is not yet payd for.

And xvj^lb of pouder to Marshfeild.
I̊t, xx^lb of pouder to Taunton.
I̊t, xvj^lb of pouder to Barnestable.
And baggs to put pōder in.

⎱ These p̃cells of pōder were remayneing of the seauenth barrell of pōder, the rest being spent by the souldiers in the last expedition.

P̃posic̃ons.

Confirmed.

‡That the townes p̃uide sufficient armes for so many men as their p̃portion wilbe to set forth, that they may be in p̃sent readynesse if any suddaine occation fall forth.‡

Confirmed.

‡That the clarke, or some one in euery towne, do keepe a register of the day and yeare of euery marryage, byrth, and buriall, & to haue 3^d a peece for his paynes.‡

P̃sentmentẽ this Court, by the Grand Enquest.

Released.

1. Wee do here p̃sent Thomas Bonney, of the towne of Duxborrow, for vnciuill carriages and lacivious actions towardẽ weomen and maydes. Released.

Released.

2. Wee do p̃sent Thomas Dexter, of Sandwich, for disobeying the Goũnors warrantẽ in conveying away his horse, being prest for the countreys use. Discharged.

Released.

3. Wee do here p̃sent Thomas Burges and Thom̃s Nicholls, for breach of the Kinges peace. Discharg^d.

4. Wee do here p̃sent Willm Brookes, of the towne of Marshfeild, for the breach of his oath, in discloseing of his fellowes counsell and his owne, wch hee through weaknes confesseth hee did, and is released.

COURT ORDERS.

5. Wee do here p̃sent John Gray, of Yarmouth, for abuseing Ann, the wife of W{m} Eldred, in an injurious manner. 1645-6.

6. We do here p̃sent M{r} Symkins for the breach of the Kings peace, w{th} strikeing of Thomas Hinckley. Released. 3 March. BRADFORD, Gov{r}.

7. We do here p̃sent Leiftennant Dimmack, of Barnestable, for neglecting to exercise their men in armes. Discharged. Released. Discharged.

*Whereas an action of slaunder and defamac̃ŏn was this Court com̃enced by M{r} John Farnyseede, and Elizabeth, his wyfe, against Thomas Bonney, by the arbitration and mediation of frendł, it was vpon the said Bonneys acknowledgment withdrawne, w{ch} was shewed in Court, and ordered to be recorded as follow{th}, viz⨝ : — [*129.]

Know all men by these p̃ntł, that whereas Thomas Bonney hath said that M{ris} Farniseede did justle him in her house; and that hee tooke it as a temptation of him vnto lust, the said Thomas Bonney doth freely and humbly acknowledḡ, vnto the glory of God and vnto his owne shame, that it was his owne base heart that caused him to make that construction thereof, hee acknowledging that hee had no sufficient reason so to conceiue, but that euell suspition arose from the corruption of his owne heart ; and although the said Thomas Bonney did further accuse her in comeing bare legged vnto him, speaking vnto him, Thomas Bonney, will you mend my shooes ? shee vtterly denyeth that euer shee came to him in any such manner, the said Thomas Bonney dareing not say but that hee might be mistaken therein ; and whateuer interpretation Thomas Bonney did make thereof, the said Thomas Bonney acknowledgeth it to arise from his owne base, lustfull heart, and doth wholly condem̃e himself frõ speakeing or thinking any euell of her, the said Thomas Bonney not dareing to say or think any other of her but that shee is a very honest, modest, and chaste weoman, both in heart, worde, and deede, and doth therefore earnestly beseech the Lord to for giue him his many and great sinns therein, & doth humbly entreate M{ris} Farnyseede, her husband, p̃entł, and frends to forgiue him these so greate wronges & injuries done by him herein, p̃miseing to acknowledḡ these his wronges (donn vnto her) in or before the congregac̃ŏn wheneuer it shalbe required of the said M{rs} Farnyseede, her husband, or frendł; and also the said Thomas Bonney doth hereby testifye, that if euer hereafter hee shall in any measure speake any thing to any pson or psons tending to her disgrace or defamac̃ŏn, that then it shalbe lawfull for the husband of the said M{ris} Fernyseede to psecute his action of slaunder and defamac̃ŏn, notw{th}standing this his acknowledgment ; the said Thomas Bonney also p̃miseing to put into the hand of the deacon of the church of Duxborrow

VOL. II. 13

1645-6. fiue shillinges, for to be by the said deacon distributed vnto the poore. In witnesse whereof the said Thomas Bonney hath subscribed his hand this second day of March, 1645.

3 March.
BRADFORD, Gou.
[*130.]

THOMAS BONI.

Witnes, John Willis.

1646.

*Richard Smyth and Ruth Bonum marryed the xxvijth March, 1646.

27 March. Edmond Freeman, Ju^r, & Rebecca Prence marryed the xxijth of Aprill,
22 April. 1646.
23 April. Andrew Ringe and Deborah Hopkins marryed the xxiijth Aprill, 1646
29 May. Thomas Pope and Sarah Jenney married the xxixth May, 1646.

---

5 May.
[*131.]

**At a Court of Assistantℓ holden the fift Day of May, in the xxijth Yeare of the now Raigne of o^r Sou'aigne Lord, Charles, by the Grace of God King of England, Scotland, France, & Ireland, Defendor of the Fayth, &c.*

BEFORE Willm Bradford, gent, Gou,   Tymothy Hathereley,
    Edward Winslow,   John Browne, &
    Willm Collyer,   Edmond Freeman, Sen,
    Miles Standish,
      Gentlē, & Assistantℓ.

VPON heareing of the cause betwixt Roger Chaundler and Kenelme Winslow, for his daughters cloathes, wch the said Kenelme detaineth, vpon p̄tence of some further service wch he required of her, whereunto the said Roger vtterly refused to consent, it is ordered by the Court, that the said Kenelme Winslowe shall deliuer the mayde her cloathes wthout any further delay.

 Kenelme Winslowe, for opprobrious words against the church of Marshfeild, saying they were all lyers, &c̄, was ordered by the Court to fynd sureties for his good behauio^r, wch he refuseing to doe, was committed to prison, where hee remayned vntill the Genall Court following.

 Vpon the petic̄on of Mr John Gilbert, of Taunton, for a p̄cell of meddow taken from him, the Court doth thinke it meete that in regard of former engagementℓ wch haue passed betwixt him and some of the ma^{trates}, the Bench do require the townsmen of Taunton to accom̄odate his sonn elswhere, that M^r

COURT ORDERS. 99

Gilbert may enjoy his meddow, puided hee resigne vp his late graunt from the towne. 1646.

Vpon informa͡cõn of an affray was made vpon Vssamequine and some of his men by Wilɫm Cheesborrow, of Seacunck, alͥs Rehoboth, and some others, the Court doth order, that a warrant shalbe forthw[th] directed to the constable of Rehoboth, to app͡hend the body of the said William Cheesborrow, and to cause him to be brought from constable to constable, to his ma[ts] goale at Plyᷠ, there to remayne vntill he shalbe thence deliuͣed by due course of law. 5 May. BRADFORD, Goᷠ.

It is also ordered, that an attachment shalbe directed to the constable of Rehoboth, to attach the body of Thomas Hitt, to fynd sureties for his app͡arance at the next Geñall Court, &c̃, to answere for haueing a hand in the said affray made vpon Vssamequin, &c̃; and also for his contempt in not appeareing this Court, according as he was appoynted by Mr John Browne, one of the Assistantɛ̃.

*May 29th, 1646. Wm Cheesborrow, of Rehoboth, blacksmith, oweth the Kinge, &c̃, ... } xx[li].
Richard Paul, of Taunton, planᷠ, ... x[li].
Aron Knap, of the same, planᷠ, ... x[li].

29 May. Released. [*132.]

The condi͡cõn, that the said Wilɫm Cheesborrow shall appeare at the next Geñall Court, to be holden at Plyᷠ the first Tewsday in June next, to answere to all such matters as on his ma[ties] behalf shalbe objected against him, concerning an affray made vpon Vssamequin and some of his people, and in the meane season to ^ towardɛ̃ o[r] said souꝰaigne lord the King and all his leigh people, and abide the further order of the Court, and not depart the same w[th]out lycence; that then, &c̃.

*The limmits and bounds of the planta͡cõn of the towne of Taunton, alͥs Cohannet, w[th]in the gouꝰment of Plymouth, bounded and ranged for length and breadth, by order of Court, by Miles Standish & John Browne, gentleᷠ, Assistantɛ̃ in the gouꝰment, the xix[th] day of June, año D[m] 1640, in the xvj[th] yeare of our souꝰaigne lord, Charles, &c̃, as followeth, vizꝰ : — [*133.]

Inpri[s] from two marked trees nere vnto Asonet, a neck of land being betweene Asonet and them, lying southerly, and from the said marked trees ranging east and by south foure miles; rangeing also from the extent of the said foure miles north and by west; also from two markt trees neere the Three Mile Riuer, lying southerly of Taunton, the rang̃ to runn foure miles west & by north; and from the extent of this last menc͡õned foure miles, the rang̃ to runn north and by west eight miles; moreouꝰ, from the extent of this eight miles range, then the range to runn on the east and by south line, to meete w[th]

1646.
29 May.
BRADFORD,
Goũ.

the former expressed north and by west lyne vpon a long square; alwayes puided, that if these ranges do not take in a place called Schadingmore Meddowes, the said Schadingmore Meddowes to be included as belonging to the aforesaid towne of Taunton, wth one thousand acrees of vpland neere and adjacent vnto the said meddowes; prouided likewise, that these lines do not intitle the said towne of Taunton to intermeddle wthin two miles of Teightaquid.

MILES STANDISH,
JOHN BROWNE.

2 June.
NEW PLYM.
[*135.]

At a Gen^rall Court holden at Plym̃ afores^d, the second Day of June, in the xxijth Yeare of the Raigne of our Sou^raigne Lord, Charles, by the Grace of God King of England, Scotland, France, and Ireland, Defendor of the Fayth, &c.

BEFORE Willm Bradford, genT, Goũ,   Captne Miles Standish,
Edward Winslow,   Tymothy Hatherly,
Thomas Prence,   John Browne, &
Willm Collier,   Wm Thomas,
Genṫ, Assistantℓ, &c̃.

MR TYMOTHY HATHERLEY and Mr John Browne were chosen comĩssioners for the United Colonies for this yeare, according to the articles of confederac̃on.

The Counsell of Warr chosen & nominated by Court for this ensuing yeare.

Mr Edward Winslow, p̃sident,
Mr Thomas Prence,
Captaine Miles Standish,
Mr Tymothy Hatherley,
Mr John Browne,
Mr John Alden,
Capṫ Willm Poole.

It is enacted by the Court, that these, or any three of them, meeting together, shall haue power and authoryty to make orders for matters of warr, and to yssue forth warrants, &c̃; but if but two of them do meete, then to haue the consent and approbac̃on of the Goũ in what they doe; and that when these do so meete together, they shall haue power to choose such psons to their counsell and assistance as they shall think good, (if they please,) so they exceed not the number of foure psons ; and if any man shall refuse to doe the service when they are so warned or called therevnto, that then such pson or psons shalbe fyned as the counsell of warr shall think meete, so it exceede not fourty shillings to the colonies use ; and that these shall haue power to determine in any offence concerneing warr, either donn before this day or after, before thend of this ensuing yeare, and for all psons, as well strangers as our selues, for any thing donn wᵗʰin this goūment, and shall power to choose a p̱sident amongst themselues, and to make orders about such thinges as shalbe needfull.

1646.
2 June.
BRADFORD, Goū.

*Captaine Miles Standish chosen Treasurer for this ensuing yeare.
Mʳ Willm Collyer coroner.

[*136.]

Freemen admitted this Court, and sworne.

Mʳ Samuell Newman,	John Washborne,
Nathaniall Bacon,	Andrew Ring,
Dolor Davis,	Oliuer Purchase,
Georḡ Partrich,	Willm Brett.

These were p̱pounded to take vp their freedome the next Court : —

Willm Wills,	Thomas Huckens,
Thomas Heyward,	James Wyatt.
Edward Jenkine,	

The Court doth order, that one of a towne, viz$, Mʳ Thomas Willet, Mʳ John Alden, Mʳ Thomas Bourne, Thomas Chambers, Thomas Tupper, Henry Andrewes, Anthony Annable, Edmond Hawes, & Steeven Payne, shall, as a comittee, consider of a way for the defraying the charges of the maᵗʳᵃᵗᵉˢ table, by way of excise vpon wyne & other thinges.

Clement Briggs, of Weymouth, made knowne to the Court that Mʳ Isaack Allerton was endebted vnto him the sum of seauen pounds, whereof he desires notice may be taken because of a late act made concerneing debtē not demaunded wᵗʰin a yeare after they are due, in some cases are hardly recoūable, and for that he cannot speake wᵗʰ Mʳ Allerton himself. Mʳˢ Fuller sayth that

*The Constables of the seūall Towneshipps for this Yeare.

[*137.]

Plymouth, . . .	Robert Paddock & Thomas Whitney.
Duxborrow, . .	Georḡ Partrich.
Sandwich, . . .	Peter Gaunt.

102   PLYMOUTH COLONY RECORDS.

1646.   Bāstable,   . . . Thomas Huckens.
  ⌣   Marshfeild, . .   Thoṁ Chillingsworth, Robte Barker.
 2 June.   Nawsett,   . . . Samuell Hicks.
BRADFORD,   Scittuate,   . . . Ephraim Kempton & John Hollett.
  Goṽ.   Taunton,   . . . Oliver Purchase.
               Yarmouth,   . . . John Joyce.
               Rehoboth,   . . . Peter Hunt.

Nawsett is graunted to be a towneshipp, and to haue all the pruiledges of a towneshipp, as other townes wᵗʰin this goũment haue.

Surveyors of the Heighwayes.

Plymouth,   . Robert Wickson, Robert Finney, and John Finney.
Duxborrow,   . Wilłm Merrick & Morris Truant.
Scittuate,   . . John Stockbridḡ & Walter Woodward.
Sandwich,   . Edmoñ Freeman, Juʳ, & James Skiff.
Taunton,
Barnestable, . Henry Rowley & Thomas Shawe.
Yarmouth,   . Yeluerton Crowe, Edward Sturges.
Marshfeild, . John Dingley & William Brooke.
Rehoboth,   . Thomas Cooper.

The Grand Enquest.

Mʳ Thomas Howes,   ⎫   Michaell Turner,   ⎫
Robte Lee,   ⎪   Phillip Delanoy,   ⎪
Nathaniell Morton,   ⎪   Thomas Heyward,   ⎪
Robte Bartlet,   ⎬ juṙ.   John Hore,   ⎬ sworn.
John Bourne,   ⎪   Thomas Raulins,   ⎪
Joseph Biddle,   ⎪   Thomas Hyland,   ⎪
Wilłm Carpenter,   ⎪   Barnard Lumbert,   ⎪
John Stronge, not swore.   ⎪   Henry Bourne,   ⎪
Georḡ Knott.   ⎭   Emanuell White,   ⎭

John Jenkine, not sworn, released of his fine.

[*138.]   *The Court doth graunt to the inhabitę of Taunton that they shall purchase the p̄cell or neck of land, or yland, lying at Namaskett Pond, or wᵗʰin the s̄d pond, wᶜʰ they desire for a calues pasture, and to haue the use of it vntill there shalbe a plantaċon erected there aboutę to whom it may be helpfull; and that then they, paying the purchase and the charḡ that Taunton inhit[shalbe at about the said pcell of land, shall haue such pt thereof as shalbe thought meete by the Court.

1646.

Whereas Willm Halloway, of Taunton, complayned that an old woeman wch hee brought out of England was chargable to him, the Court tooke it into consideracon, & do request the said Willm Halloway to deliû her to the towne, or whom they shall appoynt to receiue her, wth her cloathes and bedding, and such thinges as shee hath, and the towne to take order for her mayntenance; and if hereupon the said Halloway shall refuse to deliuer her, wth her apparell & bedding, &c, that then he appeare here the next meeting, the first Tewsday in July next, to shew reason to the contrary, except the towne & the said Halloway shall agree otherwise.

2 June.
BRADFORD, Gou.

William Cheesborrow, of Rehoboth, for mending two locks for peec[at three shillings a peece, and for his abuse of Vssamequin, as the case now stands betwixt us and him, and for his breach of ymprisonment and flying to a forraigne goûment, and leaueing this, is censured by the Court to be ymprisoned fourteene dayes, w^thout bayle or mainprize, and to pay six pounds fine to the colonies use.

Cheesborro fin^d 6^li.

Thomas Hitt, of Rehoboth, for takeing pt with Cheeseborrow in the affray made vpon Vssamequin and his men, is fined twenty shillings, & for his contempt.

Hitt fined xx^s.

The Rates agreed vpon for Excise.

‡That such strangers as haue liberty to fish at the Cape to pay fiue shillings p share.‡

Vpon euery gallon of Spanish wine drawne by retayle by such as are allowed, eight pence.

Vpon euery gallon of French wine drawne by retayle by as are allowed, foure pence.

Vpon euery hogshead of beere, two shillinges.

Vpon euery gallon of strong water, eighteene pence.

Vpon euery pound of tobaccoe retayled, j^d.

Vpon euery gallon of oyle, j^d.

This Court is adjourned to the first Tewsday in July next, when the seûall townes are appoynted to send their committees to do such businesses as are now left vndonn.

1646.
7 July.
NEW PLYM.
BRADFORD,
Goῦ.
[*139.]

*At the second Session of the Geñall Court, begun the first Tewsday in June, and adjorned vnto the first Tewsday in July following, and now holden the said first Tewsday in July, in the xxijth Yeare of the Raigne of our Sou'aigne Lord, Charles, by the Grace of God King of England, Scotland, France, and Ireland, Defendor of the Fayth, &c.

BEFORE Willm Bradford, gent, Goῦ, Miles Standish,
   Edward Winslow,   Tymothy Hatherley, and
   Willm Collyer,   Willm Thomas,
      Gent, Assistantℓ, &ĉ.

THE comittees of the seûall towneshipps :—

Plymouth,	Mr John Howland, Manasseth Kempton, John Dunham, Señ, Mr Thoṁ Willett.
Scittuate,	Humphrey Turner, John Lewes.
Taunton,	Richard Williams.
Yarmouth,	Mr Anthony Tãcher, Edmond Hawes.
Rehoboth,	None.
Duxborrow,	Mr John Álden, George Soule.
Sandwich,	Mr Edmond Freeman, Willm Newland.
Barnestaple,	Henry Cobb, Thoṁ Hinckley.
Marshfeild,	Josias Winslow, Robte Waterman.
Nowsett,	None.

In the differrence betwixt Richard Church, complaynent, and M^{ris} Jenney, widow, defeñt, the Court, vpon heareing the cause and examinaçõn of witness^s, and view taken of his booke, there appeared due vnto Richard 1 ii^s, wch the Court doth award and order the said M^{ris} Jenney to pay to the said Richard Church, saue that the said Richard Church is to hew a sett of coggs and rounds for her, according to the couenant.

In the case betwixt Teag̃ Jones and Raph Wheilden and his daughter, the Court, not fynding thinges fully cleared by reason of the absence of the said Wheildon and his daughter, it is referred to further heareing, either at the next Geñall Court or some Court of Assistantℓ before, where the said Raph Wheildon and his daughter and the said Teag̃ are required by the Court to appeare, and vpon further heareing then to be decided.

Francis Sprague, of Duxborrow, is lycensed to keepe an ordinary and to draw wyne at Duxborrow.

COURT ORDERS.

Edward Jenkins, of Scittuate, is lycensed to keepe an ordinary and to draw wyne at Scittuate.

*Edward Sturges, of Yarmouth, is lycensed to keepe an ordinary and draw wyne at Yarmouth, ꝑuided Mᵣ Thacher draw out his. Repealᵗ 20 : 8 : 1646.

Roᵬte Barker is lycensed to keepe an ordinary at Marshfeild, and to draw wyne.

1646.
7 July.
BRADFORD, Goᵥ.
[*140.]

The action betwixt Tobias Taylor, complⁿᵗ, and John Shawe, defeⁿᵗ, is referred to the ending of Mʳ Hanbury and John Lewes for John Shawe, Mʳ Alden and Thomas Clark for Tobias; and if they cannot end yt, they foure to choose a fift man vnto them, and as any three or more of them agree, so to stand.

Mʳ William Collyer, Mʳ Thomas Willett, Mʳ Anthony Thacher, and Josias Winslow are appoynted by the Court as a coͫittee to draw vp the excise into due forme of an act, and also to ꝑscribe a way and meanes how it shalbe gathered, wᵗʰ penalties vpon the delinquentꝭ, and ꝑsent it to yᵉ Court to be confirmed.

Constant Southworth is allowed by the Court to be ensigne bearrer of Duxborrow company.

Mʳ Thomas Dimmacke, of Barnestable, is allowed by the Court to bee leiftennant, to exercise their men in armes at Barnestable.

Whereas Charles Thurston, servant to Mʳ Wilᵗm Hanbury, for his former misdemeanor, and revelling, & disguised daunceing, was fined lˢ or there aboutꝭ, for wᶜʰ his said mʳ did vndertake to pay, or elȿ he should haue beene whipt at the publike post, the said Charles Thurston ꝑmised in the Court either to ꝑcure his said master security for the payment thereof, or elȿ to serue him so much longer after his tyme was out (wᶜʰ the said Charles acknowledged to be two yeares from the xxvᵗʰ of this instant July) as would satisfye his master, and for other demaunds of losse of tyme for absenting himselfe from his service wᵗʰout his said masters consent.

The Men nominated and appoynted in euery Towne to recouer the Excise & gather it.

Plymouth, . . John Finney.
Duxborrow, . John Willis.
Scittuate, . . Samuell House.
Sandwich, . . Peter Gaunt.
Taunton, . . James Wyatt.
Yarmouth, . . Edmond Hawes.
Barncstable, . Isaack Robinson.
Marshfeild,. . Roᵬte Waterman.
Rehoboth, . . ˆ
Nausett, . . ˆ

These are to be for one yeare, and to be yearely renewed.

1646.

7 July.
BRADFORD,
Goῦ.

[*141.]

*It is agreed vpon and ordered by the Court, that when the inhabitantᶜ of Sandwich haue payd a debt of xvij^{li} or xviij^{li}, oweing to the old company, and payd the charḡ & purchase of their towneship, or such a sume as Mr Thomas Prence and Captaine Miles Standish shall agree vpon, that then the comittees or vndertakers shall yeild vp the lands vndesposed of to the towne, to be giuen forth and disposed by such psons as the towne shall appoynt, and that euery inhabitant haueing lands graunted him shall pay pportionably to the s͞d paymentᶜ.

It is ordered by the Court, that the comittees of euery towne shall send the names of all their males, from xvi^{teene} yeares of age to sixty, to the Goῦ, sealed vp, by the first of August next.

Vpon complaint, by some of the inhabitantᶜ of Scittuate, that there was great want of heighwayes to be layd forth, and a form͞ jury haue beene empaneled to haue donn the same who haue not yet, for diuers yeares, recorded their verdict, that the wayes might be knowne as the Court is informed, the Court doth therefore order that a warrant shalbe directed to the constables of Scittuate, requireing them to cause a sufficient jury to be empanelled before Mr Tymothy Hatherley, who vpon their oathes shall lay forth all such wayes wth as much convenyency for the geñall, and as little p͞judice to the p͞ticulers, as may be according to the act of the Court.

This Court is adjorney vnto the next Tewsday before the Geñall Court in October next, wch wilbe the xxth day of the said month.

Memorand : that something be donn to mayntaine the libertys of the churches, wthout intermedleing or wronging eich other, according to the statutᶜ of England, that they may liue in peace.

Defects in Apᵖarence this Court by the Ma^{trates} and Comittees.

John Dunham, Señ, ...	vj^d.
Mr Edmond Freeman, . .	xviij^d.
Mr Thacher, ...	vj^d.
Edmond Hawes, ...	xij^d.
Henry Cobb, ...	vj^d.
Thom͞ Hinckley, ...	vj^d.

} iiij^s vj^d.

[Here the records cease to be in the handwriting of Mr. Souther. The following pages, as far as page 159, in the original manuscript, were written by Governor Bradford.]

COURT ORDERS.

*The 10 of December, 1646.

1646.
10 December.
BRADFORD,
Goũ.
[*143.]

John Barnes acknowledgeth himself to stand bound to oure soueraigne lord, King Charles, King of England, Scotland, France, & Ierland, Defendore of y⁰ Faith, &ĉ, for Thomas Shaue, of Bāstable, body for body, that y⁰ said Thomas Shaue shall appeare at y⁰ next Generall Courte, to be held at Plimouth for our said soueraine lord y⁰ King, the first Tuesday in March next insuing; and ther to continue till he hath answered all shuch maťers as are aledged against him by John Crocker or others.

Likwise Thomas Huckins, of Bāstable afforsaid, planter, acknowledgeth himselfe to stand bound for y⁰ aforesaid Thomas Shaue, body for body, to our soueraigne lord y⁰ King, in all respects as y⁰ said John Barnes, &ĉ.

Taken by William Bradford & Captaine Myles Standish, the day & yeare aboue writen.

Vpon the day & time abouesaid, viz⸝, the 2ᵈ of March, y⁰ pson app̄ed, & so y⁰ sureties were released, &ĉ.

**Att a Courte of Assistantℛ holden att Plimouth aforesaid, on Tewsday, the fourth of August, in y⁰ xxij*ᵗʰ *Yere of y*ᵗ *now Raigne of o*ʳ *Souraigne Lord, Charles, by y*ᵉ *Grace of God of England, Scotland, &c, King, Defendor of y*ᵉ *Faith, &c.*

4 August.
NEW PLYM.
[*144.]

BEFORE Wᵐ Bradford, genť, Goũ,   John Browne, and
Edward Winslow,   Wᵐ Thomas,
Tymothy Hatherley,
Gentł, Assistants, &ĉ.

IN the case betwixte Samuell Eddy and John Dunham, Juñ, about y⁰ said John Dunhams giving poyson to the said Samuell Eddys dogg, the Court, having taken the same into serious consideracōn, vpon hearing what could be said on both sides, the Courte doth order yᵗ y⁰ said John Dunhame shall finde sureties for his good behavioʳ vnto y⁰ next Court.

In the case betwixte Thomas Bonney, compł, and John Willis and Mʳ John Farneseede, defendˢ, for damage don in the corne and garden of y⁰ said compł, wᶜʰ damage was awarded to vijˢ by such as viewed the same, the Court, having heard the allegations of all the said p̄ties, doe determine, that the said vijˢ shalbe equally borne betwixte them, vizᵗ: ijˢ iiij a peece; yᵗ is, 2ˢ

1646.

4 August.
BRADFORD,
GOŮNOR.

4ᵈ Bonny, 2ˢ 4ᵈ John Willis, & 2ˢ 4ᵈ John Farneside, & Thomas Bonney to pay yᵉ charge of yᵉ Courte.

In the case betwixte John Barnes, compł, agˢᵗ Giles Rickett, for a bill of fiue pounds and a p̄cell of silke wᶜʰ the said compł hath bought of Samuell Harvey, the Court doth award the said Giles Rickett the p̄cell of silke for his paines taken in the busines, and John Barnes to haue the debte of 6ˡⁱ 5ˢ, & 15ˢ damage & xjᵉ charges of yᵉ suite, saue yᵗ yᵉ said John Barnes shall saue yᵉ said Giles Rickett harmeles of yᵉ said xjˢ, or pay it to him yᵗ laid the same downe for yᵉ said Harvey.

The Courte grants execuc̃on vpon the debte, &c̃.

The Court doth award execuc̃on against John Shaw to Tobias Tayler for 50ˢ, in peeces of eight, according to yᵉ ships account.

The acc̃on depending betwixte Tobias Tayler & John Shawe is referd to.

The foure aboue menc̃oned, not assenting, made choyse of Josias Winslow for the fifte man; and we whose names are vnderwritten order as followᵗʰ, that is to say, John Shawe shall pay to Tobias Taylor fifty shillings, according to the seamens account, & the cost of yᵉ Court excepting yᵉ mony given to the jury.

15 July.

James Addams & Francis Vassall married yᵉ 15ᵗʰ of Julie, 1646.

John Dunhame, Junʳ, acknowledgeth to owe the Kinge xlˡⁱ.

Released, paying his fees.

That the said John Dunhame shalbe of the good behavioʳ towards oʳ soŭaigne lord yᵉ Kinge & all his leigh people, and app̄re here at the nexte Genn̄all Court, and not dep̄te yᵉ same wᵗʰout licence; that then, &c̃.

---

20 October.
NEW PLIM.
[*145.]

*Att the third Session of the Genʳall Courte, begun the first Tewsday in June, holden the 20ᵗʰ of October, in yᵉ xxijᵗʰ Yere of yᵉ Raigne of oʳ Souʳaigne Lord, Charles, by yᵉ Grace of God King of England, &c., Defender of yᵉ Faith, &c.

BEFORE Wᵐ Bradford, genť, Goůnor,   Tymothy Hatherly,
Edward Winslow,   John Browne, and
Wᵐ Collier,   Wᵐ Thomas,
Capť Miles Standish,
Genť, Assistants.

ANTONY THACHER and George Sole were chosen a com̄ittee to draw vp an order concerning disorderly drinking of tobacco.

COURT ORDERS.

Whereas Robte Paddock complaines to this Court for and desires to haue an account of what is due vnto ⁁ by the last will & testa^{nt} of Wm Palmer, deceased, the Court desires Mr Thomas Prence either to come and giue in an account or send it vnto the Goūnor, y^t so what is due vnto ye said Paddock may be satisfied vnto him, according to ye teno^r of ye said will, as soone as wth conveniency he may, and that before this winter yf he canne.

1646.
20 October.
M^R
BRADFORD,
GOŪNOR.

The pporc̄ōn of eūy townships rates for the raising of their publike charges, as by this Court is ordered and agreed, is:—

	li s d				
Plimouth,	3 10 0	Duxborough,	ij^{li} x^s.	Scituate,	iiij^{li} x^s.
Sandwitch,	3 5 0	Tanton,	ij^{li} x^s.	Bastable,	ij^{li} x^s.
Yarmouth,	2 10 0	Marshfield,	ij^{li} x^s.	Rehoboth,	iiij^{li}.

28^{li} 15^s.

Vpon complaint of Thomas Star, of Yarmouth, about fees of Court, in an acc̄ōn psecuted in the Court att Yarmouth aforsaid agst Samuell Hincley, the Court ordereth, that the jury repay what they haue received frō the said Thomas Star as theire fees in y^t case, & that Sam̄ Hincly pay all y^e ⁁ belonging to ye clark of ye Court.

The two com̄ittees for the towne of Taunton, vizt, Richard Williams and ⁁, for theire non app^{r}ance are fined xx^s a peece.

Fine remitted
June 2^d, 1647.

Whereas the township of Taunton had a fine of 30^s given vnto them for & towards ye amending of their highwaies in c̄taine swamps; the Court, vnderstanding y^t they having received ye said fine, but not don ye said work, doth order y^t ye worke be forthwith sufficiently don, or elce that the mony be repaid by them to the Treasuror for ye Goūm^{ts} vse by March Court next. Mr Browne vndertooke y^t ye one of ye two should be don.

**Att a Genn'all Courte holden Octob^r 27th, in ye xxijth Yere of his Maties now Raigne, of England, &c.*

27 October.
NEW PLIM.
[*147.]

BEFORE Mr Bradford, Goūnor, Mr Browne, &
Mr Colliare, Mr Thomas,
Capt̄ Miles Standish,
Gent̄ & Assist̄.

JOHN TOMPSON, coming into this Court and acknowledging his fault of incontinency wth his wife before marriage, but after contract, was fined

Fine v^{li}.

1646.
27 October.
Mʀ Bradford, Goῦnor.

vˡⁱ & imprisoned according to order, but paying his fees, was released of his imprisonmᵗ.

In a case of diffrence twixte John Dunham, Juñ, and Samˡˡ Edie, the Court orders, & the said John Dunham agreed therevnto, that Mʳ Wᵐ Paddie and John Cooke, Juñ, shall heare, end, & determine all former civill differences twixte them to this ꝑsent day.

In a case of diffrence twixte Thomas Savery and William Bradford, Juñ, about a canoo, the Court ordereth, that in case he be not found yᵗ removed the said canoo frō Mʳ Attwoods by the nexte Genⁿall Court, that then the said Wilhm Bradford shall satisfie & pay yᵉ said Savery vˢ.

John Hore, Thomas Hiland, & John Jenkin, of the grand inquest, for default of appʳance at this Court, were ⚹ 20ˢ a peece, according to order.

In the case betweene Gabriell Whelding and Richard Taylor, about his daughter Ruth, the said Gabriell ꝑmiseth his free assent and consent to theire marriage.

1646-7.
5 January.
New Plim.
[*148.]

*Att a Courte of Assistants holden the vᵗʰ Day of January, in the xxijᵗʰ Yere of yᵉ Reigne of oʳ Souʳaigne Lord, Charles, now of England, &c, King, &c.

Before Mʳ Bradford, genẗ, Goῦnor,   Timothy Hatherly, &
Capẗ Miles Standish,   Wᵐ Thomas,
Genẗ, & Assisẗ, &ĉ.

WHEREAS Edward Hall compẗ agˢᵗ Capẗ Standish and Jonathan Bruster, &ĉ, for iijˡⁱ ijˢ, due to him for building, the Court ordereth, that they satisfie & pay him according to their agreemᵗ, and they to recoῦ yᵉ same againe frō yᵉ towne of Duxbury by way of distresse & sale of yᵉ goods of such as refuse to pay theire ꝑporĉŏns according to rate.

COURT ORDERS. 111

*Att a Gen'all Court holden March 2^d, in y^e xxijth Yere of his Maties now Raigne, of England, &c.

1646-7.
2 March.
NEW PLIM.
MR BRADFORD, Go𝒰nor.
[*149.]

BEFORE Mr William Bradford, gen$̃$, & Go𝒰,   Mr Hatherly,
Cap$̃$ Standish,   Mr Browne, &
Mr Colliare,   Mr Thomas,
Gen$̃$ & Assistants.

WHEREAS Abraham Sampson was p̃sented by y^e grand inquest for being drunke, he, tra𝒰sing y^e said p̃sent^{nt}, made his plea at this Court, & by verdict of y^e jury was found guilty ac$̃$ to y^e p̃sent𝔪̃t, and therevpon, ac$̃$ to order, was fined v^s & the fees of Courte. Fine v^s.

The jury for this triall were,—

John Cooke,	⎫		Gabriell Followay,	⎫	
James Hurst,			Giles Rickett,		
Joseph Rogers,	⎬ jurat̃.		Edmond Tilson,	⎬ jurat̃.	
John Finney,			Rob̃t Finney,		
Thõ Cushman,			Joshua Pratt,		
Rob̃te Wickson,	⎭		George Watson,	⎭	

Att this Court John Crocker compl̃ against Thomas Shawe for coming into his house by putting aside some loose pallizadoes on ye Lords day, about ye middle of the day, & tooke and carried out of his said house some venison, some beefe, some butter, cheese, bread, & tobacco, to the value of xii^d, wch ye said Thõ Shaw openly in publike Court confessed, submitting himselfe to ye censure of the Court; wherevpon, his sureties being released, he was com̃itted to ye marshalls charge; and ye Court censured him to make satisfacc̃on for ye goods stolen j^s, being so valued, and 13^s 4^d a peece to ye two men y^t attended on him to ye Court, and to be publikely whipt at ye post, wch was accordingly don by ye publike officer.

Vpon compl̃ of John Vassall vnto ye Court concñing John Lewis, app̃ntice to his father for iiij yeres, being ye remaine of vij yeres in wch he was bound to serue George Kenrick, the Court ordereth, y^t ye said John Lewis shall dwell with ye said Mr Vassall, and serue out ye full terme of his said indentures, as also for so long time as he hath absented himselfe wthout leaue from ye service of his said master or former masters in the foresaid seruice of vij yeres, as by indenture app̃reth.

George Wright and Joseph Tory were released paying theire fees of their bonds for the good behavior, but not of attending the Courte.

112 PLYMOUTH COLONY RECORDS.

1646-7.
2 March.
Mr Bradford, Goũnor.
Fine xli.
[*150.]

*Whereas Steven Wing, of Sandwitch, & Oseah Dillingham, were found to haue had carnall knowledge each of others body before contract of matrimony, wch the said Steven Wing, coming into the face of ye Court, freely acknowledging, he was, according to order of Court, fined in xli, and so is discharged.

Whereas George Wright was p̃sented by ye grand inquest for attempting the chastity of divs women by lacivious words & carriages, he, trafising ye said p̃scntnt, made his plea at this Court, & by verdict of a jury of 12 men was found guilty acc̃ to ye p̃sentnt. The Court, having maturely considered ye matt rs & circumstances, censured him to be bound to ye good behavior to or soũaigne lord ye King and all his leidge people vntill the next October Court, & then to app̃re and attend the further pleasure of ye Court, & so com̃itted him vntill he finde sureties.

The Jury for his Trafis.

John Finney,
Joseph Rogers,
Rich Sparrow,
John Crocker,
} jur̃.

Robte Wicson,
Gab Followay,
John Morton,
Joshua Prat,
} jur̃.

Richard Wright,
Giles Rickett,
Georg̃ Watson,
Joseph Torey,
} jur̃.

William Forde, being p̃sented for detaining and not delifling to ye owners their due weight & measure of corne frõ ye mill, is in Court admonished only for this first offence, that henceforth he be more carefull to vse diligence and faithfulnes, yt men may no more haue occac̃õn iustly to complaine, & to pvide a place for scales & weights in his milne, (being pvided by the towne,) yt so all may haue free librty to weigh their corne & meale yt will, and to put away the dogge or doggs yt frequent his milne, & carefully to keepe away sheepe or any other cattle yt may annoy mens corne & meale.

Vpon petic̃õn of Francis Crooker, who desires in marriage Mary Gaunt, kinswoman to Mr Coggin, of Bãstable, the Court, having heard both p̃ties & seriously weighed ye circumstances, doth order, yt yf ye said Crooker bring vnto ye Goũnor a c̃tificate, vnder the hands of Mr Chauncy & some other approved phisition, that that disease wth wch he is sometimes troubled be not the falling sicknes, that then he, ye said Crooker, shall in convenient time haue in marriage the said Mary Gaunt.

Antony Thacher, being returned at this Courte register keeper for Yarmouth, was approved of by ye Court.

[*151.] *Whereas Samuell Edeth, & Elizabeth, his wife, of ye towne of Plim̃ aforesaid, having many children, & by reason of many wants lying vpon them, so as they are not able to bring them vp as they desire, and out of y⁰ good respect they beare to Mʳ John Browne, of Rehoboth, one of y⁰ Assistantꞇ of this goũment, did both of them ioyntly desire yᵗ he, yᵉ said Mʳ Browne, would take Zachery, their son, being of the age of seven yeres, & bring him vp in his imploymᵗ of husbandry, or any busines he shall see meete for yᵉ good of theire child till he come to yᵉ age of one & twenty yeres ; wherevpon Mʳ Browne did, in yᵉ p̃sence of Mʳ Bradford, Goũnor, take into his service the said Zachary, & p̃miseth to p̃vide for & allow him during yᵉ said terme all necessaries convenient & fitting such a servant, according to yᵉ state & condic̃õn of yᵉ country, & doth furthʳ, of his owne will p̃vide yᵗ, yf in case he, yᵉ said Mʳ John Browne, & his wife, shall dep̃te this life before yᵉ said Zachary shall attaine to yᵉ end of his time of service, yᵗ then his eldest son, yᵗ shall haue yᵉ goũnmᵗ of him during yᵉ residue of yᵉ said time not attained vnto, shall not make sale of yᵉ said residue of time not attained vnto, nor any p̃te thereof to any pson or psons whatsoever whereby he shall or may be wronged ; and yf it shall so come to passe yᵗ those to whomsoeũ he shalbe comĩtted vnto, after the death of yᵉ said Mʳ John Browne & his wife, shall not deale well wᵗʰ him as such a servant ought to be dealt wᵗʰ, then vpon the complaint of any of yᵉ friends of yᵉ said Zachery, it shalbe lawfull for yᵉ deacons of yᵉ church of Plim̃ aforesaid, wᵗʰ the Goũnor, yᵗ then shalbe, to take him wholy away, & place him wᵗʰ whom they shall see meete, p̃vided yᵗ no sale or marchandise be made of yᵉ remaine of his time by any.

1646-7.
2 March.
Mʳ BRADFORD, Goũ.

	li	s	d
George Wright, of Rehoboth, plant̃, acknowledgeth to owe oʳ soũaigne lord yᵉ King	40	00	00
Richard Church, of yᵉ Eale River, plant̃,	20	00	00
Samuell Nash, of Duxborow, plant̃,	20	00	00

The condic̃õn, yᵗ yf yᵉ aboue bounden George Wright shall psonally app̃re at yᵉ nexte Genñall Court of oʳ soũaigne lord yᵉ King, to be holden att Plim̃, in October nexte, &c̃ ; & in the meane time to be of yᵉ good behavior towards oʳ said soũaigne lord yᵉ King and all his leigh people, and abide the further order of yᵘ Cout, & not dep̃te yᵉ same wᵗʰout licence ; yᵗ then, &c̃.

October Court, 26ᵗʰ, 1647. He not app̃ing, Richard Church and Samuell Nash had licence and libʳty granted them to bring in the aboue bounden George Wright at the nexte Genñall Courte of oʳ soũaigne lord yᵉ King, to be holden at Plim̃ aforesaid yᵉ first Tewsday in March nexte.

26 October.

1647.
4 May.
NEW PLIM.
Mʀ BRADFORD, Goū.
[*152.]

*Att a Courte of Assistants holden May 4th, in the xxiijth Yere of his Maties now Raigne, of England, &c.

BEFORE Mʳ Willm Bradford, Goū, Mʳ Hatherlie, and
Capt Standish, Mʳ Thomas,
Mʳ Colliare,
Gent, & Assist.

IT was ordered, that the now constables of Scituate be by warrant required to appre at the next Genñall Court, to giue their account concning yᵉ officers wages.

---

1 June.
NEW PLIM.
[*153.]

*Att a Genn'all Courte holden at Plim aforesaid, the first Day of June, in the 23th Yere of the Raigne of oʳ Sou'aigne Lord, Charles, by the Grace of God King of England, Scotland, France, & Ireland, Defendor of the Faith, &c.

BEFORE Willm Bradford, gent, Goūnor, Timothy Hatherly,
Thomas Prence, John Browne, and
Willm Colliare, Willm Thomas,
Capt Miles Standish,
Gent, Assistants, &c.

Freemen admitted this Court, and sworne.

Thomas Howes, Thomas Hayward,
Edward Jenkine, John Allen.

The Names of such as were ppounded to take vp their Freedome at the next Geñall Elecōn Court.

Ephraim Morton, Franc Goulder,
Henry Wood, Thomas Dunhā,
John Morton, John Bradford,
Steven Wood, James Glasse,
Richard Paul, Ephraim Heckes,
Willm Willes, Alexander Standish,
John Wood, John Browne,
Sam Dunham, John Allen,
Robert Finney, Samuell Tomkins.
Jacob Cooke,

COURT ORDERS. 115

Mr Will̃m Bradford was elected Goũnor. 1647.

Mr Edward Winslow, ⎫
Mr Thomas Prence, ⎪ 1 June.
Mr Will̃m Colliare, ⎪ M^R
Capt̃ Miles Standish, ⎬ were elected Assistants. Bradford,
Mr Timothy Hatherly, ⎪ Goũnor.
Mr John Browne, & ⎪
Mr Will̃m Thomas, ⎭

Mr William Bradford, Go^r, and ⎫
Mr John Browne, ⎬ were chosen Com̃issions ;
and the third man in elecc̃õn in case eithr of them faile, who was Mr Prence, and in case he misse, then the 4th, vizt, Mr Hatherley.

Capt̃ Miles Standish is chosen Treasurer for this yeare.

The constables chosen by the seũall townes, and p̃sented to this Court and sworne, are, —

Plimouth, . . . { Andrew Ring, } jur̃.
               { Robert Wickson, }
Duxborough, . . Will̃m Merritt.
Sandwitch, . . Thomas Dexter, Juñ.
Yarmouth, . . Tristrã Hull.
Marshfield, . . Kenelime Winslow & Peter Collimore.
Scituate, . . . Edward Jenkin & George Sutton.
Taunton, . . . Oliver Purchis.
Bãstable, . . . John Hall.
Nawsett, . . . John Smaley.
Rehoboth, . . . Wm Smith.

              Sup̃visors of the Highwaies.

Plimouth, . . .
Duxborough, . . Edward Hall & John Browne.
Scituate, . . . { John Williams, Thomas Chambers,
               { Humph Turner & Isaac Stockman.
Sandwitch, . . Joseph Holloway & George Buett.
Tanton, ... Edward Slocomb & Edward Rew.
Yarmouth, . . . Gabriell Whelding & John Darbie.
Bãstable, . . . Sam̃ Hincley & Henry Rowley.
Marshfield, . . Thomas Bourne & Thomas Tylden.
Rehoboth, . . . Rob̃te Tytus & Thomas Blisse.
Nawsett, . . . Nicolas Snow & Edward Banges.

1647.
1 June.
Mʳ Bradford, Goũ.
[*154.]

For Plimouth towne, . . . Richard Sparrow and John Barnes.
For the Eell Riuer, . . . Thoṁ Clarke.
For Joanses Riuer, . . . Jakob Cooke.

*The Grand Enquest.

William Nickerson,
Richard Church,
Giles Ricard, (cleared,)
John Morton,
Edward Tylson,
John Farnisside,
Snmuell Tompkins,
Thomas Burd,
George Russell,
John Daman,
} juř.

Anthony Snow,
John Dingley,
Thomas Tupper,
Edmond Freeman,
John Burseley,
Edw̃ Fitzrandall,
John Jenkin,
Thõ Gilbert,
John Tysdall,
} sworne.

Thõ Coop, Thõ Clifton, not sworne.

Receifts of Excise in each seũall Township.

Pliṁ, ... John Finney.
Scituate, ... Saṁ Jackson.
Taunton, ... James Wyat.
Bãstable, ... Isaac Robinson,
Rehoboth, ...
Duxbořw, ... John Willis.
Sandwitch, ... Peter Gaunt.
Yarmouth, ... Edmond Hawes.
Marshfield, ... Joseph Beedle.
Nawsett, ...

Mʳ Colliar, Mʳ Howland, Wᵐ Merrick, & George Partrich are appoynted to view an high way for yᵉ avoyding of yᵉ highway by yᵉ Goũnors meadow past Jones River to yᵉ vpper path to Mattacheesett, & make reporte of it to yᵉ Court, & appoynt it out, & yᵉ surveiors to lay it out.

James Cole, compł, agˢᵗ Thomas Pope, in an acõõn sclandʳ, daṁ 100ˡⁱ. The defend acknoledged his fault in Court, brought in his authors, who did yᵗ same wherevpon yᵉ compł let fall his acõõn, the defendˢ equally paying the charges.

Capt Miles Standish, compł, agˢᵗ Gilbert Brookes, in an acõõn of trespas vpon the case ; daṁ vˡⁱ. The jury found for yᵉ defend 2ᵈ daṁ, & charge of yᵉ Courte.

COURT ORDERS. 117

Thomas Prence, gent, compł, ag[st] Edward Holeman & Nicolas Hodges, **1647.**
def: Ac͠con, trespass vpon ye case; dam̄ 40[s]. The jury found for the plaint.
his peece & locke made good by y[e] defend, & cost of Court, and iudgm[t] therevpon was graunted.

1 June.
M[R] BRADFORD, Go⁸.

The Petty Jury for these Trialls.

John Finney,		John Allen,	
Rich Sparrow,		Joshua Pratt,	
Rob̃te Wickson,	jur̃.	Experience Michell,	sworne.
Sam̃ Nash,		Rich Higgens,	
George Soule,		George Partrich,	
Wm Wood,		Richard Wright,	

*The Com̃ittees for this Courte. [*155.]

Plym̃, ...	John Dunham,	John Howland,
	James Hust,	Wm Paddy.
Sandwitch, . .	Thõ Tupper,	Wm Newland.
Taunton, . . .	Henry Androuse,	Edward Case.
Nawsett, . . .	Josias Cooke &	Richard Higginson.
Duxborough, . .	Mr Alden,	Const Southward.
Scituate, . . .	Humphrey Turner &	John Williams.
Yarmouth, . .	Anthony Thacher,	Edmond Hawes.
Bastable, . . .	Anthõ Anable,	Henry Cob.
Marshfield, . .	Josias Winslow,	Rob̃te Waterman.
Rehoboth, . . .	Walter Palmer,	Steven Paine.

Joseph Rogers p̃posed by the towne of Nawset to this Court for lieutenant, to exercise theire men in armes, is by this Court app̃ved & established
liuetennant there. Willm Newland also liuetennant for Sandwitch.

The Courte ordereth and requesteth Mr Alden & John Washborne to view
the bounds betwixte the lands of Capt Standish & Frauncis Eaton, and sett
them at rights.

Mr Alden & Mr Paddie were chosen and appoynted a com̃ittee to take an
account of ye Treasurer for ye last yere, & make reporte thereof at ye nexte
Genñall Court.

Whereas the towne of Marshfield was p̃sented for not trayning according to order, the Court hath appoynted (vpon ye com̃ittees answer) and in-
treated Capt Miles Standish to goe of̃ and exercise the company, & vpon his
tryall finding any pson of ye company in some good measure able to exercise
ye body, to invest him wth power to do it, vntill y[ey] p̃sent to ye Court a fit man

118   PLYMOUTH COLONY RECORDS.

1647.
1 June.
Mⁿ Bradford, Goṽ.

for to be theire leader, & to attend to such further direccõns as the said capt shall giue them, & yᵉ seargeant of yᵉ band, vpon notice given him by yᵉ comĩttees, to warne a trayneing day yᵉ 16 day of this moneth, & in case yᵗ day ꝑue rayny, then yᵉ next faire day following.

It is enacted by this Courte, yᵗ yᵉ towne of Rehoboth shall haue lib̃ʳty yerely to make choyse of two freemen of yⁱʳ inhabitants to be Assistants vnto yᵉ magestrate then in being, for the examining & trying of all mattʳˢ in diffrence betwene p̃ty & p̃tie, by a jury of twelue men, not exceeding yᵉ valew of tenne pounds, reserving lib̃ʳty to any p̃ty after triall for appeale to yᵉ Genñall Courts att Plimouth, ꝑvided yᵗ yᵉ appeale be made yᵉ same day yᵉ verdict is brought in, & he yᵗ shall appeale doe giue security yᵗ yf he be cast in the Court of Plimouth, then he shall pay double damages.

And further, for the avoyding of travell & charge, the freemen of the towne of Rehoboth shall for yᵉ eleccõn of maˢᵗʳᵃᵗᵉˢ haue lib̃ʳty to send their votes by proxes, ꝑvided theire votes be orderly taken in yᵉ towne meeting, and then iɱediately sealed vp and deliũd to yᵉ comĩttees or grand iurymen who shalbe sent to attend the affaires of yᵉ Genñall Court, and deliũd in Court by them, vnles vpon other weighty occasions theire p̃sence be required by speciall warrant.

---

26 October.
NEW PLIM.
[*157.]

*Att a Gennʳall Court there holden, Octobʳ 26ᵗʰ, in yᵉ 23ᵗʰ Yere of his Maᵗⁱᵉˢ now Raigne, of England, &c.

BEFORE Mʳ Wᵐ Bradford, Goũnor,   Mʳ Tymothy Hatherley,
Mʳ Prence,   Mʳ John Browne, &
Mʳ Colliare,   Mʳ Willm Thomas,
Capt Miles Standish,

Gent, Assistants, &c.

RICHARD SARES, compl, agˢᵗ Nepoytam, Sachamas, and Felix, Indians. The Court ordered & gaue power to Mʳ Thomas Prence, accompanyed wᵗʰ Anthony Thacher, to here his complaint at his house, at Nawsett, and determine the same, & both plaint and Nepoytam in Courte agreed to yᵉ same.

Mʳ Hathʳley here in Court acknowledgeth that Helene, the wife of Kanelme Winslow, acknowledged her free assent and consent to yᵉ sale of all such lands as her said husband had sould vnto Samuell Sturdevant. Capt Miles Standish acknowledged likewise, yᵗ she, the same Helene, acknowledged her

COURT ORDERS.

free assent & consent to ye sale of all such lands as her said husband had sould to Henry Sampson.

1647.

John Floyde, paying his fees, was released frō his bonds for y^o peace; but Xtopher Winter, refusing to pay his fees, was not released.

26 October. Mr BRADFORD, Goũ.

In a case of diffrence twixte John Floyde & Jane Duglas, his serv^t, the Court ordereth y^t the said Jane, or her assignes, pay vnto ye said John, or his ass^s ye sum of iij^{li} x^s in good country pay wthin 30^{tie} dayes after sight of this order, & so she is released frō ye service of her said master, Floyde, & hath her libty to serue elcewhere.

At this Court, Wm Handbury, compł, agst Franc̄ Billington, for v^{li} xv^s, or thereabouts, it was agreed vpon by them in ye Courte, that ye said Billington shall & will satisfie & pay vnto Mr Wm Handbury, or his ass^s, two barrells of tarre, marchantable, at the house of James Cole, in Plim̄, wthin ye space of eight dayes nexte insuing, and the remaine to him or his assignes by ye 20th day of March nexte, & in case he failes of eith^r ye said paym^{ts}, it shalbe lawfull for ye said Wm Hanbury, or his ass̄, to seize into his owne hands and possession so much in one cow, wch he, ye said Billington, now stands possessed of, & hath not form̄ly ingaged ye said cow for.

Att this Court, Mr Wm Bradford, Goũ, administrator of ye goods, and chattles, & cattles of Sarah, ye wife & relict of Cutbert Godberson, deceased, gaue in an account of his said administratorship, & requiring his discharge; his accoumpt vpon view being accepted, he was likewise discharged.

*The Courte ordereth, vpon petic̄o͂n of Richard Burt, the sonne of Richard Burt, deceased, late of Taunton, that ye said Richard Burt shall make choyse of his owne gardian; & whereas he makes choyse of his vncle, James Burt, to be guardian vnto him, & to liue wth him during his minority, the Court appues of his choyse, & confirmes the same.

[*158.]

The Court ordereth, and giues full power vnto Mr Bradford, Goũ, to stay and seyze vpon all ye goods, corne, and graine y^t are in and vpon his farme by Jones Riuer, vntill his tennants haue fully satisfied and payde vnto him, or his ass^s, all such rents & oth^r dues as are due and payable vnto him frō his now tennants there.

The Courte ordereth, that for ye raysing of ye publike charge for officers wages for this last yere, to pceede according to ye rates & pportions of ye form̄ yere, only Nawset, being now to be added thereto, is now rated, & ordered to pay xl^s.

	li	s	d
James Cole, of Pliñ, acknowledgeth to owe o^r soũaigne lord ye King	40	00	00
Thomas Willett, of Pliñ, ...	20	00	00

120 PLYMOUTH COLONY RECORDS.

1647.
26 October.
BRADFORD,
Gov.

James Coall discharged of these bonds.

Antony Thacher, of Yarmouth, ... 20 : 00 : 00

The condiĉōn, y^t yf ye aboue bounden James Cole shall psonally app^{re} at ye nexte Genñall Court of o^r soũaigne lord ye King, to be holden at Pliñ in March nexte, and in y^e meane time to be of y^e good behavior tow^{ds} our said soũ lord y^e King, and all his leidge people, & to abide y^e further order of y^e Court, & not depte the same wthout licence ; y^t then, &ĉ.

John Groomes, of Pliñ, acknoledgeth to ow o^r soũ-aigne lord y^e King . . . . $\begin{cases} \text{li} & \text{s} & \text{d} \\ 40:00:00 \end{cases}$

Thomas Clarke, of y^e Yele Riuer, plant, ... 20 : 00 : 00

Thomas Little, of y^e Yele River, plant, ... 20 : 00 : 00

Mr Gromes is aquited of these bonds.

The condiĉōn, y^t yf y^e aboue bounden John Groomes shall psonally app^{re} at y^e nexte Gefiall Court of o^r soũaigne lord y^e Kinge, to be holden at Pliñ in March nexte, & in ye meane time to be of ye good behavior tow^{ds} o^r said soũ lord ye King & all his leidge people, & to abide ye further order of ye Court, & not depte ye same wthout licence ; y^t then, &ĉ.

[Here the records first appear in the chirography of Mr. Nathaniel Morton, Secretary of the Colony.]

7 December.
[*159.]
This was at a Court of Assistant(.

*New Plimouth, this 7th of December, 1647. Wheras Samuell Cutbert complaineth against Edward Doty, for y^t hee, the said Edward Doty, hath wronged the said Samuell in taking away som wood from of his land, the Court haueing heard what can bee be said on both sids, the said Court hath ordered y^t the said Edward Doty shall pay vnto the said Samuell Cutbert 7 shilt damage, & the charges of the Court.

[*160.]

*Whereas the inhabitants of Rehoboth desire liberty to make vse of a quantity of marsh lying on the west syde of Sowames Riuer, w^h they call the new meadowes, containing about one hundred accars, vntell there should bee a plantation at Sowames, leaue was graunted vnto them so to make vse of it, but no further ppriety to belong vnto them, but vntell a plantation should bee setled at Sowames ; and for the avoyding of all differences or contention amongst them about the same, it is left vnto the discretion of Mr Browne for him to dispose of it amongst them, as hee should see them stand in need.

And for such pieces of marsh lying within the fence vpon the necke of land w^h the Indians are possesed of, and doe inhabite, which doth not belong vnto the township of Rehoboth, Mr Browne is allowed to make vse of the same for himself, without molestation from the inhabitants of Rehoboth, vntell there bee a plantation at Sowames, and then to require no further ppriety therin.

COURT ORDERS.

*At a Generall Court holden the 7th of March, in the twenty third Yeare of his Maties now Raigne, of England, &c.

1647-8.

7 March.
NEW PLIMOUTH.
MR BRADFORD, GOUER.
[*161.]

BEFORE Mr William Bradford, Gouerner, Captaine Myells Standish, and Mr Prence, Mr William Thomas, Mr Coliar,

Gent, Assistants, &c.

THE millitary company of the towne of New Plimouth, haueing acording to order, proposed vnto the Court 2 men for euery espetiall offise of thair band, the Court doe alow and aproue of—

Mr Thomas Willit for capptain,
Of Mr Thomas Southworth for lieuetenant,
Of Mr Willī Bradford, Junior, for insigne.

The bridge at Joanses Riuer being dangerus to pase ouer it, both for man and beast, the Court haue ordered yt Captaine Myells Standish, Tresurer, doe see the said bridge repaired forthwith.

A bill exhibbited vnto the Court by Mr Charles Chanssy, complaining of the neglect of payment of the charges of Roger Cooke, for his diet in the time of his sicknes, and for his funerall exspences, which is required of the towne of Marshfeild, the Court hath ordered yt Josiā Winslow shall defraye the said charges, being ingaged to doe the same.

Captain Myels Standish is deputed by the Court to haue the hearing, and to put to an end all sutch differences as doe remayne in the towne of Yarmouth.

Leiuetenant Nashe and Sergant Church are respited vntell the next Court, at which Court thay are to cauese to apeere Captain Gorḡ Wright in person, for whose personall apeerance and good behauior thay stand bound.

---

*At a Court of Assistants holden the 2cond of May, 1648.

1648.

2 May.
NEW PLIMOUTH.
[*162.]

BEFORE Mr Bradford, Gouernor, Captayn Miles Standish, and Mr Thomas Prenč, Mr William Thomas, Mr William Coliar,

Gent, Assistants.

PEETER HANBERY aknowlidgeth to owe vnto our souerain lord the King . . . . } 20l.

VOL. II.   16

1648.

2 May.
NEW PLIMOUTH.
Mʳ BRADFORD, GOUERNOR.

The condition, yᵗ if the aboue bounden Peeter Hanbery shall apeere at the next Generall Court of our souerain lord the King, to bee holden at Plimouth aforesaid, the first Tusday in June next, and in the mean time prouid surtyes for his good behauiour ; that then, &c. *This bond forfited by non aper.*

John Barnes, of Plimouth, is alowed by the Court to brew and sell beere vnto comers and goers vntell the Court shall see reason to the contrary in regard of his intent to bake biscake, and for yᵗ otherwise it would bee prejeditiall vnto him.

Whereas differences are between Captaine Miles Standish and Samuell Eaton, about the bounds of thayer lands, the Court haue apoynted yᵗ Mʳ Alldin, John Washburn, Senior, Henery Sampson, and Phillip Delanoy shall viue and set at rights sutch diferences as are between them.

Wheras contreversis have been between Mʳ Gromes and Thomas Clarke, of Plymouth, about sundery acounts depending between them, the s̃d differences haueing been heard by Mʳ Bradford, Mʳ Coliar, and Captaine Miles Standish, the s̃d Mʳ Gromes couenants to pay vnto the s̃d Thomas Clarke 14 bushels of wheat, and five bushells of Indian corn, the wheat to bee payed on the 15ᵗʰ day of September next, and the Indian corne to be payed when it is marchantable ; allso, yᵗ the s̃d Thomas Clarke acsepteth of 4ˢ debt dew vnto Mʳ Gromes from Mʳ Prence, and so all mañer of debts and demaunds are cleared from the begeñing of the world to this day.

5 December.

1648, December fifte. Vpon Mʳ Coliars demaund of the aforsaid debt, ther was payed by Mʳ Gromes three pound fiue shill and 4 pence.

---

7 June.
NEW PLIMOUTH.
[*163.]

Att a Generall Court holden at Plimouth aforsaid, the 7ᵗʰ of June, 1648, in the twenty fourth Yeare of his Maᵗⁱᵉˢ now Raigne, of England, &c.

BEFOR William Bradford, gent, Gouer,
Mʳ Thomas Prence,
Mʳ William Coliar,
Captain Mils Standish,

Mʳ Timothy Hatherle,
Mʳ John Brown, and
Mʳ William Thomas,

Gent, Asistants.

FREEMEN admited this Court, and sworne : —

Isaak Stedman,
Robert Caruer,

Robert Titus,
William Cheesburow,

COURT ORDERS.   123

John Morton,   Ephraim Hicks,   1648.
Ephraim Morton,   Alexander Standish,   7 June.
John Wood,   Samuell Tomkins,   Mʳ
Henery Wood,   John Aldin,   BRADFORD,
Samuell Dunham,   James Wyate,   GOᵾNOR.
Robert Finny,   Nicolas Hyde,
Jakob Cooke,   Josepth Tory.
James Glaŝe,

This Court Mʳ William Bradford was elected Gouerñ.

Mʳ Edward Winslow,
Mʳ Thomas Prence,
Mʳ William Coliare,
Captain Mylls Standish, } elected Assistants.
Mʳ John Brown,
Mʳ Timothy Hatherlee,
Mʳ William Thomas,

This Court Mʳ William Bradford, Gouerner, and Mʳ John Brown weer elected comissioners for the Vnited Colynies.

Captain Myls Standish elected Trēsurer for this yeare.

*The comittees for this Court weer —   [*164.]

For Plimouth, . .   { Mʳ John Howland,   Mannasses Kemton,
                     { Mʳ William Pady,   John Cooke.
For Duxbery, . .   Mʳ John Alldⁿ,   William Basset.
                     { sent none this Court. John Williams and
Seteaat, ...   {   Thomas Chambers, being present, serued
                     {   in the rom̄e of comityes.
For Sandwidḡ, . .   Thomas Tupper and   Thomas Burgis.
For Yarmouth, . .   Lieutenant Palmer and   Mʳ Edmond Hawes.
For Barnstable, . . Mʳ Thomas Dimake and   Thomas Hincklee.
For Taunton, . .   Richard Williams,   Edward Case.
For Marshfeild, . . Thomas Chillingsworth, Robert Waterman.
For Rehoboth, . .   Robert Titus,   John Dogged.
For Naussit, . . .   Nicolas Snow,   Samuell Hicks.

*The Cunstables of the seuerall Townes.   [*165.]

For Plimouth, . .   Ephraim Morton, sworn.
For Duxbery, . .   Thomas Heward, sworn.

1648.

7 June.
Mʀ Bradford, Gouernor.

For Seteaat,	. .	{ Thomas Hyland, not sworn, and Isaake Stedman, sworn.
For Sandwidg̃,	. .	James Skiffe, sworn.
For Taunton,	. .	Mʳ Thomas Gilbert, sworn.
For Yarmouth,	. .	John Marchant, to bee sworn at home.
For Barnstable,	. .	Mʳ Thomas Allin, to bee sworn at home.
For Marshfeild,	. .	{ John Gorum and } both sworn. Thomas Tildin,
For Rehoboth,	. .	John Allin, to bee sworn at home.
For Naussit,	. .	Jobe Cole, to bee sworn at home.

The Grand Inquest.

Jury sworn.
{ John Dunham, Señ,
Isaak Wells,
Peeter Gant,
Mʳ Thomas Burne,
Isaake Robinson, absent,
Robert Finny,
Henery Wood,
‡Ephraim Hicks,‡
James Walker,
James Wyat,
Loue Brewster,
William Paybody.+ }

sworn.
{ John Barker,
Josepth Colman,
John Stokbridg̃,
John Allin,
Thomas Bordman, absent and fiñd,
‡Thomas Bursell,‡
James Bursell, absent,
Josepth Tory,
Robert Sharpe,
Mycaell Blackweell,
Daniell Cole. }

[*166.]   *Servayors for the Hyewayes.

For Plimouth,	. .	{ Richard Sparow, John Barnes,	Thomas Clarke, Jakob Cooke.
For Duxbery,	. .	Francis Sprage,	Abram Sampson.
For Seteaat,	. .	{ John Willis, Thomas Chambers,	Humfry Turner, Thomas Burd.
For Sandwidge,	. .	Thomas Dexter,	John Fishe.
For Taunton,	. .	John Dean,	Richard Stasy,
For Yarmouth,	. .	Richard Tayler,	Francis Baker.
For Barnstable,	. .	Thomas Burman,	Gorge Lewis.
For Marshfeild,	. .	John Russell,	Robert Barker.
For Rehoboth,	. .	John Miller,	John Pellum.
For Naussit,	. .	Josias Cooke,	Robert Vixon.

COURT ORDERS. 125

The names ^ those y{t} are to take vp the excise weer these : —

    For Plimouth, . . . John Finny.
    For Duxbery, ... John Willis.
    For Seteaat, ... Samuell House.
    For Sandwidḡ, ... Peeter Gaunt.
    For Taunton, ... James Wyat.
    For Yarmouth, ... M{r} Edmond Haws.
    For Barnstable, ... Isaake Robinson.
    For Marshfeild, ... Josepth Beddle.
    For Rehoboth, ... John Dogged.
    For Naussit, ... Nicolas Snowe.

1648.
7 June.
M{r}
BRADFORD,
GOUERNOR.

Constant Southworth alowed to sell wine at Duxbery.
Richard Sillis alowed to sell wine at Seteaat.
Josias Cooke alowed to sell wine at Nausset, and to be regester keeper for the towne.

*The names of those y{t} weer absent this Court y{t} should haue taken vp thaire freedom. [*167.]

    Richard Paull,   John Bradford,
    William Phillips,   John Browne,
    Francis Goulder,   Thomas Dunham.

The names of those y{t} stand propounded vnto the Court to take vp thair freedom are these : —

    John Dogged,   John Gorum,
    Obadia Holmes,   Thomas Burd,
    Thomas Clifton,   John Daman.

Samuell Mayo complains against John William, Señ, in an action of tresspas vpon the case, to the damage of fourty pounds.

Samuell House complains against Gowin White, in an action vpon the forfiture of a bond, in a mater of arbetration, to the damage of fiue pound.

Samuell House complains against Gowin White, in an action of tresspas vpon the case, to the damage of twenty pound.

Gowin White complayns against Samuell House, in an action of tresspas vpon the case, to the damag of tenn pound.

These foure actions aboue written weer all non suted by reason of the plaintifes not apeering to prosecute, and the charges of the Court awarded to bee payed by the plaintiffes.

1648.

7 June.

Mʳ BRADFORD, GOUERNER.

Sertain debts demaunded of the ouerseers of the will of Thomas Howell, deseased, which the said Thomas Howell ought in his life time.

Vpon the demand of a debt by Captain Harding, the jury find for the plaintife the debt and the charges of the Court.

Vpon the demand of a debt of one pound 5 shill, by John Barker, the jury find for the plaintife 16 shilling and the charges of the Court.

[*168.]

*In the action of debt dew from Thomas Howell to Simon Suton, the jury find for the plaintife the debt and the charges of the Court.

The jury for these trialls weer these foloing :—

Jury sworn.
{ Mʳ Thomas Howes,
‡Samuell Nash,‡
Christofer Waddsworth,
Experience Michell,
Phillip Delanoy,
Joshua Prate,
Richard Sparow,
Barnard Lumberd, }

jury sworn.
{ Thomas Chambers,
Robert Carver,
James Skiffe,
John Washburn,
Robert Bartlit a part of the time, & being nessesitated to depart, John Thomson was put in his rome. }

Mʳ Edmond Haws presenting a parssell of waights to the Court, to bee the standerd for the waights of Yarmouth, the Court doe alow them so to bee.

The Court hath ordered, concerning the estate of Mʳ Winchester, for the well disposing therof, for the good of his children, that Mʳ Brown doe treat with the superuisors of his will and teastament, and to doe in yᵗ behalfe what shall bee needfull.

Further, wheras it doth apeer by the late will and testament of Mʳ Alexander Winchester, desseased, yᵗ hee hath made his wife the sole executris of his will aforsaid, it is ordered by the Court, yᵗ if Mʳ Brown and the towne of Rehoboth shall see it needfull to make choise of another vnto himselfe and the superadvissers, for the well disposing of the aforsaid estate in the behalfe of the children of the aforsaid Mʳ Winchester.

[*169.]

*Nicolas Hyde petissions to the Court for a childs portion of the estat of Thomas Blisse, desseased, and the Court haue promised to take it into consideration.

That som one of the grandjurymen of Yarmouth doe keep a trew standerd to tryall waights in the townshipe by.

The Court doe alow a fine of fiue pound dew from John Tomson to the towne of Plimouth, towards the mending of the causway at Joansses Riuer.

The Court doe alow and request Mʳ Howland, William Merrick, and John

COURT ORDERS. 127

Roggers to stake out the hyeway from Joansses Riuer Bridge to Massachussets Path, by William Mericks aforesaid.

1648.
7 June.
Mᴿ Bradford, Gouerner.

The inhabytants of the Eell Riuer haue proposed to the Court ether to haue thaire bridge now in building to bee a toalle bridg, or to haue som healpe towards the charge. The Court haue promised to take it into consideration vntel the next Court.

The Court have ordered yᵗ Nausset pay by rate fourty shilling for the last yeare, and fourty for this present yeare; and soe añually forty shillings.

And further, yᵗ the seueral townships are to pay thair rates acording to the same proportion thay did the last yeare.

That by retaile of tobacco is to bee ment all yᵗ sell it by retaile, whether in roule or any other wise, yᵗ onely exsepted which men raise by planting at home.

*Wheras it doth apeer yᵗ ther is a debt of fiue pound and 8 shill apertaining vnto Gorg Wright, in the hands of John Dogged, of Rehoboth, the Court haue ordered, yᵗ the said debt remayne atached in the hands of John Dogged aforsaid, for the vse of Leiuftenant Nash and Sergeant Church, in consideration of the damage befaling them by the abouesaid Gorg Wright, the breaking of his bands for the good behavior.

[*170.]

Lres of administration are graunted vnto Edmond Weston, to administer vppon the estate of Thõ Howell, desseased, and to pay his debts as fare and by equall pporsions as the estate will amount vnto, and Phillip Delanoy and Robert Carver with him.

Josia Winslow, Junier, is alowed and aproued of by the Court to bee insyne bearer of the trayne band of Marshfeild.

The Court haue ordered, yᵗ what the exsyse shall not defray of the charges by the magestrats table shall bee satisfyed by the fines, and yet if ther bee want, the cuntry to make it vp.

Mʳ Howland and Mʳ Alldin to bee aded to the Tresurer, to take an account of the trade of Cenebecke, and to yeild a trew account to the Court therof, betwext this and the sixteenth of July next.

Richard Burton, being acused for stealling of a calfe, and the same acussation orderly proued against him, was sensured by the Court to pay vnto the owener of the calfe sixteene shillings, and to bee publickly whipte, the later whearof acordingly was performed.

Mʳ Hatherle requesting to haue liberty to set vp an iron mille, the cuntry doe reffer it to bee determined by the Gouerner and Asistants at the next Court of Asistants.

Differences depending between William Sherman and John Barker about

1648.

7 June.
Mʳ
Bradford,
Gouerner.
14 May.
[*171.]

the bounds of thayer lands, the Cŏrt doe apoint and requeste Captaine Myles Standish and Mʳ Aldin, and to bee acŏmpanied with Joshua Prat, to set at rights sutch differences as are betwext them.

*At Yarmouth, the xiiijth day of May, 1648, by Captain Standish, who was authorised by the Court holden at Plimouth, the 7th of March, 1647, to haue the hearing, and to put an end to all differences as doe remayne in the towne of Yarmouth.

It is ordered by the said Captaine Standish, y^t Thomas Payne shall inioy the first eight acars of land granted to him in the west feild, which hee denied to lay downe, and for the other twenty eight acars or therabouts, hee shall relinquish to the comõns, as was formerly agreed vnto by the towne.

Also, y^t Mʳ Hawes shall enjoy 8 acars of vpland or therabouts, in the west feild, which hee bought of Goodman Chase.

Item, y^t Robert Dennis shall enjoy 12 acars of vpland in the west feild, which hee bought of Peeter Worden, and 10 acars of Mʳ Hawes, and 7 acars of Mʳ Hallott, and 4 acars there giuen him by the towne.

Also, y^t Thomas Flawne shall enjoy 13 acars of land, or therabouts, in the west feild, giuen him by the comittes.

Also, y^t Andrew Hallott shall relinquish eight acares of land granted to him in the west feild, and to take it vp in somẽ other place conuenient.

Also, y^t Mʳ Hawes shall relinquish eight acares of land granted to him in the weste feild, and take it vp in somẽ other conuenient place.

Also, it is ordered, y^t the towne shall enjoy and posses the necke of land comõnly called Nobscussett Necke, aŀs Sasuet Necke, both vpland and medowe, notwithstanding all former graunts and sales of any part therof, exsepte what haue been graunted to Mʳ Gray, about 6 yeares sence, being 10 acars of vpland and 4 acars of meadowe lying there, betwext the great rocke and harbors mouth, the vpland and the creeke.

Whereas Mʳ Thatcher, Mʳ Howes, and Mʳ Crow, comittees of this plantation of Yarmouth, in consideration of thayer charges about the discouering, purchaš, and other charges by them disbursed, about the same, haue clāmed and taken vp, vizß, Mʳ Thatcher, 130 acars of vpland, and twenty six acars of meadowe for a farme, and Mʳ Howes 100 acars of vpland, and 20 acars of meadowe for his fearme, or great lot, and Mʳ Crow one hundred acars of vpland, and twenty acares of meadowe, for his farme or great lot,— the towne hath aŀowed Mʳ Thatcher an hundred and tenne acares of vpland, and his twenty-six acares of meadowe, and hee hath layed downe to the towne the other twenty acares of vpland, and likewise the towne haue graunted vnto Mʳ

COURT ORDERS.

Howes fourscore acars of vpland, and twenty acares of meadow, and hee hath layed downe to the towne, in liew of the other twenty acares of land by him taken vp in his great lot, twenty acars lying in Rock Furland, next on the west side to Edward Sturges land, bought of Gabriell Wheildin; and lickwise the towne hath allowed vnto Mr Crow 4 score acars of vpland, and twenty acars of meadowe, wherof som part is taken vp allredy, and the rest to bee taken vp by him where hee shall find it conuenient, and twenty acars hee remits to the towne, which the towne accepts, and is satisfyed in full in respecte of any differences y^t hath been betwext the towne and them, and every one of them, in respecte of theire farmes or great lots, or any greewances about the laying out of lands from the begining of the plantation to this 13th day of May, 1648, aforsaid.

1648.

14 May.
M^R
BRADFORD,
GOUERNER.

*Also, Mr Thatcher and Mr Howes hath layed down to the vse of the town, viz$, Mr Thatcher 12 acares of vpland neare the Great Basse Pound, and Mr Howes hath layed downe 10 acares of vpland in Nobscussett, lying there in a furland called Rabbits Ruine, in liew of 12 acares a peece claimed by them, and taken vp heertofore, in consideration of charges about the laying out of lands in the winter 1638, which apeers in thayer acompte given into Court, año 1640, which the towne hath otherwise satisfied vpon agreement.

[*172.]

Item, it is ordered, y^t Richard Templar shall enjoy his fiue acares of land at Nobscussett, layed out there in Snakes Furland, next the hyeway buting vpon Mr Mathues land.

Item, it is ordered, y^t Goodman Clarke shall enjoy three acares of vpland at Nobscussctt, in the playn furland next beyonde fiue acars late Thomas Hatches, and next vnto the fearme.

Item, it is order, y^t Robert Dennis shall enjoy 2 acares of vpland in Nobscussett there, in affurland called Rabbets Reuine, betweene Mr Lumkins and Goodman Prichards, and abbuting vpon the Coy Ponde.

Item, it is granted vnto Mr Nickerson to haue tenne acars of vpland, and 8 acares of meadow towards the South Sea, which is not for the present to the prejudice of the towne.

Item, it is graunted allso to John Darby to haue six acares of meadow in the Easteren Swan Pond Meadowe, in lewe of 4 acars dew to William Chase, for a debt the town owed him.

It is ordered, y^t Richard Hore shall haue tenne acares of meadow in the Easterne Meadows in the Swan Pond, and in the easterne end therof

It is lickwise granted y^t Mr Howes shall haue 17 acars in the Eastern Meadow, and at the easterne end in the Swan Ponds, in liewe of 17 acars of meadow Mr Howes hath taken vp in Nobscussett, a^{ls} Sassuett Necke, and

1648.
14 May.
Mʀ BRADFORD, GOUERNER.

sould to Thomas Burman : hee hath layed downe to the townes vse 7½ acars of meadowe, late Mʳ Hallotts, lying at the lower end of the rocke tree furland, and eight acares of meadow, late William Chases, lyeing next vnto Edward Sturges meadow, between the riuer and Mʳ Simkins necke.

It is ordered, yᵗ Mʳ Miller bee sufficiently accomodated.

It is ordered, yᵗ euery inhabytant haue his land, both vpland and meadow, suffitiently bounded in convenient time with stones.

15 May.
[*173.]

*The 15ᵗʰ day of May, 1648. It is agreed by Captaine Standish, Mʳ Crow, Mʳ Thatcher, and Mʳ Howes, the comittees of this plantation of Yarmouth, and Richard Hore, Mʳ Hawes, William Nicorsone, William Pallmer, and Robert Dennis, in the behalfe of the towne, that Mʳ Staare, William Nichorsone, and Robert Dennis shall bee joyned to the comittees for this p̃sent yeare, and thence after by the towne : thay haue thayer liberty to choose other three to the comittees aforsaid, so yᵗ the comittees shall not heerafter dispose of any lands, either vplands or meadow, without the conssent of those three or tow of them, and if any difference arise between them which they cannot compose themselues, yᵗ thay repayer to Captain Standish for his dyrection.

Wheras at a towne meeting, March 22ᶜᵒⁿᵈ, 1647, Mʳ Thatcher freely layed downe and renounced all right, title, and interest to any manner of vpland as his dew by way of proportion, excepting 40 acars of vpland, more or lesse, lying and being about his dwelling house betwext Mʳ Hawes and Mʳ Millers, and the cart path to Barnstable, excepte allso 20 acars giuen him by free gifte, commonly called the Reward, which hee acknowlidgeth this fifteenth day of May, 1648, to stand vnto. Hee allso demaunds 8 acares of vpland in West Feild, which hee bought of Thomas Hatch, and which is to bee layed out next vnto Mʳ Hawes 8 acares of land there, which hee bought of Goodman Chase, vnto which the towne consenteth, and other vpland hee claimeth not.

17 May.

An agreement made the 17ᵗʰ of May, 1648, betweene Paupmunnuck, with the consent of his brother, and all the rest of his associats on the one part, and Captaine Myles Standish in the behalfe of the inhabitants of Barnestable on the other part, as followeth, viz͠ : —

That the said Paupmunnucke hath, with the free and full conssent of his said brother and associats, freely, fully, and absolutly bargãned and sould vnto the s̃d Captaine Myles Standish, in the behalfe and for the vse of the inhabytants of Barnstable aforsaid, all his and thayer right, title, and intereste in all his and thayer lands lying and beeing within the p̃cincts of Barnstable affor̃said, faring vpon the sea, comonly called the South Sea, buting home to Janno his land eastward, and a little beyond a brooke, called the First

Hearing Brooke, weastward, and to Nepoyetums and Seaqunneks lands north- 1648.
ward, exsepting thirty acars which hee, the said Paupmunnick hath retained to
the pper vse and behoofe of himselfe, his brother, and assosiates, for and in con- 17 May.
sideration of 2 brasse kittells and one bushell of Indian corn, to bee dewly and M^R
trewly payed vnto him, the s̄d Paupmunnuck, by the said inhabytants of Barn- BRADFORD, GOUERNER.
stable, between the date heerof and Nouember next inseuing ; allso, one halfe
part of so mutch fence as will fence in the thirty acars of land affoŕsaid for
the said Paupmunnuck, to bee dewly and trewly made by the laste of Aprill
next insewing the date heerof; allso, the said Paupmunnuck and his asociates
shall haue free leaue and liberty to hunt in the said lands, provided thay giue
notice to the said inhabitants *before thay sett any trappes, as allso fully and [*174.]
dilligenttly to see all thair trappes eury day, y^t soe in case any are taken or in-
trapped therin, thaye shall speedyli lett them out, and ãquaint the said inhabytants forthwith therof; as allso to ãquainte them if thay shall perceiue any
cattell to haue broken out of thayer trapps before thay come vnto them.

In wittnes of all and singuler the preemises heerof, thay haue heervnto
sett thayer hands the day and yeare aboue written.

All which conditions, in case thay doe not dilligently obserue, thay shall
pay whatsoeuer damage comes to any mans cattell through thayer default
heerin.

---

*Att a Court of Asistants holden att New Plymouth, the first of   1 August.
August, 1648.

BEFORE Mr William Bradford, Gouernor,   Capptayn Myles Staandish, and
Mr William Colyar,   Mr William Thomas,
Genť, Asistants.

ATT this Court it was ordered, y^t Thomas Cushman shall haue and enjoy,
without disturbance, the one third part of all the English corn due
vnto Mis Combe, for her part, from William Spooner, for this p̃sent yeare, excepting the rye, wherof hee is to haue the one halfe, and one part of fiue of the
Indian corn, and the one half of the frute, and the one half of the hempe.

The said Court haue further ordered, concerning the children of the said
Mis Combe, now being with William Spooner, y^t the said Spooner keepe them
for the p̃sent, and not dispose of them for the future, without further order
from the Court.

Wheras it doth appeer, that Mr John Combe was indebted to the estate

1648.

1 August.
Mʀ
Bʀᴀᴅғᴏʀᴅ,
Gᴏᴜᴇʀɴᴇʀ.

Of this see more the 2ᶜᵒⁿᵈ page forward of this booke; the assignment being there entered.

of Cudbert Godbersom, as appeers by the account of the Goñ, Mʳ William Bradford, administrator of the said estate, which said estate was debtor a considerable sumē to Mʳ Isacke Allerton, marchant, whoe by a letter of attorney doth giue the said debt to his son in law, Mʳ Thomas Cushman, and impowered him to the receiueing therof, whoe desires healp of the Court; and they finding that the said Combe was indebted to the abouesaid Mʳ Allerton, they graunted, by way of extent vpon the lands of the said Combe, that a p̄te of the encrease therof for some time should bee payed to Mʳ Cushman aforsaid, to whom the moneyes was due, which accordingly being done as farr as they could judge, the said Combe stood indebted to the estate of the aforsaid Cutbert Godbersom by any thinge that did then appeer, the land was freed from any further extent vpon that account.

[*175.] *These sheweth, that on July the 22ᶜᵒⁿᵈ, 1648, wee, whosse names are vnderwritten, were sworne by Mʳ Bradford, Gouerner, to make inquiry of the death of the child of Allis Bishop, the wife of Richard Bishope.

Wee declare, yᵗ coming into the house of the said Richard Bishope, wee saw at the foot of a ladder wʰ leadeth into an vpper chamber, much blood; and going vp all of vs into the chamber, wee found a woman child, of about foure yeares of age, lying in her shifte vppon her left cheeke, with her throat cut with diuers gashes crose wayes, the wind pipe cut and stuke into the throat downward, and a bloody knife lying by the side of the child, with wʰ knife all of vs judḡ, and the said Allis hath confessed to fiue of vs att one time, yᵗ shee murdered the child with the said knife.

JOHN HOWLAND,	JAMES COLE,
JAMES HURST,	GYELLS RICKARD,
ROBERT LEE,	RICHARD SPARROW,
JOHN SHAWE,	THOMAS POPE,
FRANCIS COOKE,	FRANCIS BILLINGTON,
JOHN COOKE,	WILLIAM NELSON.

Rachell, the wife of Josepth Ramsden, aged about 23 yeares, being examined, saith that coming to the house of Richard Bishope vppon an ērand, the wife of the said Richard Bishope requested her to goe fetch her som̄ buttermilke at Goodwife Winslows, and gaue her a ketle for that purpose, and shee went and did it; and before shee wente, shee saw the child lyinge abed asleepe, to her best deserning, and the woman was as well as shee hath knowne her att any time; but when shee came shee found her sad and dumpish; shee asked her what blood was that shee saw at the ladders foot; shee pointed vnto the chamber, and bid her looke, but shee perseiued shee had ki̇led her child, and being afraid, shee refused, and ran and tould her father and mother. Moṙouer, shee saith the reason yt moued her to thinke shee had ki̇led her child was yt when shee saw the blood shee looked on the bedd, and the child was not there.

1648.
1 August.
Mᴿ Bʀᴀᴅғᴏʀᴅ, Gᴏᴜᴇʀɴᴇʀ.

Taken vppon oath by mee,   WILLIAM BRADFORD,
The day and year aboue written.

At a Court of Aṡistants holden at New Plymouth, the first of Aguste, 1648, before Mʳ Bradford, Goueṙ, Mʳ Coliar, Captain Miles Standish, and Mʳ William Thomas, gent̃, Assistants, the s̃d Allice, being examined, confessed shee did com̃ite the affoṙsaid murther, and is soṙy for it.

*An Assignment appointed heer to bee recorded.   [*176.]

Know all men whom these p̃sents may any waies concerne, that I, Isacke Allerton, of New Amsterdam, in the prouince of the New Netherlands, marchant, doe, by vertue heerof, absolutely, freely, and of my owne accord, assigne, giue, and make ouer from mee, my heires and exequitors foreuer, vnto my welbeloued sonne in law, Thomas Cushman, of New Plymouth, in New England, his heires, exequitors, administrators, or assignes for euer, all my right, title, interest, and claime I can any waies make or pretend vnto a certaine debt of one hundred pound sterling due vnto mee from John Combe, gent̃, and for which the land adjacent to the said New Plymouth, and appertaining to the said Mʳ John Combe, was engaged to mee, as by the records may appeer, the said sum̃e of one hundred pounds sterling, more or lesse, being due vnto mee, the said Isacke, as may appeer by seuerall accounts, giueing and granting, and by vertue heerof I doe giue and graunt full power and authoritie vnto my said son in law to vse all lawfull meanes for the recouery of the said debt vnto the proper vse and behoofe of my said sonne in law, or his heires, with as large and ample power as is or may be giuen by vertue of any letter of attorney or assignment, and as much as if myselfe were pʳsonally p̃sent, ratifying, ałowing, and confeirming any acte that shalbee lawfully dõn by my said son in law, for the recouery of the said debt against myselfe, or any other claiming for or vnder mee. In witnes wherof I haue heervnto sett my hand and seale, this twenty seauenth of October, 1646.

                 ISACKE ALLERTON, and a   (Seale.)

Sealed and deliuered in the p̃sence of
     Gorge Baxter,
     Thomas Willett,
     Gorḡ Woolsey.

1648. *Att the Generall Court of our Soueraine Lord the King, holden at Plymouth aforsaid, the 4th of October, 1648.

4 October.
NEW PLYMOUTH.
Mʀ BRADFORD, Goῦ.
[*177.]

BEFORE Mʳ Bradford, Gouerner, Mʳ Timothy Hatherle, and
Mʳ Thomas Prence, Mʳ William Thomas,
Captaine Miles Standish,
Genṯ, Assistants.

ATT this Court, Allice Bishope, the wife of Richard Bishope, of New Plymouth, was indited for felonius murther by her comīted, vppon Martha Clark, her owne child, the frute of her owne body.

The names of the grand inquest that went on triall of the aforsaid bill of inditment, weer these : —

    John Dunham, Señ,   John Barker,
    Isaake Weels,   Josepth Colman,
    Mʳ Thomas Burne,   John Allin,
    Robert Finny,   Thomas Bordman,
    Henery Wood,   James Bursell,
    Ephraim Hickes,   Josepth Tory,
    James Walker,   Micaell Blackwell,
    James Wyat,   Daniell Cole.
    Loue Brewster,

These found the bill a trew bill.

The petty jurys names that went vppon her tryall were these : —

    Josias Winslow, Senī,   Gyells Rickard,
    Thomas Shillingsworth,   John Shaw, Señ,
    Anthony Snowe,   Steuen Wood,
    Richard Sparrow, } sworn. William Mericke, } sworne.
    Gabriell Fallowell,   William Brete,
    Joshua Prat,   John Willis,

These found the said Allice Bishope guilty of the said fellonius murthering of Martha Clarke aforsaid ; and so shee had the sentence of death pronounced against her, vizṱ, to bee taken from the place where shee was to the place from whence shee came, and thence to the place of execution, and there to bee hanged by the necke vntell her body is dead, which acordingly was executed.

COURT ORDERS.

*Presentments of the Grand Enquest.

Christofer Wadsworth, Nicolas Robbins, John Roggers, John Willis, Samuell Eaton, Jonathan Brewster, Arther Haris, Thomas Gannet, being presented for being deffectiue in ladders, vppon thayer now being better prouided of them, are cleared.

4 October.
Mʀ BRADFORD, GOUERNER.
[*179.]

The towne of Seteaate haueing been presented for not chusing milletary offecers aĉording to order, Mʳ Hathelē promising the Court to see the milletary company of the towne aforsd exercise in armes at times apointed vntell thay can conueniently make choise of offecers, are clered of this presentment.

The seruayors of Seteaate haueing been presented for not mending ther hyewayes aĉording to order, vppon redresse therof are cleared of this presentment.

Seteaate presented for not puiding armes for publicke seruis aĉording to order, respeted vntell the next Court.

8ᵗʰ June, 1648.

The towne of Taunton was presented for not mending the hiewayes between Taunton and Plymouth, wᶜʰ thay are ordered by the Court to doe, or to returne the xxx shillings finne of Francis Doughty allowed them for yᵗ end.

The seruayors of Duxbery, haueing been presented for not mending the hyeway at Iland Creeke, vppon thayer sence mending therof, are cleared of this presentment.

These aboue written presentments weer presented vnto the Court on March the 7ᵗʰ, 1647, but examined on the third of October, 1648.

Christofer Winter and his wife haueing been presented, the 8th of June, 1648, for haueing knowlidḡ each of other before publicke mariage, the said Christofer, deliuering a bill vnder his hand vnto Captain Standish, Trēsurer, for the payment of his finne, is cleared of the said presentment.

Thomas Dexter, Junier, miller, of Sandwidḡ, haueing been presented for not haueing a toale dish sealled acording to order, vppon the hearing of his deffence, was cleared.

*James Walker, of Taunton, informing against William Hedggis, for yᵗ the s̄d Hedgges, knowing of one yᵗ that hath traded shote vnto the Indians, and refusing to declare who it is, by a sommons sent vnto him is required to apeer at the next Generall Court; aĉordingly hee did, and was cleared.

[*180.]

Gorḡ Pitcocke, of Siteaate, being wholy deffectiue in respecte of armes, is to prouide armes compleat for one man, and constantly to pay his finnes, for yᵗ hee beareth not armes.

Wheras differences haue been betwext Loue Brewster and Samuell Eaton about the bounds of theire lands, the Court hath ordered and doe requeste Mʳ

1648.
4 October.
Mʀ Bradford, Gouerner.

Alldin, Henery Sampson, and Phillipe Delanoy to range out thayer lands betwexte them, begiñing at the lower end, and make report therof to the Court how thay find it.

The Court haue ordered, concerning Thomas Dunham, that hee abstaine from coming att or sending vnto Martha Knote, of Sandwidge, from this p̄sent day vntell the first Tusday of Desember next, vntell the Court can better deserne the treuth of his pretended contracte with the s̄d Martha Knot, vnles the Gouerner, vppon clearing of thinges, shall giue him leaue.

1648-9.
6 March.
New Plymouth.
[*181.]

*At the Generall Court of our Souerain Lord the King, holden at Plymouth aforsaid, the sixt of March, 1648.

Beffore Mʳ William Bradford, Gouerner, Mʳ Timothy Hatherle,
Mʳ William Coliar, Mʳ John Browne, and
Captaine Miles Standish, Mʳ William Thomas,
Genȶ, Assistant.

Fine.

CONCERNING William Cheesburow and William Palmer, of Rehoboth, the Court haue ordered, that for thaire contempt of the Court, maniffested by theire p̄seeding in the dispossing of the children of Mʳ Winchester, contrary to order from the magestrats, and other miscarriages about the s̄d children, thay are fined tenn pound.

Whereas fiue shillings was demaunded and retained by William Cheesburow as a leggasy giuen by Mʳ Winchester, the Court find it not due, and appoint him to returne it to them yᵗ haue the disposing of the children of the aforsaid Mʳ Winchester.

Whereas William Cheesburow and William Palmer did demaund twenty shillings charges for a jury to Plymouth about busines for the children of Mʳ Winchester, the Court haue aƚowed vnto William Palmer tenn shilƚ, but vnto William Cheesburow thay haue aƚowed nothing, because it apeered yᵗ the said William Cheesburow cam to Plymouth at yᵗ time vpon other oc̄ations.

Concerning the bridge at the Eele Riuer, the Court haue ordered, yᵗ wheras there hath been longe neglect and complaint for yᵗ the said bridge was not built ac̄ording to order of Court held the 4ᵗʰ of September, 1638, thay haue thought good to signify vnto the townes whom it perticulerly concerns, — viz𝔰, Yarmouth, Barnstable, and Sandwidḡ, — yᵗ ac̄ording to the

said order, thay ought at least to beare a considerable part of the charg̃ arise- 1648-9.
ing by the bridg̃ now built by the inhabitants of the Eel Riuer aforsd ouer
the riuer aforsaid, and the rather because it is found by late and com̃on expe- 6 March.
rience y^t trauellers doe make vse of the s̃d bridge as finding the way leading MR BRADFORD,
therunto most com̃odius for theire jurniing to and fro; and y^t the townes GOUERNER.
aforsaid should consider of the perticulars aforsd against the next Generall
Court, y^t thay may giue answare therunto, and make payment for the charge
of the bridg̃ as aforsd.

*William Bassit, of Duxbery, Senĩ, haueing been presented at the Gen- [*182.]
erall Court holden at Plymouth aforsaid the 4th of October, 1648, for not Fined.
mending of guns in seasonable time, ac̃ording to order of Court, is fined for
his neglect heerin fiue shillings.

The Court haue graunted liberty vnto John Morton to draw and sell wine
by retaile at Plymouth, and to lodg̃ and entertaine straingers and trauellers
to bead and bord, for dew concideration for the same.

The Court haue graunted liberty vnto John Lewis to keep an ordinary,
and to draw and sell wine, at Seteaat, or any other whom the towne of Seteaat
aforsaid shall alow of, if the said John Lewis shall thinke meete not to
keep it.

The Court alow vnto Mr Leueridge for foure witnesses subpenaed by him
this Court 3 shill a peece, in all twelue shillings.

And vnto Mr Thatcher, being subpenaed by Mr Dexter, 4 shillĩ.

And vnto Mr Dillingham and Richard Bourn, being subpenaed by M^r
Dexter, 3 shillings a peece.

*Presentments of the Grand Inquest. [*183.]

Wee p̃sent Mr William Hedge, of the towne of Yarmouth, for leting of Cleared.
an Indian haue a gun, and poulther, and shot.

Wee p̃sent Mr Crow, Senĩ, for receauing stollen goods. Cleared.

Wee p̃sent the wife of Mr Hedge, of Yarmouth, for receaueing of stolen Cleared.
goods.

Wee p̃sent the wife of Hugh Norman, and Mary Ham̃on, both of Mary Hamon
Yarmouth, for leude behauior each with other vpon a bed. Of this more is cleared with
entered in the conclusions of the Court held the 2^{cond} of October, 1650, p. 226. admonision.

Wee p̃sent Richard Bishope, of Plymouth, for stealing of a spade from
Andrew Ring. Hee was sentenced to sit in the stocks, and to pay a new spade
to Andrew Ring before the next June Court, or otherwise to bee publickli whipt.

Wee p̃sent the way wardens or survayors of Taunton for neglecting to Cleared.
mend the hyewayes.

1648-9.
6 March.
Mʀ Bradford, Gouerner.

Fined.

Wee p̱sent Peregrin White, and Sara, his wife, both of Marshfeild, for fornication before marriage or contract. Cleared by paying the fine. Fined.

Wee p̱sent William Sabin, the miller of Rehoboth, for not returning mens corn vnto them by two quarts in a bushell, allowing their toule. Cleared.

Robert Padduk, of Plymouth, and William Clark, of Duxbery, were both p̱sented June the 4ᵗʰ for being drunk, and sence both cleared by the paiment of theair fine.

1649.
6 May.
New Plymouth.
[*185.]

*At a Court of Assistants holden at Plymouth aforsaid, the first of May, 1649.

Before Mʳ William Bradford, Gouerner,   Mʳ Timothy Hatherlee,
Mʳ William Coliar,   Mʳ John Brown, and
Captain Miles Standish,   Mʳ William Thomas.
Gent, Assistantȩ.

RICHARD BISHOPE, for stealing of a spade from Andrew Ringe, was sentenced to sit in the stocks, and to pay vnto the said Andrew Ring a new spade before the next Generall Court, or otherwise to bee whipt.

The Court haue ordered yᵗ John Churchill, of Plymouth, shall haue the disposing of the house and land yᵗ was Gorḡ Clarks for the vse and good of Abigaell Clarke, daughter vnto the said Gorḡ Clarke, either to let or sell the said house and land with the Courts consent.

Wheras a sheepe of Captain Standishes was worried by a doge of Beniamin Eatons, the Court haue ordered, that the said Beniamin Eaton shall pay vnto Captaine Standish thirty shillings for the s̃d sheepe.

It is ordered by the Court, yᵗ Beniamin Eaton abouesaid shalbee at his owne disposing vntell the next October Court, and in the mean time to provide himselfe a service; if not, the Court to provid him one, and what bargan hee shall make with any man in this behalfe is to be brought and the conditions therof to bee recorded.

Execution graunted vnto Thomas Burd, of Sittuaat, against Gorḡ Russell for fifty ʆhilling damaḡ and the charges of the sute, ‡and yᵗ the said Gorḡ Russell is to make go ˄ , ˄ pay the charges of the said execution.‡

*At the Generall Court holden at Plymouth, aforsaid, the sixt of June, 1649.

1649.
6 June.
NEW PLY.
BRADFORD,
GOUERNER.
[*187.]

BEFORE Mr William Bradford, Gouerner,   Mr Timothy Hatherle,
Mr Thomas Prence,   Mr John Browne, and
Mr William Coliar,   Mr William Thomas,
Captaine Miles Standish,
Gent, Assistants.

THE whole body of freemen of the coliny of Plymouth aforsaid, or the maine part of them, being mete together, it was vnanimusly concluded, that wheras things are mutch vnseteled in our natiue cuntry in regard of the affairs of the state, wherby the Court cannot so clearly prosseed in election as formerly, all offecers, wether magestrats or inferior offecers, shall continew in thaire places with as full power and authority as thay had the yeare last past for the space of a full yeare for the year foloing, vnles som spesiall intellegent or order com ouer w^h shall at any time within the year aforsaid ocation the calling the body of fieemen together for a new election.

This Court, Mr Bradford, Gouerner, & Mr John Browne, were requested by the Court to continew comissioners for this psent yeare; and acordingly thay condesended thervnto.

Servayors of the Hiewayes.

Plymouth, ... Mr Howland, Mr Paddy, Mr Willit.
Duxber, ... John Staare, John Washburn.
Seteaate, ... Walter Briggs, Edward Jenkins.
Sandwidge, ... William Newland, Peeter Wright.
Taunton, ... James Wiate, Gorge Maasse.
Yarmouth, ... Samuell Ryder, Richard Templer.
Barnstable, ... Thomas Lumbert, Mr Lennit.
Marshfeild, ... Josias Winslow, William Brooks.
Rehoboth, ... Richard Bowin, Robert Sharpe.
Nawset, ... John Smalley, Thomas Williams.

*Presentments of the Grand Inquest. [*189.]

Wee psent Gorg Russell, of Settuate, for plowing and blocking vp the hieway, y^t men cannot conueniently pase.   Cleared.

Wee psent the servayors of Seteaat for not repairing the hieway ouer a marsh called Rotten Marsh.   Cleared.

1649.
6 June.
BRADFORD,
GOUERNER.

Wee p̃sent the seruayors of Plymouth for not repaireing the hiewayes at Joanses Riuer and at Wellingsla. Cleared.

Wee p̃sent John Shaw, Junier, for profaining the Lords day for atending on the tar pits.

John Shaw was sentenced this Court to sit in the stocks for this, which accordingly was executed.

Also wee p̃sent Steven Bryant for carriing a barrell to the said pits on the same Lords day. Steven Bryant, with admonission, is cleared.

Wee p̃sent the towne of Sandwidḡ for not trayning for one whole yeare last past.

Cleared.

Wee p̃sent Edward Bobbit, of Taunton, for receaueing pay for stollen wampom.

Cleared.

Wee p̃sent Thomas Gillbert, cunstable of Taunton, for letting goe of one whom hee knew to haue stollen a quantity of wampampege, and was suspected of other things.

Fined.

Wee present Thurstrum Clark for leting an Indian to haue a gun, pouder, & shott; the said Thurstrum Clark is fined for this 2^s.

[*190.]

*Wee p̃sent Mr Samuell Newman, teacher of the church of Rehoboth, for dilliuering such things in publick preaching as tend to the defamation of the magestrats of this colony. For this see more in the 13th page forward in this booke. P. 207.

William Sabin, the miller of Rehoboth, was p̃sented on the sixt of March for not returning mens corn vnto them by two quarts in a bushell, allowing thaire toule.

This Court, the said William Sabin did trauerse this p̃sentment, & by verdit of the jury was cleared.

This Court, John Shaw, Jun$\tilde{\text{i}}$, and Steven Bryant, weer p̃sented for profanation of the Lords day; thay lickwise trauised theire p̃sentments, & weer found guilty & sentenced, as on the other side this leafe is spesified.

The jurys names y^t tried these p̃sentments weer these foloing :—

| Sworne. | Josias Winslow, James Hust, Henery Cob, Barnard Lumbert, John Fenney, Joshua Prat, | sworne. | Gorḡ Lewis, Phillip Delanoy, Experience Mechell, Henery Howland, Henery Sampson, Josias Cook. |

This Court, John Damman, of Settuaat, requested y^t hee might orderly inioy his right in the lands of Mr William Gillson, desseased; his proposition or request was refered vnto the jury aboue written, which said jury found the said John Damman the lawfull heaire aparent vnto all the lands of Mr William Gillson, desseased. Of this see more in the fifte page forward in this booke.

1649.
6 June.
BRADFORD, Gouʋnor.

Liberty is graunted vnto the townsmen of Plymouth to make vse of the land att Sepecan for the hearding & keeping of cattell, & wintering of them there as they shall see cause.

*Payed by Josias Cooke vnto Elizabeth Dean her full portion in a cow valleued at fiue pound.

[*191.]

John Read allowed to draw and sell wine and strong waters, & to keep an ordenary, at Rehoboth.

John Crocker is allowed to keep an ordinary at Barnstable.

Edward Sturgis allowed to draw and sell wine at Yarmouth.

The Names of those who weer propounded to take vp thair Freedom.

John Crocker,	Mr Thomas Gilbert,
John Chipman,	James Walker,
John Smith,	William Hedgges.

Mr Coliar, Captain Standish, Mr Hatherle, Mr Browne, & Mr Thomas was ordered to arbetrate a difference betwixt John Crabtree & Edmond West, as the executer of Thomas Howell, desseased; & thay order Edmond West aforsaid to pay vnto the said John Crabtree six pound eleuen shilł & 10 pence.

Captaine Standish & Mr Browne weer ordered by the Court to view the lands & set out the bounds of Rehoboth, according to the trew entent of the first graunt.

John Hoare acknowlidgeth to owe vnto the Court the soṁ of . . . . } twenty pound. Released.

Mr Thomas Tart the soṁ of . . . . 10ł.
Mr James Cudworth the soṁ of . . . . 10ł.

The condition y^t if the said John Hoare shall bee of good behavior towars all maner of psons, and apeer at the next Generall Court, and not depart the said Court without licence; y^t then, &c̃.

*Wheras complaint was made concerning the lands of John Hazell, of Rehoboth, the Court hath ordered, y^t the said John Hazell shall inioy without interuption all his former graunts of lands, and bounded as foloweth: His home lot, containing twelue acares, bounded on the east with the towne green, on the southwest with the mill coue, on the northwest with the land of James Ridway, on the southwest with the Gouerners lot, his salt marsh, containing

[*193.]

1649.

6 June.
BRADFORD,
GOUERNER.

fouer acars, bee it more or les, with an iland in it, and a little vpland as it lyes now within his fence, bounded on the east with the oxe pasture, surrounded on the west, north, & south with Patucet Riuer; four acars of fresh meadow, bee it more or les, now within his occupation, bounded on the east with the brook, on the west and north with his owne land, on the sowth bounded with a linne y^t runs between the towne land and his other allotment, being six hundred acars, bounded on the east with his fresh meadow & a litle run of water and a ceader swamp, on the west with Patucet Riuer, on the north with the woods, on the sowth with the towne land, only the iland & litle vpland aboue mensioned is part of the six hundred acars.

That the remainder of the cuntryes stock vndisposed of bee imployed by the Trēsurer for the procuring of powlder to bee keep in stock for the cuntries vse.

That the Gouerner & Captain Standish doe concider of a conuenient place to keep the cuntries stock of powlder in, wher it may bee in safty.

Concerning the differenc̃ betwixt Richard Chadwell & Mr Thomas Dexter about the breach of the mater of arbetration, the said Dexter is to pay vnto the said Chadwell six shillings, & so the mater is ended.

8 June.

The Oath of Mr Thomas Dexter, taken in open Court the 8th of June, 1649, concning a p̃sell of Corn receaued for a Barke sould by the said Dexter.

This I testifye, y^t the barke y^t was betwixt Richard Chadwell & myselfe I sould to Maior Gibbens for an hundred & fourty bushell of Verginnia corn, at fiue shilling a bushell, and no more.

Wittnes my hand this 8th of June, 1649.

THOMAS DEXTER.

[*195.]

*This Court, John Damman, of Seteaat, required y^t hee might inioy his right in the lands of Mr William Gillson, of Seteaat, aforsaid, desseassed.

To clear vp the aforsaid right, these folowing writings weer openly read & aproued vpon oath : —

Wee, whose names are heer vnderwritten doe giue testimony, vnder our hands, this 7th day of June, 1649, y^t wheras William Gillson, late of Seteaat, desseased, in his life time did require earnestly of the townsmen aforsaid seuerall p̃cells of land for accomõdation of the s̃d William Gillson, but being required of him by vs whose names are heer vnderwriten the reason of his desire of so mutch land, being ancient & haueing no isew of his body to inherite the same after him, his answare was, y^t hee had brought ouer with him into New England two of his sisters children from thaire parrents, and was

COURT ORDERS.

bound in conscience both to take care & to guide for them as if thay weer his owne; and wee conceaue y^t the land was graunted vnto him according vnto his desire in y^t behalfe.

1649.
8 June.
BRADFORD, GOUERNER.

HUMFRY TURNER, HENERY ROWLY,
HENERY COBB, BARNARD LUMBERT.

Vpon the oathes of Humphry Turner, Henery Cob, &c.

Further, I, Humfry Turner, being a townsman at y^t time, & sence so remayning in Seteaat aformentioned, doe further testify y^t William Gillson, desseased, did say vnto mee y^t I aske this land y^t my kinsfolks may inioy it when I am dead.

Wittness my hand, HUMFRY TURNER.

Vpon the oath of Humfry Turner.

The 24th of May, 1649. These p̱sents testifyeth to whom it may concern, y^t I doe remember that Mr Gillsons plea with vs for land was, y^t allthough hee had no children of his owne, yet y^t hee had two of his sisters children, w^h hee looked vpon as his owne, & so did desire to leaue them som̄thing after his dayes was ended; and so for John Damman I haue heard Mr Gillson say y^t hee should haue his land after his wiues dayes weer ended; and I haue lickwise heard Mr Gillsons wife acknowlidḡ it, & further y^t shee would not wrong the said John & Hanna of what was her husbands will about the lands, yet shee would not for som̄ reasons haue the said John & Hanna know her husbands will in y^t busines for the p̱sent. Thus mutch for the p̱sent I doe call to mind to my remembrance, and can safly testify.

24 May.

P mee, ISAACK ROBENSON.

Concerning the abouesaid John Damman, for the clearing of his right and title vnto the abouesaid land of Mr William Gillson, desseased, see more in the fift page bakward of this booke, p. 190.

*Mr Hatherle was ordered by the Court to set at right such thinges as concern Thomas Rawlins & John Damman, by reason of & concerning som̄ cost & charges bestowed by the said Thomas Rawlins vpon the lands of the aforsaid Mr Gillson.

[*196.]

This Court, allso, open proclamation was made y^t if any could lay any just claime or title to the lands of William Gillson, desseased, y^t thay should com̄ in and should bee heard; but no claim or title was challinged.

Wheras sundery psons of Setuaat, viz̧, Humfry Turner and others, find themselues agreeued concerning som̄ lands of thaires lying on the north side of the North Riuer, for y^t thaire land marks are lost, and sundery errors weer

1649.
June.
BRADFORD,
GOUERNER.

in the laying out of the said lands, the Court haue ordered, y^t it shalbee lawfull for the psons aforsaid to hyer a seruayor to measuer the said lands, begiñing at ye rundlit of water called Stony Coue vnto the vttermost extent westward so fare as any lots weer giuen; and to set at rights sutch bounds as are misplaced, y^t so euery of the psons aforsaid may haue his proportion of marsh according to the number of the acars of vpland allowed to each pson, as is expressed in the towne book of Setuaat aforsaid.

The first Tusday in July is apointed for those to meet together w^h are apointed to treat & order the letting of the trade.

The comittee apointed are Mr Coliar, Captaine Standish, Mr Hatherlee, Mr Brown, and Mr Thomas, Mr Allden, Mr Cudworth, Constant Southworth, & Robert Waterman.

This Court is aiurned vnto the fift day of the last full weeke in October, and the foloing Court to bee the next 2^{cond} day after.

[*197.] *The Names of the Comitties of the seuerall Townships y^t serued at this Court and the Aiornments thereof.

Plymouth,	{ Mr Howland, Mr Paddy, { Mannasses Kemton, John Dunham, Senī.
Duxbery,	Mr John Alden, Constant Southworth.
Settuaat,	‡William Hatch,‡ James Cudworth, Thomas Clapp.
Sandwidḡ,	Mr John Vincent, William Newland.
Taunton,	Mr Henery Andrews, Edward Case.
Yarmouth,	Leiutenant Palmer, Mr Edmond Hawes.
Barnstable,	Mr Thomas Dimmack, Thomas Hinckle.
Marshfeild,	Kenelme Winslow, Robert Waterman.
Rehoboth,	Steuen Payne, Robert Titus.
Nawset,	Mr John Done, Samuell Hicks.

8 June.
[*199.]

*At the Generall Court holden at New Plymouth the 8th of June, 1649, a comittee was apointed in the behalfe of the cuntry to treat of and let out the trad at Keñebeck, which accordingly, on the 4th of July folowing, thay did as foloeth:—

Those y^t weer apointed by the Court aforsaid to let the trade at Kenebeck,—viz⌊, Mr William Coliar, Captaine Miles Standish, Mr Timothy Hatherlee, Mr John Browne, Mr William Thomas, Mr James Cudworth, and Constant Southworth; Mr John Alden and Robert Waterman being absent,—the 4th of July, 1649, did let and set the said trade of Keñebeck vnto Mr William Bradford, Mr Edward Winslow, Mr Thomas Prence, Mr Thomas Willet, and

Mr William Paddy, vpon the like conditions as formerly thay haue had it, as is expressed in indentures formerly passed betwixt the p̄ties aforsaid for the full tearme of three yeares, and couenants to bee drawne betwixt them as formerly.

1649.
8 June.
BRADFORD,
GOUE^R.

**At the 2^{cond} Session of the Generall Court, begun the sixt of June, holden the twenty fift of October.*

25 October.
[*201.]

BEFORE Wiłłam Bradford, gent̃, Gouer^r,   Timothy Hatherley,
         Wiłłam Colyar,   John Browne, &
         Captaine Miles Standish,   Wiłłam Thomas,
                 Gentlemen, Assistants.

IT is ordered by the Court, y^t the com̄itties of Scittuaat shall take a view of the timber vpon or neare the range betwixt the Massachusetts & vs, & to make report therof vnto the next Court of Assistants, & for such timber as ap̄eers vndoubtedly within the pattent, to forbid such as are without the gouerment to make vse therof.

Wheras a request is made vnto the Court, by Mr Paddy & others, of the towne of Plymouth, in the behalfe of sundry of the said towne, for a tract of land to supply theire wants & nessesities, lying ouer against Aquetnet Iland, the Court haue ordered Captaine Standish and Mr Browne to take a view of the s̃d lands, & vpon theire viewall therof doe graunt it vnto them of Plymouth aforsaid, for the supply of them in want as aforsaid, if vpon theire viewall therof thay find it not preiuditiall to the colyny ; and the said Captaine Standish & Mr Browne are to set the bounds therof ; and the said Court doe further order the Gouer̃, Mr Paddy, Captain Willet, Mr Howland, Elder Cushman, John Dunham, Sen̄, and Leiuetennant Thomas Southworth, to order & dispose the said lands as thay shall see meetest for the ends aforsaid.

Wheras diuers sad, iniurius practises to the murthering of sum of the English haue been com̄ited by the natiues to the westward, against the said English at Stanford & other places, with diuers insolent & threatening speaches by them allso spoken, wherby the com̄issioners for the Vnited Colinyes are ocationed to vse theire best endeauors for the rectifying of the said abuses ; and being vncertaine whether there may bee need of a warr with the said natiues for y^t end, & haue therfore signifyed vnto the seuerall Vnited Colinyes y^t thay may bee in a redines if ocation should bee.

It is therfor ordered by the Court, y^t forthwith due puision bee made,

1649.
25 October.
BRADFORD,
Gov.

both of men and amunition, with poulder & shot, & victailes, and other nessesaryes for fourty men for the space of three monthes, sutable for such an ocation, & y^t euery towne respectiuely prouid for theire owne men.

The Court haue generally nominated and voted Captaine Standish to bee vnder the concideration of a generall offecer, or comissary generall, to haue the ouersight of the seuerall millitary companies within this gouerment, both for the viewall of theire armes, & to comaund the said companies vpon spetiall ocations; & Captaine Standish aforsaid doth condecend therunto.

The Court haue graunted vnto Mr Bradford, Gouer^r, a pcell of meadow esteemed about as much as will winter ten head of cattell lying vpon the further side of Raged Playne, westward of the path going from Plymouth to Waymouth.

The abouesaid pcell of meddow granted to Mr Bradford, Seni^r, with another pcell of meddow lying att the end of John Faunces land, and his att Joaneses Riuer, which said latter mentioned pcell of meddow was sometimes the meddow of Josepth Rogers and Stephen Tracye; these two pcells of meddow the said Mr William Bradford, Seni^r, did in the time of his sicknes freely giue and make ouer vnto his son, Mr John Bradford, to him and his heires foreuer, and was alsoe ratifyed and confeirmed vnto him by Mis Allice Bradford, Seni^r. See Booke of Sales and Giufts of Lands, anno 1658.

---

29 October.
[*203.]

At the Generall Court holden at New Plymouth, the 29th of October.

BEFORE William Bradford, gent, Gouern^r, Timothy Hatherley,
William Colyare, John Browne, &
Captaine Miles Standish, William Thomas,
Gent, Assistants.

WHERAS Richard Berry acusseth Teage Joanes of sodomy, and y^t the said pties were both bound ouer vnto this Court, to answare the aforsaid acussation, the Court haueing heard what can bee said in the case for psent, for want of further euidence, haue refered it for further hearing vnto the next Generall Court, & haue taken bonds for the apeerance of the aforsaid pties.

Released.

Edward Sturgis acknowlidgeth to owe vnto the Court the som of . . . . } 20^l.
Richard Berry the som of . . . . 20^l.

COURT ORDERS.

The condition, y^t if the said Richard Berry doe apeer at the Generall Court to bee holden at New Plymouth the first Tusday in March next, & not depart the said Court without lycence ; y^t then, &c̄.

Emanuell White acknowlidgeth to owe vnto the Court the soม̄ of . . . . } 20^l.

Teage Joanes the soม̄ of . . . . 20^l.

The condition, y^t if the said Teage Joanes doe apeer at the next Generall Court, to bee holden at Plymouth aforsaid, the first Tusday in March next, & not depart the same without lycence ; y^t then, &c̄.

Obadia Hullme,
Wilłam Carpenter, } are bound one for another in the soม̄ of ten pound a peece.
Joseph Tory,

The condition, y^t if the said parties doe apeere at the next Generall Court of Election, to bee holden the first Tusday in June next, & not depart the same without lycence ; y^t then, &c̄.

1649.
29 October.
Bradford, Gouer^r.
Released.

Released.

*Presentments by the Grand Inquest.   [*204.]

Wee p̃sent Wilłam Halloway and Peregrin White, both of Marshfeild, for fighting.

Wee p̃sent John Hathawey, of Taunton, for lending a gun to an Indian.

Concerning the bridge at the Eel Riuer, the Court haue ordered y^t a pposition bee made vnto the three townes, viz⁋, Yarmouth, Barnstable, and Sandwidḡ, y^t if thay will make payment of the soม̄ of fiufteen pound in good & currant pay vnto the inhabitants of the Eel Riuer aforsaid, towards the charḡ by them expended in the biulding of the aforsaid bridḡ, the said fifteen pound to bee paid by eich of the three townes aforsaid proportionable to theire rates in publick charges ; y^t then the said inhabitants shall accept of the said soม̄ towards the charḡ aforsaid ; or otherwise the said inhabitants to haue libertie to cōmence suit against the townes aforsaid, in respect of the perticular aforsaid as thay shall see reason.

The Court haue ordered Mr Alden, Phillip Delanoy, & Henery Sampson to measure Samuell Eatons land at the vper end, & to make report therof vnto the Court.

Lr̃es of administration are graunted vnto Mis Abigail Coggin, of Barnstable, to administer vpon the estate of her husband, & to pay the debts as fare as the estate will amount vnto, by equal pportions, & is bound to the Court to doe it, & Mr Thomas Dimack & Thomas Hinckley with her.

Cleared, with admonission to take heed for the future.

1649. The Accoumpt giuen in by the Treasurer at this Court.

29 October.
BRADFORD,
GOUERⁿ.

	l : s : d
The companye are indebted to the cuntry,	38 : 19 : 08
The cuntry indebted to the company for building of the house at Keñebeck, for the purchase of land with the Indians, and a barrell of poulder,	^
Reconed with the Treasurer for all accoumpts during the time of his being Treasurer, and rests due to the cuntry from the Treasurer,	10 : 00 : 00
Rests in the Treasurers hands in beads,	10 : 00 : 00
Edward Jenkins indebted for excise,	06 : 00 : 00
Christofer Winter, for a fine,	05 : 00 : 00
‡Constant Southworth, for excise,‡	01 : 14 : 02
Samuell Cutbert indebted,	01 : 00 : 00
William Paybody indebted,	01 : 01 : 00

This 1li 14s 2d payed by Constant Southworth to Captaine Standish.

Memorandum: to giue accoumpt for James Coles excise, out of which to set of the comitties charges for this Court.

[*205.] *Att the Generall Court holden att New Plyṁ, the sixt of March, 1649.
6 March.

BEFOR William Bradford, gent, Gouer, & William Colliar, & Captaine Miles Standish,
Gent, Assistants.

WHERAS, att the Generall Court, holden at Plymouth aforsaid, the 29th of October, 1649, Richard Berry acussed Teage Joanes of sodomy, & other vnclean practisses allso with Sara, the wife of Hugh Norman, & for y^t cause the said pties were both bound ouer to answare att this Court, & accordingly appeered; the said Richard Berry acknowlidged before the Court y^t hee did wrong the aforsaid Teage Joanes in both the aforsaid pticulars, & had borne false wittnes against him vppon oath; and for the same the said Richard Berry was sentenced to bee whipte at the poste, which accordingly was performed.

Lres of adminestration are graunted vnto Mrs Margeret Hicks, to adminester vppon the estate of Ephraim Hicks, & to pay the debts as fare as the estate will amount vnto by equall pportions, & is bound to the Court to doe it, & M^r Thō Willet with her.

The fourth of Aprell, 1650. Thõ Wallen, Richard Carle, Gorḡ Way, Katheren Warner, and Mary Mills were apprehended at Barnstable, in the jurisdiction of New Plym̃; and on the eight day of Aprell, aforsaid, they being examined before Willam Bradford, gent, Gouer, Willam Collyar, and Willam Thomas, gent, Assistants, confessed y^t they, the said Thõ Wallen, Richard Carle, & Gorge Way did healpe away Katheren Warner & Mary Mills, who were run away from theire husbands; and for y^t purpose y^t Richard Carle aforsaid did steale his fathers boat, which they came away in; it was therfore ordered by the Gouer & Assistants aboue mensioned, that the aforsaid Gorḡ Way, Katheren Warner, & Mary Mills should bee sent from constable to constable to the place from whence they came, w^h is a place called Winter Harbor, near Richmans Iland to the eastward; and y^t Thõ Wallen & Richard Carle aforsaid bee com̃itted to ward; all which accordingly was forthwith pformed.

1650.
4 April.
BRADFORD,
GOUER^R.

---

*Att the Court of Asistants holden att Plym̃, the 7th of May, 1650.

7 May.
[*206.]

BEFORE Willam Bradford, gent, Gouer, and
Willam Collyar,
Captaine Miles Standish,
  Gent, Asistants.

Timothy Hatherley, and
John Browne,

WILLAM SHEPHERD, of Taunton, haueing confessed y^t hee hath purloyned & stolen certaine goods from his mother in law, was sensured to returne the said goods vnto his said mother in law againe, and to bee whipt at the post; the latter of which accordingly was forthwith performed.

An execution graunted vnto Edward Doty against James Shaw and John Shaw, Juni͂, for thirty fiue shillings damage and the charge of the suit, wherof the said James & John Shaw is convict by course of law.

New Plym̃, the 3^d of October, 1650.

3 October.

According to an order of Court the day and yeare aboue written, that wheras John Alden, Senior, and Miles Standish, Senior, by order of the Court in the year 1640, were to lay out lands and meddows to John Cooke, Francis Cooke, and John Rogers, and sence sould by the said p̃ties to Thõ Tilden, Moris Truant, and Willam Maycomber, and difference falling out betwixt the aforsaid Thomas Moris and Willam, by order aforsaid, wee, the

1650.

3 October.
Bradford,
Gouer^r.

said John and Miles, doe thus declare our entents when wee first layed out the said land and meddow; that the vpland range with the first trees that were marked : further, wee thuse expresse our selues for the meddow, that it rang from the bound trees vpon the same range to ye North Riuer ; the reason was because wee did not then know, neither yet doe, that ther was any meddow graunted to the two ilands, which, if it appeer by former graunt, wee must confese our ignorance. And wheras by the said order that wee should establish the bounds to continnew to future times, wee therfore order, that as wee find wee layed out the meddow that halfe the meddow before the land layed out to John Rogers bee equally deuided between Wiłłam Maycomber and Moris Truant; and Thŏ Tilden the other halfe of the said meddow. Wee, therfore, by these p̃sents, doe request and order Mr Richard Garrett, according to the mutuall agreement between Wiłłam Maycomber, Moris Truant, and Thomas Tilden, assenting to the same afterward, to pay the said Richard Garrett for his paynes for the same, and that hee lay it out according to the mannifestacions of our entencions at our first laying out of the said lands and meddow abouesaid ; which done, the said bounds to stand for the future and to continew. Wee haue vpon the place shewed the said Richard Garrett the first bounds. Wittnes our hands this 13th of March, 1650.

MILES STANDISH,
JOHN ALDEN.

[*207.]

P. 190.

*Att the Generall Court holden att New Plym̃ the 29th of October, 1649, Obadia Hullme complained against Mr Samuell Newman, in an action of slander to the dammage of an hundred pound ; but the suite was not tried by jury, though ended as vnderneath is expressed.

Obadia Hullme, plaintife, & Mr Newman, deffendant, in an action of slander : the said Hullme complained y^t Mr Newman had reported him to haue taken a false oath in the Court at Plym̃ ; and in the examining the matter before the Gouer^r and Asistants, Mr Newman said hee could not charge him with it of his owne knowlidg̃, but as hee had receaued information from som̃ others, which, not being true, hee did in the Court acknowlidg̃ hee had done him wrong, & promised to pay his charges. And the said Hullme rested satisfyed ; and thervppon Mr Newman deliuered into the Court a wrighting, subscribed vnto by Thŏ Cooper, Stephen Payne, Robert Sharpe, Jonathan Blise, Thŏ Wilmoth, & Wiłłam Sabin, the p̃ties from whom hee had his information. Hullme desired the Court to keepe the wrighting, saing y^t it had been red in theire owne towne in the p̃sence of many straingers, to his great reproch, yet said if those men would but as openly acknowlidg̃ they had

COURT ORDERS. 151

done him wrong as Mr Newman had then done, hee would rest therin; the Court aproving of his willingnes to rest in so easie a satisfaction, and knowing the wrighting to bee false & scandalus, advised Mr Newman to declare in som publick meeting in the towne, att his coming home, how those men had abussed him; for the said Hullme had not giuen in the Court any such testimony as y^t wrighting did import, & vppon his request the Court thought it just to record his clearing.

1650.
29 October.
BRADFORD,
GOUER^R.

Charges allowed vnto Obadia Hullme by the Court in Respect vnto the Suite aboue mensioned.

	s	d
It, to himselfe,	012 :	00
It, to Wiłłam Carpenter, wittnes,	012 :	00
‡It, to the clarke,	02 :	00‡

*Thō Cooke, aged about twenty yeares, late of Ipswidge, trauelling towards Equednett, accompanied with a youth about twelue yeares of age, both of them lodging att the ordenary att Taunton the 2^{cond} day of May, 1650, and vppon the 10th day of the said month the body of the aforsaid Thō Cooke was found dead in the riuer of Taunton, about six miles from the towne. Whervppon a jury of twelue men was impannelled to inquire how and by what meanes hee came by y^t vntimly death. The p̃ticular names of the jury are heer vnder expressed.

[*208.]

Henery Andrewes, foreman of the jury.

Wiłłam Parker,	Richard Stacy,
Richard Williams,	James Bortt,
Walter Deane,	John Tisdall,
John Deane,	Anthony Slocom,
Hesekiah Love,	Nathaniell Woodward.
Thō Linkon,	

The eleuenth day of May the jury brought in theire verdict y^t the youth, by the aduise of the said Tho: Cooke, did take a cannowe, without the knowlidge of the owener therof, and making hast away lest hee should bee pursewed, did stand in the end of the canoowe to paddle it away, and did fall into the riuer, and so by y^t accident was drowned and came to his end.

HENERY ANDREWES, Forman.

June the 9th, 1650. M^r Wiłłam Hedge and Robert Denis are respited vntell the next aiornment of the Court holden the day and yeare aboue said, to make John Besthope to apeere, for whose p̃sonall apeerance they stand bound.

9 June.

1650.
9 June.
[*209.]

*The acknowlidgment of Strong Furnell, of Boston, concerning reproch by him cast vppon M{r} Prence and the towne of Nawset.

June the 9th, 1650. If it may please the honored Court now assembled to take a favorable concideration of these few linnes : —

Wheras there hath been entered an action of slander to the vallew of two hundred pound damage, and partly proceeded in, by the reverent and truely respected M{r} Prence, against mee, Strong Furnell, of Boston, —

I, Strong Furnill aforsaid, doe by these few words declare and testifye to this honored Court now p{r}sent assembled, and to all other psons whersoeuer, y{t} notwithstanding my former psistance in this euell of slandering, it beeing justly charged vppon mee vppon due conviction of my guiltines in this great transgression, I desire therfore to adresse my selfe to remoue my great offence according to my power and the p{r}sent apprehensions I haue of this offence, and hope y{t} for the future I shall more sensably concider of the nature of my offence. I, Strong Furnell abouesaid, doe freely confesse my great transgression being directly against the Holy Scripture and the rules therof, & y{t} agreuated, it being against a ruler in place of justice, and a man of whom I am reuerently perswaded of, and doe not onely now, but haue seen his faithfullnes and integrity; wherfore I am very sorry y{t} I should so justly offend against his pson, against his honored office, so iniure the Bench and the whole honored Court assembled, confessing y{t} allthough M{r} Prence for his owne part hath so humbly expressed his lenity and redynes to take satisfaction, yet I am not in my owne apprehension able to make this p{r}sent and honered Court satisfaction according to the nature of my offence and wrong done vnto them neither by word or deed; but my endeauors and humble desires are y{t} M{r} Prence will bee pleassed to continew his willing acceptance of this my weake acknowlidgment, and y{t} this whole Court assembled wilbee pleassed to accept therof as y{t} which may bee the least y{t} can bee done on my part in a transgression of this nature; and for my owne part I doe further promise heerafter to looke better to my tongue, as the Scripture teacheth, and also heer and els where to put forth my endeauors to regaine and promote the honer of both M{r} Prence, who doeth more imediately suffer by my vngouerned tongue, and also this honored Court and corporation; from whom, if I find this smale tender of myne to find acceptance, I cannot adiudge y{t} I haue, and shall so acknowlidḡ y{t} I haue, found more favour then I should haue found elswhere vppon such a transgression, and shall so acknowlidḡ it, not onely now, but heerafter; further I doe acknowlidḡ y{t} I know no vnfaithfullnes in the towne of Nawset in the p{ti}culars aforsaid.

By mee,   STRONG FURNILL.

COURT ORDERS.   153

The Court, on the day and yeare aforsaid, did order concerning Strong Furnill aforsaid, that hee beare and defray all the charges arising by the suite of Mʳ Prence against him as aforsaid ; and yᵗ if hee, the said Strong Furnell, shall at any time reuiue the aboue said reproches & slanders againe, Mʳ Prence hath his libertie to procecute against him as hee shall see reason.

1650.
9 June.

*Att the Generall Court of Election holden att Plym̃ aforsaid, the fourth of June, 1650.

4 June.
NEW PLYM.
[*211.]

Mᴿ WILL͠AM BRADFORD elected Gouernor, and sworne.

Mʳ Edward Winslow,
Mʳ Thõ Prence,
Mʳ Will̃am Collyar,
Captain Miles Standish,
Mʳ Timothy Hatherley,
Mʳ John Brown,
Mʳ Will̃am Thomas,
Mʳ John Alden,
} chosen Assistants, and sworn.

Mʳ Thõ Prence and Mʳ John Browne chosen com̃issioners for this yeare to treat with the com̃issioners of the Vnited Colonies according to the articles of confederation att the time and place appointed.

The Cunstables chosen by the seuerall Townships, and p̃sented to this Court and sworne, vizſ : —

Plym̃, ...	John Tompson.
Duxbery, . . .	Francis Sprague.
Scittuate, . . .	Gorg̃ Russell, John Williams, Junĩ.
Sandwidge, . . .	Edmond Freeman.
Taunton, . . .	Gorg̃ Maasy.
Yarmouth, . . .	Mʳ Will̃am Hedge.
Barnstable, . . .	Nathaniell Bacon.
Marshfeild, . . .	Joseph Bedle, Moris Truant.
Rehoboth, . . .	John Read.
Nauset, ...	Gorg̃ Chrispe.

VOL. II.   20

1650.

4 June.
BRADFORD,
GOUERNER.

Freemen admited this Court.

Francis Goulder,   John Bradford,
John Gorum,   John Crocker,
Thō Burd,   . James Walker.

The Names of such as stand ppounded to take vpp theire Freedom.

M^r Thō Robenson,   Thō Cooper,
John Stockbridḡ,   Robert Sharpe,
James Bates,   Wilł Paybody,
Ephraim Kemton,   Mr Miller,
Samuell Mayo,   Edward Sturgis,
Robert Wixon,   Robert Dennis,
John Read,   William Nicarson,
John Churchill,   Josiah Winslow.

[*213.] *The comitties of the seuerall Townes that serued at this Court, and the aiornment therof, were as foloeth : —

Plymͥ, ...
{ Mr Paddy, absent,
  Mr Howland,
  Mannasses Kemton,
  John Dunham, Senī.

Duxbery, ...
{ Gorḡ Soule,
  Constant Southworth.

Scittuate, ...
{ Mr James Cudworth,
  Humphry Turner.

Sandwidḡ, ...
{ Mr John Vincent,
  Thō Tupper.

Taunton, ...
{ Richard Williams,
  Oliuer Purchase.

Yarmouth, ...
{ Leiutenant Palmer,
  Richard Hore.

Bāstable, ...
{ M^r Thō Dimacke,
  Anthony Anable.

Marshfeild, ...
{ Kanelme Winslow,
  Robert Waterman.

Rehoboth, ...
{ Steuen Payne,
  Robert Titus.

Nauset, ...
{ Mr John Done,
  Nicolas Snow.

COURT ORDERS.

Survayors for the Hiewayes.

1650.

Plyṁ,	. . . . . .	Captaine Willett, Mr Howland, Mr Paddy.
Duxborrow,	. . . .	John Stare, John Washburn, Juñ.
Scittuate,	. . . . .	Peeter Collimore, Richard Curtis.
Sandwidḡ,	. . . .	Thõ Dexter, Micaell Turner.
Taunton,	. . . . .	Thõ Linkcolne, Edward Case.
Yarmouth,	. . . .	Andrew Hallot, Richard Templer.
Bāstable,	. . . . .	Gorge Lewis, Abraham Blush.
Marshfeild,	. . . .	John Bourne, Richard Beare.
Rehoboth,	. . . .	Walter Palmer, Peeter Hunte.
Nauset,	. . . . .	Edward Banges, Gyels Hopkins.

4 June.

BRADFORD, GOUERNBR.

Receuers of the Exsise.

Plyṁ,	. . . .	Richard Sparrow.
Duxberry,	. . . .	Wilł Paybody.
Scittuate,	. . . .	Henery Meritt, Senr.

The Names of those who are deputed by the Court to marry in each Towne.

For Taunton,	. . . .	Mr Wiłłam Parker.
For Bāstable and Yarmouth,	. . .	Thõ Hinkley.
For Sandwidḡ,	. . . .	Thõ Tupper.

*The Grand Inquest. [*215.]

Mr Thõ Robenson,		Thõ Falland,	
Mr Thõ Cooper,		Edward Sturgis,	
Edward Case,		John Tisdall,	
Gyels Rickard,		Henery Howland,	
Henery Sampson,		Gorḡ Buett,	
Thõ Burman,	sworne.	Wiłłam Gifford,	sworne.
John Crocker,		Steuen Wood,	
Thõ Chillingsworth,		Robert Wixon,	
John Dingley,		Andrew Ringe,	
Robert Sharpe,		Ephraim Kemton,	
Edward Jenkens,		Jacob Cooke.	

Presentments by the former Grand Inquest, June the fift, 1650.

June 5.

Wee present Thõ Tilden, the cunstable of Marshfeild, for not deliuering the two prisoners coṁitted vnto his charge to the cunstable of Scittuate, but gaue them the warrant in theire hand, and let them depart.

Tho: Tilden fined 1ˡⁱ 10ˢ.

1650.
5 June.
BRADFORD,
Gov.

Wee p̃sent Edward Hunt, of Duxburrow, for shooting vpon the Lords day at deare. Fined 2ˢ.

Wee p̃sent John Barnes, of Plym̃, for being drunke. Cleared by paying the fine.

Lres of adminestration are graunted vnto Mʳ Thõ Howes and Samuell Mayo to adminnester vppon the estate of Samuell Hallot, and to pay the debts as fare as the estate will amount vnto by equall proportions.

Lres of adminestration are allso graunted vnto Sara, the wife of Thõ Blossom, to administer vppon the estate of the said Thõ Blossom, and to pay the debts.

And, further, the said Sara, the wife of Thõ Blossom aforsaid, doth by these p̃sents make ouer vnto her child that shee had by her said husband, whom shee calleth Sara, fiue pound sterling out of the estate aforsaid, to belong and appertaine vnto the said child as its owne p̃per right foreuer.

Obadia Hullme and Joseph Tory are bound one for an other in the sum of tenn pound a peece.

Cleared by apeerance att the said Court.

The condition, yᵗ if the said Obadia & Joseph doe appeer at the Generall Court to bee holden at Plym̃ the first Tusday in October next, and not depart the same without licence; yᵗ then, &c.

4 June.
[*217.]

*Att the 2ᶜᵒⁿᵈ Session of the Generall Court, begun the 4ᵗʰ of June, 1650, and held the 10ᵗʰ of June aforsaid.

BEFORE Wiłłam Bradford, Gouᵉʳ,
Thõ Prence,
Wiłłam Collyare,
Captaine Miles Standish,
Timothy Hatherley,
Wiłłam Thomas, and
John Alden,
Gent̃, Assistants.

WHERAS Mʳ Hatherley hath made a motion to the Court to haue libertie to sett vpp an iron mill, and for that purpose hath requested a p̃cell of land lying betwixt Namassakeeset and Indian Head Riuer, lying aboue the path, the Court haue graunted vnto Mʳ Hatherley aforsaid, according to his desire, all the land lying betwixt the path and the ponds betwixt

the two riuers aforsaid, with all and singulare the appurtenances and priui- 1650.
lidges belonging thervnto; to haue and to hold vnto the said Mr Timothy
Hatherley, with all and singulare the appurtenances, to him, his heaires, and
assignes foreuer, vnto the onely proper vse and behoof of him, the said M^r
Timothy Hatherley, to him, and his heaires, and assignes foreuer, prouided,
that the said Mr Timothy Hatherley doe sett the said iron mill to work within
the space of three yeares next ensewing the date heerof, or otherwise the said
lands are to returne againe vnto the colonie.

10 June.
BRADFORD,
Go??.

  The Court haue ordered y^t a jury bee forthwith impanelled, or as soone
as conueniently maybee, by Captain Standish, six wherof are to bee out of
Plym̃, and six out of Duxburow, to lay out the way from Joanses Riuer to
the Massachusits Path, so as it may bee most conuenient, and lest preiuditiall
to any; and if it so fall out y^t it doe or may so bee laid out as it shalbe preiuditiall to either Mr Bradford or John Rogers, that they, or either of them, so
damnifyed, shall haue full satisfaction for the same.

Of this see
more the fift
page forward
of this booke

  That an accoumpt bee giuen by the cunstables of Marshfeild that were
1646 how theire rate was payed that yeare.

  Pecunke, Ahivmpum, Catscimah, Webacowett, and Masbanomett doe all
afferme, that Chickatawbutt his bounds did extend from Nishamagoquanett,
near Duxbery mill, to Teghtacutt, neare Taunton, and to Nunckatatesett, and
from thence in a straight linne to Wanamampuke, which is the head of Charles
Riuer; this they doe all sollomly afferme, saing, God knoweth it to bee true,
and knoweth theire harts.

  Dated the first of the fourth month, 1650.
  Wittnes: Encrease Nowell,
     John Eliot,
     John Hoare.

  Josiah Wampatuke, Indian, sagamore of the Massachusits, and Nahatan,
the sonne of Jumpum, cam̃ to Plym̃ the 7th of June, 1650, and there did testifye, that the land, according to a drauft in the keeping of Mr Hatherley and
others, and the perticulars therin specifyed, was the onely pper lands of
Chickatawbutt, father to Josiah Wampatuke aforsaid; and this hee acknowledged before Captain Standish, Mr William Thomas, and Mr John
Alden.

  Mr Hatherley and others with him haue bought so much of the land
aboue mensioned of the said Josiah Wampatuke as concerned them to
buy.

158   PLYMOUTH COLONY RECORDS.

1650.

10 June.
[BRADFORD,
GOVERNOR.]

[*219.]

Seale.

*A Copie of the Comission from the Gouerment of the Massachusets.

To our trusty and wellbeloued frinds, Captain Humphry Atherton and Captaine Eliazer Lusher.

You, being chosen comissioners by the Generall Court in psent being, haue full power and authoritie, and are heerby inabled in theire names, to consult, agree, and determine with the Generall Court at Plym concerning the title of land called Shawwamett and Pautuxit, and protection of the English and Indians there according to our engagements, repayering all priuat iniuryes according to law and justice.

Att a Generall Courte held att Boston the first of June, 1650.
Thõ Dudley, Gouer.

Wheras a comission was giuen to Captain Humphry Autherton and Captaine Eliezer Lusher by the Generall Court of the Massachusets, bearing date the first of June, 1650, and sealled with theire comon seal, giueing them full power and authoritie to treat, debate, and determine with the Generall Court of Plym about the controuersie concerning the title to the lands called Shawwamett and Pautuxet, and the protextion of the English and Indians, &c, as appears more att larg by a copie of the said comission.

The aforsaid Generall Court of Plym, the sixt of June, 1650, chose William Bradford Gouer, Mr Thõ Prence, Mr William Collyar, Assistants, and Mr Howland, Mr Dimack, Mr Cudworth, Mr Josiah Winslow, freemen, for a comittie, and gaue them full power and authoritie in theire names, and on theire behalfe, to treat with the aforsaid comissioners, and to determine and conclude the abouesaid controuersye, and to put a full end thereunto in any way yt should seem best vnto them.

The conclusion and agreement therabouts was as followeth on the 2cond page forward.

Mr William Bradford,	Mr James Cudworth,
Mr Thõ Prence,	Mr Thõ Dimack,
Mr William Collyare,	Mr Josiah Winslow.
Mr John Howland,	

[*220.]   *June the 7th, 1650. Forasmuch as there hath beene for some long time past some question depending betwixt the jurisdictions of the Massachusetts and New Plym, concerning a certaine tract or tracts of land called Shawwamett and Pautuxett, and some places therabouts; and yt hath pleassed the honored Court of the Massachusetts to graunt a comission, vnder the hand and seale of the said Court, vnto Captaine Humphry Autherton and Captain

Eliezer Lusher, enabling & investing them with full power and authoritie to treat, consult, and determine together with the honered Court of Plymͥ aforsaid in all cases whatsoeuer doe or may concerne the tracts of land before specified; the Generall Court of Plymͥ haueing, in conciderstion of the p̅mises, as allso for the preseruing of mutuall loue, frendshipe, and amitie with theire naighbors of the Massachusetts, haueing chosen and deputed Mr Willam Bradford, Gouer, Mr Thͦ Prence, and Mr Willam Collyare, Assistants, Mr John Howland, Mr Thͦ Dimack, Mr James Cudworth, Mr Josiah Winslow, freemen, as a comͥittie of the said Court, and authorising and enabling them with full power for them and in theire behalfe likwise to debate, resolue, and fully to determine together with the aforesaid comͥissioners of the Massachusetts all and euery of the cases or questions about or concerning the land aforsaid, which said comͥittie, vppon due conciderstion as aforsaid, doe resolue, conclude, and determine as foloeth, videlicet : —

1650.

10 June.
[BRADFORD, GOVERNOR.]

That they doe fully and foreuer relinquish and yeild vpp vnto the gouerment of the Massachusetts aforsaid all their right, title, or claime whatsoeuer the said gouerment or jurisdiction of Plymͥ haue or might haue had, any way or by any meanes whatsoeuer, vnto yͭ whole tract or tracts of land knowne by the name of Shawwamett and Patuxett aforsaid, being such as are or were the just rights of Pumham & Socanoco, or either of them, att yͭ time that the said sachems subiected themselues and theire lands to the jurisdiction of the Massachusetts aforsaid; theire said rights being or to bee cleared according to euedent and aparent demonstration; and wee, the said comͥittie, by the authoritie aforsaid, doe in like manor relinquish vnto the jurisdiction of the Massachusetts all our rights, claime, or title vnto the lands justly and lawfully posessed by Willam Arnold, Robert Coale, and such of the other English as att that time together with themselues did in like manor subiecte to the Massachusetts as aforsaid; prouided, that this shall in no sort hinder or p̅jeduce the due acͦomplishment of the order of the honered comͥittie of Parlement in any other thing or case therin concerned; and allso prouided alwayes, that the bounds of these aforsaid lands shall not extend further towards Cowessett then the true, knowne, and approued limits of the lands of Pumham did extend at the time of theire subiecting to the jurisdiction of the Massachusetts as aforsaid; and allso further with *this prouiso and condition, that what lands soeuer haue bene allredy or heerafter may bee made to ap̅eere to belong to the towne or inhabitants of Prouidence vnto this day by any just title shall not bee included in this relinquishment aboue specifyed, but shall notwithstanding remayne and wholy belonge to the inhabitants of Prouidence, freely to inioy as formerly they haue done; and allso yͭ this jurisdiction of Plymͥ bee not

[*221.]

1650.

10 June.
[BRADFORD, GOVERNOR.]

in any thinge heerby put to more trouble or charge then any other of the two confederate jurisdictions, videlicet, Conictacott and New Hauen.

WILLAM BRADFORD,   JOHN HOWLAND,
THO: PRENCE,   THO: DIMACK,
WILLAM COLLIARE,   JAMES CUDWORTH.

According to our order, wee haue found out and marked a new way from Joaneses Riuer to the Massachusetts Path through John Rogers his ground, and are all agreed the said way by vs marked out to bee most convenient and least preiuditiall.

Wittnes our hands heere vnder written.

This jury was impanelled according to an order extant in the fifte page bakward of this book, p. 217.

JOHN HOWLAND,   THO: HEWARD, Senĩ,
FRANCIS COOKE,   JOHN WASHBURNE, Senĩ,
JOSHUA PRATT,   HENERY SAMPSON,
JOHN WOOD,   GORG: PARTRIDGE,
SAMUELL STURTIVANT,   THO: LETTIS,
HENERY HOWLAND,   WILLAM PAYBODY.

All sworne.

---

7 August.
[*222.]

**Att a Court of Assistants holden att New Plym̃ the seauenth of August, 1650.*

BEFORE Willam Bradford, gent, Gouer,   Tymothy Hatherley,
Willam Collyare,   William Thomas, and
Captaine Standish,   John Alden,
Gent, Assistants.

WHERAS Isaake Buke, of Scittuate, did att this Court acuse John Hewes yt hee, the said Hewes, had stolen from him fouer hoes; the Court could not proseed against the said Hewes for want of further euedence; and therfore haue ordered, yt the cunstable of Scittuate doe keepe the said hoes in his custedie vntell further euedence can bee prodused for the clearing of the case, and then such order to bee taken therin as shall bee thought meet; and that the said Isaake Buke needeth not to apeere any more psonally about yt matter.

Isaake Stedman, the younger, for breaking into a house and from thence stealing out cheese and other things, was sentanced by the Court to bee publikly whipte att Scittuate att the descretion of Mr Hatherley.

COURT ORDERS.

Nathaniell Stedman, for purloining of an handkerchife, was onely admonished and cleared.

1650.

Edward Doty is ordered by the Court to pay vnto Edward Gray and Samuell Cutbert each of them a bushell of Indian corn for damage done by the calues and other cattell of the said Edward Doties in the corn of the sd Edward Gray and Samuell Cutbert.

7 August.
[BRADFORD, GOVERNOR.]

An execution graunted the 2cond of September, 1650, vnto Mr Thō Robenson against Isaak Stedman, Senī, for twenty pound damage and the charge of the suit, wherof the said Isaake Stedman is convict by course of law.

*Att a Generall Court holden att New Plym̄ the 2cond of October.

2 October.
[*224.]

BEFORE Willam Bradford, gent, Gouerr, Thō Prence, Willam Collyare, Captaine Miles Standish, Timothy Hatherley, Willam Thomas, and John Alden,

Gent, Asistants.

IT was ordered, that wheras John Stone, of Hull, hath had leaue giuen him by the Gouer to make vse of our lands att Cape Cod these diuers yeares for basfishing, vntell such time as hee should haue any order from vs to the contrary, hee carriing himselfe peacably there, wee, hearing of sundry miscariages this yeare past, and haueing now sundry of our owne that purpose to sett vpon the said basfishing, thought meet to giue order that the said John Stone bee forthwith warned to desist from making any vse of any of our lands there for yt purpose, that so our owne may without disturbance goe on in theire intended basfishing.

2condly. Wheras Mr Thō Prence and Mr Willam Paddy haue desired leaue to sett vppon a constant course of basfishing att Cape Cod, supposeing that if God please to blese theire proceedings, in time it may proue very beneficiall to this jurisdiction, the Court, hauing taken this theire motion into serius concideration, thought good for p̄sent, therfore, to condecend to theire motion, and therfore haue judged it fitt to giue leaue to Mr Thō Prence, Captaine Miles Standish, and Mr Willam Paddy, with such other of the three townes of Plym̄, Duxburrow, and Nawsett as shall joyne with them vppon the said basfishing, and to that end to make vse of any of the lands, creeks, timber, &c, vppon the Cape land, in such convenient places as they shall chuse for yt purpose.

1650.

2 October.
[BRADFORD, GOVERNOR.]

And wheras wee are informed y** two companies, with nett, boats, and other craft, is as much as the place can beare, it is therfore graunted y* the p̄ties abouesaid, for the better managing of the said voyage, may suit themselues the most conuenientest they can for the seuerall companies out of the three townes, or any two of them, for fitt seting vppon the work intended; and y* the first companie may make choise of the place to build vppon, and the 2*cond* companie to make choise when they are fitt, that so a due orderly course may bee obserued in the managing of it.

Furthermore, M*r* Thō Prence is apointed by the Court to purchase what lands yet remaineth on y* side Cape Cod vnpurchased from the true propriators of them for the vse aboue mensioned, and to make returne of his proceeding to the Court in June next, y* then the said Court may dispose of such p̄cells of the said land to the aboue mensioned p̄ties for the ends proposed as aforsaid.

The 9*th* of June, 1651. The aboue mensioned p*r*uilidge is confermed vnto the aboue mencioned p̄ties, together with M*r* Wiltam Bradford, in the behalf of the aforsaid townes, for the tearme of three years from the next October, and then to returne to the cuntrys disposeing.

[*225.]

2 October.

*Presentments by the Grand Inquest.

October the 2*cond*, 1650. Wee, whose names are heer vnder written, being the grand inquest, doe present to this Court John Hazaell, M*r* Edward Smith and his wife, Obadia Holmes, Joseph Tory and his wife, and the wife of James Man, Wiltam Deuell and his wife, of the towne of Rehoboth, for the continewing of a meeting vppon the Lords day from house to house, contrary to the order of this Court enacted June the 12*th*, 1650.

THO: ROBENSON,	THO: COOPER,
HENERY SAMPSON,	THO: BURMAN,
JOHN CROKER,	EDWARD JENKENS,
HENERY HOWLAND,	ROBERT WIXON,
JOHN TISDALL,	THO: FALLAND,
ROBERT SHARP,	ANDREW RING,
EPHRAIM KEMPTON,	GORG BUIT.

Cleared.

Wee present James Cole, of the towne of Plym̄, for making of a batterie vppon Wiltam Shirtley, of the aforsaid towne.

Cleared, with admonision.

Likwise wee present Thō Shereue, of the towne of Plym̄, for pilfering corn in Richard Sparrows barne, of the aforsaid towne.

Cleared.

Further, wee present Richard Sparrow, of the towne of Plym̄, for concealling of the aforsaid acte of Thõ Shereue, vppon an ingagement so to doe vnlesse called before authoritie.

Wee p̃sent the bridge vppon Joanes Riuer for being defectiue and very dangerus for cattell to goe ouer.

1650.
‿
2 October.
BRADFORD,
GOUER^R.

Wee present the townes of Plym̃, Duxburrow, Marshfeild, & Nawset for want of sufficient pounds.

THO: ROBENSON,	EDWARD JENKINS,
HENERY SAMPSON,	ROBERT WIXON,
JOHN CROKER,	THO: FALLAND,
HENERY HOWLAND,	ANDREW RINGE,
JOHN TISDALL,	GORGE BUITT,
ROBERT SHARPE,	GYELS RICKETT,
EPHRAIM KEMTON,	STEUEN WOOD,
THO: COOPER,	THO: CHILLINGSWORTH,
THO: BURMAN,	JACOB COOKE.

*Wheras a sertaine skife came on drift out of the Massachusetts Bay, sup̃osed to bee one y^t ap̃ertaineth to Mr Hucheson, of the said Massachusetts, and taken vpp by Zacariah Soule, of Duxburrow, —

[*226.]

The Court haue ordered, that the said Zacariah Soule deliuer the said skife vnto Mr Wilł̵am Paddy, who was ap̃ointed to demaund the said skife in the behalfe of the said Mr Hucheson, and y^t Mr Paddy doe pay the said Zacariah Soule for his paines about the said skife.

Wheras the wife of Hugh Norman, of Yarmouth, hath stood p̃sented diuers Courts for misdemenior and lude behauior with Mary Hammon vppon a bed, with diuers lasiuious speeches by her allso spoken, but shee could not ap̃eere by reason of som̃ hinderances vntell this Court, the said Court haue therfore sentanced her, the said wife of Hugh Norman, for her vild behauior in the aforsaid p̃ticulars, to make a publick acknowlidgment, so fare as conueniently may bee, of her vnchast behauior, and haue allso warned her to take heed of such cariages for the future, lest her former cariage come in remembrance against her to make her punishment the greater.

Thõ Clarke is alowed to draw and sell a cask of strong waters.

Captaine Standish is ordered by the Court to impannell a jury when hee shall see convenient time, for to view and lay out a way to a peece of meddow belonging to Constant Southworth, which was som̃times Mr Collyars, lying ouer against Duk Hill, so as it may bee most convenient to Constant Southworth and and least preiuditiall to Phillip Delanoy.

Ordered, that wheras Captaine Miles Standish and Mr John Alden were

1650.
2 October.
BRADFORD,
GOU.

soṁtimes ordered by the Court to lay out sertaine lands and meddows att North Riuer vnto Francis Cook, and John Cook, and John Rogers, the Court doth therfore further order the said Captaine Standish and Mr Alden to manifest what were theire intents about the bounds of the said lands and meddows when they formerly layed them forth, and to sett and establish the bounds of the said lands and meddowes soe as to continew for the futucr.

Mr Josepth Peck is ordered by the Court to administer the ordinance of marriage att Rehoboth, in case Mr Browne can not bee parswaded thervnto.

1650-1.
4 March.
[*227.]

*At the Generall Court holden at New Plyṁ the 4th of March, 1650.

BEFORE Wiłłam Bradford, genṫ, Goũ, Timothy Hatherley,
Wiłłam Collyar, Wiłłam Thomas,
Miles Standish, John Allden,
Genṫ, Assistants.

WHERAS M^r Wiłłam Bradford, the 7th of March, in the 18th yeare of the late Kings raigne, was graunted libertie to seeke forth a place to place soṁ of his children vpon; and when the Court doth know it, that it shalbee confeirmed to him; hee hath now found a p̄cell of land within the bounds of Barnstable, soṁtimes belonging to Napiatam, deseassed, and soṁ of his frinds, the Court doth graunt and confeirme vnto the said Mr Bradford the said p̄cell of land, with all and singular the appurtenances therunto belonging, to haue and to hold vnto the said M^r Wiłłam Bradford, his heires and assignes, foreuer; allso, if any of the Indians should bee yet liueing that can make any claime to any part therof, they giue him power and authoritie to buy the same of them, or otherwise to compound with them in the best sort hee may for the vse aforsaid.

Wheras a p̄cell of land about fourty or fifty acares, bee it more or lesse, was reserued by the Court within the liberties of Yarmouth vndesposed of; and wheras Captaine Miles Standish hath been at much trouble and paines, and hath gone sundry jurnies vnto Yarmouth aforsaid in the said townes busines, and likly to haue more in that behalfe; in respect wherunto the Court haue graunted vnto the said Captaine Standish the aforsaid p̄cell of land, with all the meddow lying before it or any way belonging therunto, of any kind, with all and singulare the appurtenances thervnto belonging, to haue and to

COURT ORDERS. 165

hold vnto the said Captaine Standish, to him and his heires and assignes foreuer. 1650-1.

4 March.
[BRADFORD, GOVERNOR.]

Presentments by the Grand Enquest.

Wee, of the grand enquest, doe p̃sent, —

Imprimus, John Palmer, of the towne of Scittuate, for lending of a gun and som̃ powder and shot to an Indian. This was answared.

THO: ROBENSON,
EPHRAIM KEMTON.

Wee present Gowin White and Zacharie Hick, of the towne of Scittuate, for traueling from Weymouth to Scittuate vpon the Lords day. This was cleared.

EDWARD JENKENS.

Wee present Robert Waterman, of the towne of Marshfeild, for offering an attempt of boddyly vncleanes to Sara Pittney, of the aforsaid towne. Fined fifty shill., or to suffer bodily punishment.

JOHN DINGLEY.

*Wee present Ralph Chapman, of the towne of Marshfeild, for striking of Ferman Haddon. [*228.]

Wee present John Starre and John Washburne, Senĩ, of the towne of Duxburrow, for neglecting the mending of the highwaies. Cleared.

JOHN DINGLEY.

Wee present Emanuell White, of the towne of Yarmouth, for villifying of Mr John Miller, minister of the aforsaid towne. Fined fiue shill., according to order.

Wee present Robert Allen, of the towne of Yarmouth, for villyfying of Mr John Millers minnestry.

EDWARD STURGIS.

The grandiurymen of Rehoboth and the grandiurymen of Nawsett are all absent.

Att the Court of Assistants holden at New Plym̃, the 4th of May, 1651. 1651.

4 May.

BEFORE Willam Bradford, gent, Gouer^r,   Timothy Hatherley,
Willam Collyar,   Willam Thomas, and
Miles Standish,   John Alden,
   Gent, Assistants.

166 PLYMOUTH COLONY RECORDS.

1651.
4 May.
[BRADFORD, GOVERNOR.]
Released, paying his fees.

JOHN ROGERS, of Marshfeild, acknowlidgeth to owe vnto the Court the sum of twenty pound.

James Cole, ... the sum of ten pound.
Henery Howland, ... the sum of ten pound.

The condition, that if the said John Rogers shalbee of good behavior towards all manor of psons, and appeere at the Generall Court to bee holden att Plym aforsaid the first Thursday in June next, and not depart the same without lycence; that then, &c.

The said John Rogers is, att the Generall Court holden the 7th of June, 1651, fined fiue shilt for villifiing the minestry.

---

5 June.
[*229.]

At the Generall Court of Election holden at New Plym, for the Jurisdiction of New Plym, the fift of June, 1651.

BEFORE Wiltam Bradford, gent, Gouer,   Timothy Hatherley,
Tho Prence,   Wiltam Thomas, and
Wiltam Collyar,   John Alden,
Miles Standish,

Gent, Assistants.

MR WILLAM BRADFORD elected Gouernor, and sworne.

Mr Tho Prence,
Mr Wiltam Collyar,
Captaine Miles Standish,
Mr Timothy Hatherley,
Mr John Browne,
Mr John Alden,
Captaine Tho Willet,
} elected Assistants, and all sworn except Mr John Browne and Captaine Willet.

Captaine Standish remaineth Treasurer for this yeare.

Mr John Browne and Mr Timothy Hatherley chosen comissioners for this psent yeare to treat with the comissioners of the United Collonies according to the articles of confederation at the time and place appointed.

Freemen admited this Court, and sworne.

Richard Bowin,   Robert Vixon,
Edward Sturgis,   Mr Josia Winslow,

COURT ORDERS.   167

Wiłłam Paybody,	Anthony Snow,	**1651.**
John Churchill,	John Burne,	5 June.
Wiłłam Wills,	Wiłłam Hedgis,	BRADFORD,
John Smith,	M⁽ʳ⁾ Thõ Gilbert,	GOUER⁽ʳ⁾.
Roger Goodspeed,	Peeter Hunt.	

Ppounded to take vp theire Freedom.

Thõ Huckens,	John Whetcom,
Tristrum Hull,	John Woodfeild,
Abram Blush,	Rodulphus Elmes,
M⁽ʳ⁾ John Freeman,	Isack Chettenden,
Leiuetenant Perigren White,	Richard Beare,
Wiłłam Merrick,	Elisha Besbee,
Nathaniell Mayo,	John Barker.
Wiłłam Twining,	John Williams, Junī,
John Willis,	John Daman,
Wiłłam Foard,	John Here,
Thõ Ensigne,	Richard Silvester,

*The Constables of the seuerall Townshipes.   [*231.]

Plym̃, ...	John Lettice.
Duxber̃, ...	John Vobes.
Scittuat, ...	Peeter Collymore, Gorg̃ Petcock.
Sandwidg, . . .	Nathaniell Fish.
Taunton, ...	William Hedges.
Yarmouth, . . .	Andrew Hallot.
Barnstable, . . .	Gorg̃ Lewis.
Marshfeild, . . .	John Burne and Jeremiah Burrows.
Rehoboth, . . .	M⁽ʳ⁾ Thõ Cooper.
Eastham, ...	Wiłłam Twiney, Junī.

The Com̃itties of the seuerall Townshipes.

Plym̃, ...	{ M⁽ʳ⁾ John Howland, Mannasses Kemton, Leiuetenant Southworth, Thõ Clark.
Duxber̃, . . .	{ Gorge Soule, Constant Southworth.
Scituate, . . .	{ M⁽ʳ⁾ James Cudworth, Humphry Turner.

168   PLYMOUTH COLONY RECORDS.

1651.   Sandwĩ, ...   Mʳ John Vencent, Thõ Tupper.

6 June.   Taunton, ...   { Mʳ Oliuer Purchase,
BRADFORD,   { Richard Williams.
GOUERᴿ.
              Yarmouth, ...   { Mʳ Anthony Thacher,
                                  { Mʳ Edmond Hawes.

              Barnstã, ... { Anthony Annable,
                                  { Isaak Robenson.

              Marshfeild, ... { Kanelme Winslow,
                                  { Josiah Winslow.

              Rehoboth, ...   { Richard Bowin,
                                  { Steuen Payne.

              Eastham, ... { Mʳ John Done,
                                  { Josiah Cook.

                    The Survayors for the Hiewaies.

              Plymouth, ...   { James Cole,   Samuell Sturtivant,
                                  { Thõ Pope,   Josepth Warren.
              Duxb̃, ...   Thõ Gannet,   John Aimes.
              Scituate, ... Thõ Pinchon,   John Turner, Senĩ.
              Sandwĩ, ... Nicholas Wright,   Jonathan Fish.
              Taunton, ...   Hezekia Hore,   John Gallop.
              Yarmouth, ...   Wiłam Clarke,   Edward Sturgis.
              Barnstable, ... Mʳ Thõ Allen,   Samuell Hinckley.
              Marshfeild, ... Anthony Snow,   Perigrin White.
              Rehoboth, ...   John Read,   Wiłam Smith.
              Eastham, ...   Edward Banges,   Richard Higgens.

[*233.]   *The Grand Enquest.

                  { Mʳ Joseph Tilden,   { Roger Goodspeed,
                  { Mʳ John Bradford,   { Richard Tayler,
                  { Mʳ John Freeman,   { Gorge Maacy,
                  { Edward Tillson,   { John Gorum,
                  { John Willis,   { Elisha Besbey,
         sworne. { John Wood,   sworne. { Walter Palmer,
                  { Walter Briggs,   { Peeter Hunt,
                  { Samuell Hickes,   { John Ellis,
                  { John Ellis,   { Peeter Wright,
                  { Peeter Wright,   { Peeter Worden,
                  { John Smith,   { Wiłam Hailston.

COURT ORDERS.

Liberty is allowed vnto the Gouer to make choise of and to depute any one of the Assistants whom hee shall think meet to bee in his rome, when hee is ocasioned to bee absent, as a deputie Gouer.

1651.
5 June.
BRADFORD, GOUERR.

Mr Olliuer Purchase is allowed and approued by the Court to bee ensigne bearer of the milletary companie of Taunton.

To the rates. Wheras Rehoboth was formerly rated 4 pounds, it is now by the Court rated 4 pound and ten shillings, Barnstable the sum of 2ł 15s, and the towne of Plym̃ the sum of 2 pound and 15 shillings.

Liberty is allowed vnto Mr Hatherley to proue the will of Thõ Lapham, deceassed, at Scittuate, in regard the widdow Lapham, through weaknes, is not able to com̃ to the Court.

That the Gouer hath authority to lycence som̃ whom hee shall think meet to keepe victalling houses at Court times in the towne of Plym̃ for the releife of such as are in nessesity at such times.

Wheras a petition was formerly p̃ferred vnto the Court by Mr Hanbery against Mr Browne, wherin the said Mr Browne was much wronged, it is ordered, that if the said petition can bee found on any of the files, it shalbe deliuered to him.

It was afterwards found, and deliuered to him, & burned.

*Wheras a promise was made vnto Mr Collyar to consider him in that which might tend to his support in the way of maiestracy, and that it hath not hetherto bene pformed, the com̃itties haue therfore engaged in the behalfe of the seuerall townshipes to make good vnto the said Mr Collyare the sum of twenty pound, to bee paied, as soone as conueniently may bee, in good and currant cuntry pay, and to bee raised vpon the seuerall townes pportionable to other publick charges.

[*234.]

Wheras by a letter from Newhauen aide by them was requested and required in settleing a plantation at Delaware against such as doe oppose them in that respect, the Court, hauing considered therof, think it not meet to answare theire desire in that behalfe, and will haue no hand in any such contreuersy about the same.

Wheras a request was made the last winter by a messenger from the French at Canada to assist them against the Mowhakes, or at lest to haue libbertie to goe vp through these p̃ts for theire more com̃odius encountering with the said Mowhakes, the Court declare themselues not to bee willing either to aide them in theire designe, or to graunt them libbertie to goe through theire jurisdiction for the aforsaid purpose.

Wheras, by former order of Court, the children of Mr Allexander Winchester were desposed of, to bee vnder the care and guidance of Richard Bowin

VOL. II. 22

1651.
5 June.
BRADFORD,
GOUER^R.

and John Hazell, and that it doth appeere that the said John Hazell, through age and other deabillitie of body, is vncapable of answering the ends of the Court in that behalfe, the Court haue therefore ordered the aforsaid Richard Bowin and Steuen Payne, both of Rehoboth, to haue the ouersight of the aforsaid children of the said Mr Winchester, deceassed; and the Court doe request and appoint Mr Browne to bee healpfull in way of aduise vpon all ocacions, vnto the abouesd pties, in the behalfe and for the good of the said children.

For the continuall support of the townshipe of Plymouth, for the place and seat of gouerment, to pvent the despersing of the inhabitants therof, it is ordered, that Sepecan bee graunted to the towne of Plym̃, to bee a generall healp to the inhabitants therof, for the keeping of theire cattell, and to remayne for the common vse and good of the said township, and neuer to bee alianated by the townshipe from the same to any other vse, and no pson or psons to inioy any right or benifit therby but the inhabitants of the towne of Plym̃ onely, except such as are the com̃on heardsmen for the said townshipe; and the bounds therof to extend itselfe eight miles by the sea side, and four miles into the land, puided it bee bounded by   ⋀   next.

8 June.
[*235.]
This answered to by Mr Hatch.

*Presentments by the Grand Inquest, June the 8th, 1651.

Wee present Wilłam Randall, of the towne of Scittuate, for lending a gun to an Indian. Witnes, Ephraim Kemton.

Henory Samson gaue euidence to this.

Wee present John Shaw and James Shaw, Samuell Cutbert and Beniamin Eaton, of the towne of Plym̃, and Goodwife Gannett, and Martha Haward, and Wilłam Snow, of the towne of Duxburrow, for vaine, light, and laciuius carriage at an vnseasonable time of the night.

Of this and ye next aboue it, see more ye fift page forward of this booke.

Wee present Gorḡ Russell and Isack Stedman, of the towne of Scittuate, for incroaching vpon the com̃on vndeuided lands of Scittuate. Peeter Collymore, Thomas Robinson, Walter Woodward gaue in euidence to this.

This was ordered to be taken of.
This cleared.

‡Wee present John Varssell, of the towne of Scittuate, for disturbing the churches peace. Edward Jenkins gaue euidence heervnto.‡

Wee present the grandiurymen of Taunton for being absent from this Cort.

Lycence is graunted vnto Mr Prence to proue the inventory of the estate of John Yates, deceassed, at home at Eastham.

Lr̃es of administracion graunted vnto Mary Yates, to administer vpon the estate of John Yates, deceassed.

John Bumpas, for idle and laciuius behauior, was sensured to be whipt, and accordingly pformed.

Walter Baker, haueing bene suspected to haue murthered John Winter, and thervpon com̃itted to ward by Mr Hatherley, was examined this Court

COURT ORDERS. 171

and cleared; onely to put in security for his appeerance, if the Court shall see 1651.
reason againe to call him in question at any time within*in* a twelumonth,
which accordingly hee did. 8 June.
Gorge Allen, of Sandwidge, fined 20ˢ for refusing to serue on the grand BRADFORD, GOUER^R.
inquest.

*The Court recciueing an answare from the Generall Court of the Massa- [*236.]
chusets, how they were willing to resigne againe to this gouerment, according to
the aduise of the commissioners, Showamet, as it was yeilded to them by an
acte of this Court, bearing date June 7ᵗʰ, 1650, but on condicion to engage
themselues to protect the English and Indians there, that haue submited
themselues to theire jurisdiction, and to pform theire engagements vnto them,
— they, vpon consideracion heerof, finding themselues vnfitt to take such a
burthen vpon them as the pformance of those engagements of theires, and for
somĩ other waighty reasons, thought better to let it remaine as it was, and
pased theire vote for that end, and soe desired an answare to bee returned; as,
allso, that they desired that all faire and gentle meanes might bee vsed towards
the inhabitants, that loue and peace might bee continued.

At a Court of Asistants holden at New Plym̃, the 4ᵗʰ of August. 4 August.

BEFOR William Bradford, gent, Gouer, Timothy Hatherley, and
William Collyar, John Alden,
Captaine Standish,
Gent, Asistants.

IT was ordered, that wheras a peticõn was pferred vnto the Court holden at
Plym̃ aforsaid, the 4ᵗʰ of June last past, by sundry of the inhabitants of
Scittuate, wherin they request that wheras certaine lands were formerly
graunted vnto them in a towne meeting in Scittuate aforsaid, and that they
could not haue the said lands layed out vnto them according to the aforsaid
graunt, that the Court would take somĩ order about it, which accordingly the
Court did, and sent vnto those whom it conserned, requiring them either to
lay forth such lands as were formerly graunted vnto the aforsaid pties as aforsaid, or otherwise to send theire reasons to the Court why they doe not.

Warrents were signed and directed to the cunstables of seuerall townes
for to leuy the fines for the defects in armes.

A warrent directed to require Ralph Allen, Senĩ, psonally to appeer, to
answare vnto such misdemeanors as wherof hee is accused.

1651.

7 October.
[BRADFORD, GOVERNOR.]
[*237.]

*At the Generall Court holden at New Plymͥ, the 7ᵗʰ of October, 1651.

BEFORE Wiltam Bradford, genᵗ, Goũ, Miles Standish, &
Thõ Prence, Timothy Hatherley,
Wiltam Collyare,

Genᵗ, Assistants.

GORGE RUSSELL, of Scittuate, was bound ouer vnto this Court to answer for his vnciuell and vnreasonable beating of Katheren Winter; and for the same was sensured by the Court to pay twenty shillings forthwith vnto the cunstables of Scittuate, for to bee imployed for the good of the said Katheren.

And wheras bond was taken for his good behauior vntell this Court, the Court haue released him of the said bond, paying his fees.

And wheras the said Gorḡ Russell, at the Generall Court holden the 8ᵗʰ of June last past, was p̃sented for encroaching on the vndeuided lands of Scittuate, hee is enioyned by the Court to demolish whatsoeuer fence hee hath on the said comͫons that haue stoped the hiewayes, and soe is cleared of this p̃sentment.

Isack Stedman was allsoe for the like encroachment p̃sented at the said Court, and is likwise enioyned by the Court to reforme the said wrong to the satisfaction of such of his naighbors as are offended therat.

Wheras, at the Generall Court holden the 8ᵗʰ of June last past, John Shaw and James Shaw, Samuell Cutbert, and Beniamine Eaton, Goodwife Gannett, Martha Haward, and Wiltam Snow were p̃sented for vaine, light, and lacivious carriage at an vnseasonable time of the night, the Court, not finding them alike faulty, haue fined James Shaw and Goodwife Gannett thirty shillings apeece, to be payed by the next Court of Assistants, & themselues then p̃sonally to ap̃eere, or otherwise to receaue corporall punishment by whiping.

And Samuell Cutbert, Wiltam Snow, Beniamine Eaton, and Martha Haward are released, with admonishion to take heed of such euell carriages for the future.

And as for John Shaw, hee is lyable to punishment when oppertunitie serueth.

[*237ᵃ.] *At this Court Walter Palmer and Peeter Hunt, grandiurymen of Rehoboth, were fined for non appeerance, (according to the order of Court,) each twenty shillings.

[*238.] *Att this Court Ralph Allin, Senᵢ, of Sandwidḡ, and Richard Kerbey were summoned to answare for theire deriding, vild speeches of and conserning Gods word and ordinances: they are bound ouer vnto the next Generall Court to make theire appeerance, and in the mean time to bee of good behavior towards all manor of psons, & not depart the said Court without lycence accordingly, as followeth:—

1651.
7 October.
BRADFORD, GOUERNOR.

Ralph Allin, Senior, of Sandwidg, acknowlidgeth to owe vnto the Court the sum of . . . . } 20 : 00 : 00   Released.

Mr Thõ Dexter, Senior, the sum of . . . . . . 10 : 00 : 00
William Basset, the younger, the sum of . . . . 10 : 00 : 00

The condicion, that if the said Ralph Allen shalbee of good behauior towards all mannor of psons, and appeere at the Generall Court to bee holden at Plym the first Tusday in March next, and not depart the Court without lycence; that then, &c̃.   Released.

Richard Kerbey acknowledgeth to owe vnto the Court the sum of . . . . } 20 : 00 : 00

Thõ Launder, the sum of . . . . 10 : 00 : 00
Ralph Allen, Senior, the sum of . . . . 10 : 00 : 00

The condicion, that if the said Richard Kerbey shalbee of good behavior towards all mannor of psons, and appeer at the Generall Court, to bee holden at Plym the first Tusday in March next, and not depart the said Court without lycence; that then, &c̃.

The Court doe allow and approue of James Wyate to bee in the office of a leiuetenant in the milletary companie of Taunton.

Mr James Cudworth and Humphry Turner are allowed 25^s for charges of attendance at June Court last past. It, for fiue daies, videlecet, from Fryday vntell the Tusday following, 2^s 6^d p day.

*Presentments by the Grand Enquest.   [*239.]

Wee p̃sent Samuell Hinckley and Jonathan Hatch for hiering land of the Indians.

Samuell Hinckley freed. Jonathan Hatch cleared.

Wee further p̃sent Ralph Allen, Senior, and his wife, Gorge Allen and his wife, William Allen and Richard Kerbey, Peeter Gaunt and his wife, Rose Newland, Edmond Freeman, Senĩ, and his wife, Goodwife Turner, and widdow Knott, all of the towne of Sandwidg, for not frequenting the publick worship of God, contrarye to order made the 6th of June, 1651.

These were refered to confer- ance and further considera- c̃on.

Wee further p̃sent the wife of Richard Knowles, of the towne of Plym, for retailing of strong waters contrarye to order.

Wee further p̃sent Elizabeth Eeddy, Senĩ, of the towne of Plym, for laboring, that is to say, for wringing and hanging out clothes, on the Lords day, in time of publicke exercise.

Fined 10^s; but sence remited.

1651.

7 October.
BRADFORD, Goῦ.

Fined 1ˡⁱ 10ˢ.

Refered to confernnce and further admonished to labore to walk inofensiuely.

Released, with admonition. See more March Court, 1651.

Released and aquite.

Wee futhor p̄sent the wife of Richard Knowles, of the towne of Plym̄, for retailing of strong waters contrarye to order.

Wee further p̄sent Goodwife Knowles for selling strong waters for fiue or six shillings a bottle that cost but 35ˢ the case. Fined 10ˢ; to bee bestowed on yᵉ poore of Plym.

Wee further p̄sent Gorge Pidcocke, of Scittuate, for taking a false oath.

Wee further p̄sent Arther Howland, of the towne of Marshfeild, for not frequenting the publicke assemblyes on the Lords daies.

Wee further p̄sent Goodwife Ramsden for lacivius goeing in the companie of young men. Sence cleared with admonition.

Wee further p̄sent Samuell Eaton and Goodwife Halle, of the towne of Duxburrow, for mixed daunsing.

Wee further p̄sent Nathaniell Bassett & Josepth Pryor, of the towne of Duxburrow, for desturbing the church of Duxburrow on the Lords day.

Wee further p̄sent Edward Halle for felling of timber and selling of it out of the colloney, which timber is on the townes com̄ons.

10 June.
[*240.]

*Taunton, June the 10, anno 1651. The verdict of the inquest in the towne of Taunton, conserning the death of John Slocume, of Taunton, the sonn of Anthony Slocume, of Taunton, as followeth, vizᵗ : —

Wee, whose names are heervnto subscribed, being, the day and yeare abouesaid, mett together to enquire and consider of the death of the said John, doe find as followeth : —

Imprimis, that on the 25ᵗ of Febreuary last, the said John, goeing with a companie of p̄sons, to the number of twenty, vnto a pond called the Fowling Pond, about two miles from the towne, to gather cramberies, in his returning, made som̄ stay behind yᵉ said companie, about a mile from his home, vpon confidence of his knowlidge of the way home, being nine yeares of age, but mising of the path, strayed in the woods, and returned not againe.

Item, that immediately vpon the mise of him, his father went to the place wher hee made his stay to seeke for him ; and when hee could not find him, nor heare his voyce neare and of a good distance about, hee returned home, hoping that hee had taken som̄ other path home ; but then finding him not, hee went againe about the woods, and yet not coming to any knowlidge of him, hee raised the towne, and with a considerable companie the whole night following, with drum, guns, and loud voyces, and 3 daies after with great dilligence sought him, but could not find him.

Item, the 5ᵗ of January, that John Lincolne, in his following the heard of cattell, found the skull of the said John, haueing the braine not wholly consumed ; and January the 9ᵗʰ, hee found som̄ other parts of the corpse, with p̄te of his clothes scattered in smale peeces about the place by a certaine pond at the head of the Mill Riuer, 3 miles from the towne, and two miles from the said Fowling Pond.

1651.
10 June.
BRADFORD, GOUERN^R.

Item, wee considering that the said John being thinly clothed because the day of his lose was temperate, and the next day stormy, and very cold, and soe likwise the fourth, and vpon view beholding a certaine place containing the length and breadth of his body, which was moist and black, and the weeds turned backward euery waies, and his clothes torne into smale peeces, and despersed into diuers places, as allsoe certaine bones found in sundry places, and in one place sofi part, as wee conseue, of his bowells not quite consumed, wee doe apprehend that the said John, when hee strayed away, wandred with much labour, and being spent with wearines and cold, perished among the brushy shrubs, and was devoured and torne, and the p̄ts of his carkeis despersed with rauenus creatures.

And heervnto wee subscribe our hands.

WILL̃AM PARKER,	JONAH **A** AUSTIN,
GORGE HALL,	JAMES WYATE,
EDWARD CASE,	JOHN DEANE,
WALTER DEANE,	NATHANIELL WOODWARD,
RICHARD **R** PAULE,	JAMES BATES,
WILLAM HAILSTONE,	HENERY ANDREWES, Junier.

*The Information of the Inhabitants of Taunton concerning the Death of Willam England, about the age of ten Yeares, Seruant to Joseph Wilbor, of Taunton.

[*241.]

Wee, whose names are heervnder subscribed, on the enquiry of the death of the said Willam, find as followeth : —

Imprimis, that the said Willam, on the sixt day of September, being the last day of the weeke, tooke a great cannoo towards the euening, to fetch home sofi wood from the further side of the riuer called ye Great Riuer, within a call of his masters house, as hee was accustomed, and not returning seasonably, his dame called to him, and not hearing his voyce nor seeing the cannoo, soe soone as his master came home, shee acquainted him with it, who im̃ediately sought for him, but could not find him ; but about a quarter of a mile from the place wher hee was vsed to fetch wood, hee found the cannoo adrift, with the seazye and stick fastened to it lying in the cannoo.

The next morning, being the Lords day, hee, with diuers others, sought on the riuer for him, and found him not ; but James Walker and Richard Burt, pasing vp the riuer towards meeting, found the said Willam floating on the water, who made it known, and caused him to bee taken vp.

1651.
10 June.
BRADFORD,
GOUERNR.

Vpon view of his corpse, wee found no wound, but conseaue that the said Willam, striuing in the ordering of his cannoo, did fall ouer the said vessell, and soe perised in the water.

WILLAM OTWAY, alīs PARKER,	JAMES BATES,
EDWARD CASE,	WILLAM HARUY,
OLIUER PURCHASE,	ANTHONY SLOCUM,
JAMES WYATE,	RICHARD STACY,
RICHARD PAULE,	THO: CASWELL.
JAMES WALKER,	
WILLAM HAILSTONE,	

[*242.] *In the difference betwixt Samuell Cutbert and Steuen Bryant, about a cow the said Cutbert sould to the said Bryant, and the difference betwixt Samuell Cutbert and Samuell King, about an heifer the said King sould vnto the said Cutbert, the said Steuen Bryant engageth to lend vnto the said Samuell Cutbert 2 bushells of Indian corn, and 2 barrells of tarr, to satisfy the said Samuell King, according to bargan for his heifer; and the said Cutbert is to haue the said heifer deliuered vnto him; and wheras there is som ouerplus due from Samuell King to Samuell Cutbert, when as the aforsaid corn and tarr is paid, the said King is to pay vnto the said Cutbert the 2 bushells of Indian corn the next haruist, that soe the said Bryant may bee satisfyed his corne hee hath lent according to promise made vnto him, and soe all differences amongst the said pties are ended by mutuall consent.

The pticulars payed to the said Kinge were,—

	£ s d
It, in broadcloth, ...	01 : 05 : 00
It, in holland, ...	00 : 12 : 04
It, in stuffe, ...	01 : 14 : 00
	03 : 11 : 04

[*243.] *Memorandum: that wheras Kanelme Winslow, of Marshfeild, somtimes inhabitant of the towne of Plym, at the time of his mariage with Ellenor Adames, (somtimes wife vnto John Adams, deceassed,) did put in securitie to pay vnto James Adames, sonn of the said John Adams, the som of fiue pounds when hee should come to bee of age, these psents wittnesseth that James Adams aforsaid did come before the Gouerner, and did acknowlidg that hee hath receued from the said Kanelme Winslow the said fiue pound; and 26 December. accordingly on the 26th of December, 1651, it was ordered to bee entered vpon publicke record as payed and receiued as aforsaid.

COURT ORDERS.

The Names of the Purchasers. [*244]

Mr Wm Bradford,	Abraham Pearse,
Mr Thoṁ Prence,	Steeven Tracy,
Mr Wm Brewster,	Joseph Rogers,
Mr Edw̃ Winslow,	John Faunce,
Mr John Alden,	Steeven Deane,
Mr John Jenney,	Thoṁ Cushman,
Mr Isaack Allerton,	Roḃte Hicks,
Capṫ Miles Standish,	Thoṁ Morton,
Mr Wm Collyer,	Anthony Annable,
Mr John Howland,	Samuell Fuller,
Manasseth Kempton,	Franc̃ Eaton,
Francis Cooke,	Willm Basset,
Jonathan Brewster,	Francis Sprague,
Edward Banges,	The Heires of John Crackstone,
Nicholas Snow,	Edward Bumpas,
Steven Hopkins,	Willm Palmer,
Thomas Clarke,	Peter Browne,
Raph Wallen,	Henry Sampson,
Willm Wright,	Experience Michell,
Elizabeth Warren, widdow,	Phillip Delanoy,
Edward Dotey,	Moyses Symonson,
Cutbert Cutbertson,	Georg̃ Soule,
John Winslow,	Edward Holman,
John Shaw,	53.
Josuah Pratt,	Mr James Shcrley,
John Adams,	Mr Beauchampe,
˰ Billington,	Mr Andrewes,
Phineas Pratt,	Mr Hatherley,
Samuell Fuller,	Mr Wm Thomas.
Clement Briggs,	In all 58.

VOL. II.   23

GENERAL INDEX.

GENERAL INDEX.

Acconquesse, alias Acockcus, ... 10
Accord Pond, ... 54
Acockcus, ... 10
Acokcus, one of the plantations of old comers, . . 5
Acquiat, ... 19
Acquind, alias Acquiat, ... 19
Acqussent River, ... 5
Adams, Ellenor, ... 176
Addams, Adames, James, ... 76
   receives money for Mr. Shirley, ... 76
   married, ... 108
   discharges Kanelm Winslow, ... 176
   John, ... 177
   his heirs, their land at Plain Dealing, . . 28
Adey, Webb, presented for disorderly living, . . 36
   committed to prison, ... 42
Adford, Henry, married, ... 66
Agawem Path, ... 29
Aimes, Aymes, John, married, ... 88
   John, ... 168
Alden, Elizabeth, married, ... 79
Alden, Aldin, Alldin, Allden, John, 9, 52, 55, 58, 85,
   88, 96, 100, 101, 104, 144, 150, 156, 157,
   160, 161, 163—166, 171, 177.
   one of Duxbury committee, 16, 40, 46, 63, 72, 75,
                 94, 95, 117, 123, 144
   an Assistant, ... 153, 166
   one of the council of war, ... 100
   John, Jun., admitted a freeman, ... 123
   John, Sen., ... 149
   Mr., 42, 83, 88, 105, 117, 122, 127, 128, 136, 144,
                          147
Alkerman's Field, ... 25
Allen, George, ... 24
   one of Sandwich committee, . . . 16, 40, 57
   bound for Edward Dotey, ... 18

Allen, George, licensed to cut hay on the Commons, ... 76
   fined for not serving as grand juror, ... 171
   and wife, presented for absence from public
     worship, ... 173
   John, ... 83, 117, 124, 134
   propounded a freeman, ... 95
   admitted a freeman, ... 114
   Ralph, Sen, ... 171
   prosecuted for absence from public worship, ... 172, 173
   Robert, ... 90
   prosecuted for defamation, ... 165
   Thomas, ... 72, 124, 168
   propounded as freeman, ... 34
   William, presented for absence from public
     worship, ... 173
Allerton, Isaac, ... 101, 133, 177
   assignment to Thomas Cushman, ... 133
   his claim against Godbertson satisfied, . . . 132
   Mr., ... 95
Almy, Almey, William, his goods attached, . . . 28
Alney, William, ... 18
Amees, John, James Torey vs., ... 80
   See Aimes, John.
Ammunition procured for soldiers, ... 47
Andrewes, Henry, ... 16, 101, 151
   his complaint against Gilbert, ... 67
   one of Taunton committee, 46, 57, 59, 68, 117,
                         144
   Henry, Jun., ... 175
   Mr., ... 177
Annable, Anable, Anthony, . . 28, 65, 85, 101, 177
   one of Barnstable committee, 16, 40, 46, 57, 63,
                68, 72, 75, 94, 117, 154, 168
   married, ... 80

(181)

GENERAL INDEX.

Annable, Hannah, married, ... 80
Applegate, Thomas, suit against William New-
    land, ... 18
Apportionment of rates and soldiers, ... 64
    See Rates.
Aquetnet Island, petitioned for by Plymouth, . . 145
Arms procured for soldiers, ... 65
    to be provided by each town, ... 96
    persons fined for not being provided with, . 171
Arnold, William, ... 159
Assistants, 8, 15, 33, 40, 52, 56, 59, 71, 83, 115, 123,
    153, 166
Attachments, ... 23, 24, 28, 30, 32, 75, 77, 81
Atherton, Humphrey, ... 158
Atkins, Thomas, ... 4, 5
    presented and censured for extortion, . . . 4
Austin, Jonah, ... 175
Atwood, John, ... 7, 25, 29
    one of Plymouth committee, 16, 31, 40, 45, 57, 59
    Treasurer, ... 34
    grants of land to, ... 9, 26
    Mr., ... 23, 26, 32
Bacon, Nathaniel, ... 84, 153
    propounded a freeman, ... 84
    admitted freeman, ... 101
Baker, Francis, ... 124
    to dwell at Yarmouth, ... 17
    married, ... 19
    Nicholas, petitions to settle at Seacunck, . . 43
    Walter, complained against for murder, . . 170
    William, his lease from John Barnes, . . . 13
Bangs, Banges, Edward, 5, 7, 31, 34, 69, 73, 115, 155,
    168, 177
    grants of land to, ... 25, 48
Bark built at Plymouth by contribution, ... 31
Barker, John, ... 124, 126, 127, 134
    fined for misdemeanor, ... 54
    propounded as freeman, ... 167
    Robert, ... 84, 102, 124
    his claim for ferriage, ... 89
    to keep ordinary at Marshfield, ... 105
Barnes, Mary, ... 38
    John, 25, 31, 32, 38, 50, 53, 54, 72, 73, 116, 124
    presented for extortion, and discharged, 5, 12
    his lease to William Baker, ... 13
    bound to appear at Court, ... 107
    his suit against Giles Rickett, ... 108
    licensed to sell beer, ... 122
    fined for drunkenness, ... 66, 156
    Joshua, ... 20, 29, 31, 36
    propounded as freeman, ... 17
    bound to be of good behavior, and re-
        leased, ... 41
Barnstable, ... 22, 44, 105
    town officers, 9, 15, 34, 40, 53, 72, 83, 84, 102,
    115, 116, 124, 125, 139, 153, 155, 167, 168

Barnstable, committees, 16, 40, 46, 57, 59, 63, 68, 72,
    75, 94, 95, 104, 117, 123, 144, 154, 168
    rates, ... 18, 92, 109, 169
    soldiers from, ... 90
    bounds settled with Yarmouth, ... 19, 21
    agreement with Indians, ... 22
    town presented for not repairing ways, . . . 60
    to make military regulations, ... 62
    military officers, ... 63, 105
    fortification, ... 65
    courts held there, ... 73
    purchases land of Paupmunnuck, ... 130
    ordinary, ... 141
Bartlett, Bartlit, Robert, . . 60, 71, 73, 84, 102, 126
Bass fishing, privileges granted to Messrs. Prence
    and Paddy, ... 161, 162
Bassett, Basset, Bassit, Nathaniel, presented for
    disturbing church, ... 174
    William, ... 9, 42, 58, 177
    one of Duxbury committee, 46, 57, 60, 68, 123
    fined for not mending guns, ... 137
    the younger, ... 173
Bates, James, ... 175, 176
    propounded as freeman, ... 154
Baxter, George, ... 133
Beare, Richard, ... 155
    propounded as freeman, ... 167
Beauchampe, Mr., ... 177
Bennett, Edward, propounded as freeman, . . . 84
Berry, Richard, ... 147
    his complaint against Jones, ... 146
    punished for defamation, ... 148
Besbey, Besbee, Elisha, ... 168
    bound to appear at Court, ... 45
    propounded as freeman, ... 167
Besbeech, Beesbeach, Thomas, ... 34
    fined for not serving as juror, ... 42
    his bounds settled, ... 39, 52
    one of Duxbury committee, ... 57
Besthope, John, ... 151
Betts, William, propounded as freeman, ... 17
Bewyt, see Buett.
Biddle, Bedle, Beedle, Beddle, Bidle, Joseph, 9, 102,
    116, 125, 153
Billington, Christian, ... 6, 38, 58, 59
    Elizabeth, apprentice to John Barnes, . . . 38
    Francis, ... 38, 58, 59, 81, 119, 132
    prosecuted and fined, ... 87
    mortgage to Caleb Hopkins, ... 78
    land granted to, ... 26
    bound for appearance, and released, . . . 81
    and wife, to give possession of land to Jon-
        athan Brewster, ... 6
    Joseph, a runaway servant, ... 58
    ———, ... 177
Bishop, Bishope, Bushop, Alice, ... 134

GENERAL INDEX. 183

Bishop, Alice, tried, condemned, and executed, for
   murdering her child, ... 132—134
   John, propounded as a freeman, ... 17
   Richard, ... 6, 132, 134
   married, ... 79
   prosecuted for stealing, ... 137, 138
Black Brook, ... 26
Black Water, ... 8
Blackwell, Blackweell, Michael, ... 124, 134
Blindman, Richard, propounded as freeman, . . 8
Blise, Jonathan, ... 150
Blisse, Thomas, ... 115
   propounded as freeman, ... 84
   settlement of his estate, ... 126
Blossom, Sarah, ... 156
   Thomas, settlement of his estate, ... 156
Blush, Abraham, ... 53, 56, 84, 155
   propounded as freeman, ... 17
   Abram, propounded as freeman, ... 167
Boardman, Bordman, Thomas, ... 124, 134
   surveyor of highways, ... 72
Boatfish, Boatefish, Botefish, Robert, . . . 9, 28, 71
   licensed as retailer, ... 75
Bobbit, Edward, presented, ... 140
Bonney, Boni, Thomas, ... 53, 72
   suit against Willis and others, ... 107
   presented for lewdness, ... 96
   his acknowledgment to John Farniseed and
     wife, ... 97, 98
Bonum, George, ... 6
   married, ... 79
   Ruth, married, ... 98
Boreman, Thomas, married, ... 80
Bortt, James, ... 151
Bound Brook, ... 19
Bourne, Henry, ... 12, 34, 41, 72, 102
   one of Barnstable committee, ... 59, 68, 75
   John, ... 102, 155, 167
   propounded a freeman, ... 45, 95
   admitted a freeman, ... 167
   Richard, ... 85, 137
   bound for William Newland, ... 18
   one of Sandwich committee, . 16, 40, 68, 94
   Thomas, ... 66, 101, 115, 124, 134
   one of Rexhame committee, ... 16
   suit against John Chandler, ... 42
   one of Marshfield committee, ... 40, 94
Bowers, Bower, George, ... 7, 31
   prosecuted for several offences, . . . 11, 18
   his suit against Bonum, ... 6
Bowin, Bowine, Richard, ... 139, 169, 170
   propounded a freeman, ... 84
   admitted a freeman, ... 166
   one of Rehoboth committee, ... 168
Bowman, Nathaniel, suit against Morris Truant, . 95
Brackenberry, William, ... 14

Bradford, Allice, Sen., ... 146
   John, ... 125, 146, 168
   propounded as freeman, ... 114
   admitted a freeman, ... 154
   William, 3, 5—8, 10—12, 14, 15, 23, 25, 27, 29,
     30—33, 37—39, 43—45, 48—52, 55, 56, 58,
     59, 63, 66—68, 71, 74, 75, 77, 79, 80, 87, 89,
     94, 98, 100, 104, 106, 107—111, 113, 114,
     118, 121, 122, 131—134, 136, 138, 139, 142,
     145, 146, 148, 149, 156, 158—161, 164—166,
     171, 172, 177.
   Governor, 8, 15, 33, 40, 52, 56, 83, 115, 123,
     153, 166
   his surrender of the colony, . . . 5, 8—11
   money granted to, ... 10
   one of the council of war, ... 47
   an Assistant, ... 71
   president of the council of war, ... 64
   commissioner of the United Colonies, 115, 123,
     139
   complains against his tenants, ... 119
   and others, hires Kennebeck trade, . . . 144
   lands granted to, ... 54, 146, 164
   engaged in bass fishery, ... 162
   William, Jun, ... 110
   ensign of Plymouth company, ... 121
   Mr., ... 157
Bray, Thomas, Francis Linceford vs., ... 27
   punished for adultery, ... 28
Brett, Brete, William, ... 84, 88, 134
   propounded as freeman, ... 95
   admitted a freeman, ... 101
Brewen, Obadiah, propounded as freeman, . . . 8
Brewster, Jonathan, 9, 23, 29, 39, 42, 43, 52, 66, 73,
     85, 96, 135, 177
   one of Duxbury committee, 16, 40, 46, 63, 72, 75
   his claim against Billington and wife, . . . 6
   controversy with John Ford, ... 6
   presented for neglecting ferry, ... 5, 18
   land granted to, ... 88
   Love, ... 6, 44, 53, 56, 73, 79, 124, 134
   his suit against Samuel Eaton, ... 135
   Mary, married, ... 94
   William, ... 79, 90, 177
   administration of his estate, ... 73
Bridge at Eel River, by whom made, . 127, 136, 147
   at Joanes River out of repair, . . . 121, 163
Briggs, Clement, ... 177
   his demand against Isaac Allerton, ... 101
   John, administration of his estate, ... 18
   Walter, ... 139, 168
Brooks, Brooke, Brookes, Gilbert, ... 83, 116
   William, ... 71, 102, 139
   a grand juror presented for disclosing coun-
     sel, ... 96
Brough, Edward, ... 58

GENERAL INDEX.

Broughton, Thomas, his suit against William
    Thomas, ... 86
Brown, Browne, John, 8, 12, 15, 19, 39, 43—45, 49,
    52, 55, 59, 63, 68, 71, 74, 78, 85, 87, 89, 98
    —100, 107—109, 111, 113—115, 118, 122,
    125, 136, 138, 139, 141, 144—146, 149
    one of the council of war, ... 47, 100
    an Assistant, 8, 15, 33, 40, 52, 56, 59, 71, 83,
        115, 123, 153, 166
    a commissioner of the United Colonies, 71, 83,
        100, 115, 123, 139, 153, 166
    propounded as freeman, ... 114
    Mary, agreement with John Doane, ... 76
    Peter, ... 89, 177
    Priscilla, agreement with John Brown, . . . 89
    Mr., ... 82, 126, 164, 169, 170
    licensed to use lands at Sowames River, . 120
Bryant, John, ... 5
    presented for drinking tobacco in highway, . 12
    Stephen, ... 176
    presented for several offences, . 81, 87, 140
Buckley, Mr., admitted a freeman, ... 71
Buett, Buit, Bewyt, George, . 83, 115, 155, 162, 163
Buke, Isaac, complaint against John Hewes, . . 160
Bumpass, Bumpas, Edward, ... 54, 177
    John, punished, ... 170
Bundy, John, ... 90
Bunting, Thomas, apprentice to John Cooke, Jun., 78
Burd, Byrd, Thomas, ... 116, 124
    a runaway servant, ... 30
    propounded a freeman, ... 125
    admitted a freeman, ... 154
    his execution against Russell, ... 138
Burgis, Burges, Thomas, ... 84, 90
    one of Sandwich committee, . . 40, 75, 94, 123
    presented for breach of peace, ... 96
Burne, see Bourne.
Burman, Thomas, ... 124, 130, 155, 162, 163
Burrowes, Burrows, Jeremiah, ... 90, 167
Bursell, James, ... 84, 124, 134
    Thomas, ... 124
Bursley, John, ... 83, 116
Burt, James, ... 84, 119
    Richard, his guardian, ... 119
Burton, Richard, presented for stealing, . . . 127
Byrd, see Burd.
Cade, James, propounded as freeman, ... 3
Callicutt, Richard, land taken from him, ... 81
Campion, Clement, ... 73
Cape Cod, bass fishing at, ... 161
    lands there granted to Mr. Prence and
        others, ... 162
Carew, John, married, ... 79
Carle, Richard, ... 149
Carpenter, William, ... 85, 102, 147
    admitted a freeman, ... 84

Carpenter, William, bound to appear at Court, &c., 147
Carver, Robert, ... 53, 126, 127
    propounded as freeman, ... 52, 69, 95
    his suit against Hiller, ... 43
    admitted a freeman, ... 122
Case, Edward, . . . 41, 53, 56, 85, 155, 175, 176
    one of Taunton committee, . . 117, 123, 144
Caseley, Casley, John, and wife, presented and
    punished for fornication, ... 37, 42
    Alice, ... 42
Caswell, Thomas, ... 176
Caughtacanteist Hill, ... 25
Cauken, Hugh, propounded as freeman, ... 8
Causumpsit Neck, ... 5
Chadwell, Richard, ... 53, 56, 72
    one of Sandwich committee, ... 46
    suit against Thomas Dexter, ... 142
Chambers, Thomas, ... 9, 17, 101, 124, 126
    bound to appear at Court, &c., ... 14
    one of Scituate committee, . . . 57, 68, 115
Chapman, Ralph, ... 5
    presented for pound breach, ... 165
    land granted to him, ... 54
Charles I., ... 10
Chase, William, ... 91, 129, 130
    his bond to appear at Court, &c., ... 9
    his settlement with Sympkins, ... 20
    Goodman, ... 128, 130
Chauncey, Chanssy, Charles, ... 45
    land granted to him, ... 9
    his claim against Marshfield, ... 121
    Mr., an approved physician, ... 112
Chaundler, Chaundlor, Edmund, one of Duxbury
    committee, ... 60, 68
    John, ... 39, 42
    Nathaniel, ... 90
    Roger, suit against Kanelm Winslow, . . . 98
Checkett, Josiah, ... 34, 40, 66
Cheesborrough, Cheesborow, Cheesburow, Chees-
    burrow, William, propounded a freeman, 84
    Ussamequin's complaint against him, . . . 99
    admitted a freeman, ... 122
    punished for sundry offences, . . . 103, 136
Chettenden, Isaac, propounded as freeman, . . 167
    Thomas, vs. Christopher Winter, ... 24
Chickatawbutt, his bounds, ... 157
Chillingsworth, Shillingsworth, Thomas, 55, 60, 77, 84,
        102, 134, 155, 163
    propounded as freeman, ... 69
    admitted a freeman, ... 71
    one of Marshfield committee, ... 123
Chipman, John, propounded as freeman, . . . 141
Chrispe, George, ... 153
Church, Richard, . . 34, 41, 53, 60, 87, 113, 116
    his execution against Fuller, ... 50
    his suit against Mrs. Jenney, ... 104

GENERAL INDEX.

Church, Sergeant, ... 127
   bound for Captain Wright, ... 121
Churches, their liberties to be maintained, . . . 106
Churchill, Churchall, John, married, ... 79
   licensed to sell Clark's land, ... 138
   propounded a freeman, ... 154
   admitted a freeman, ... 167
Clapp, Thomas, ... 83
   propounded a freeman, ... 71
   admitted a freeman, ... 84
   one of Scituate committee, ... 144
Clark, Alice, married, ... 79
Clark, Clarke, Thomas, 34, 40, 50, 53, 72, 77, 105, 116,
                   120, 122, 124, 177
   his land laid out, ... 7
   his suit against Matthew Fuller, ... 37
   his suit against William Powell, ... 73
   licensed as retailer, ... 163
   one of Plymouth committee, ... 167
Clarke, Abigail, ... 138
   George, ... 29, 33
   his land to be sold, ... 138
   Martha, ... 134
   Thurston, ... 30, 32, 38, 48
      land granted to, ... 26
      presented for lending gun to Indian, . . . 140
   William, ... 9, 90, 168
      fined for drunkenness, ... 138
   Goodman, land granted to him, ... 129
Clerk's salary, twenty pounds, ... 34
Clifton, Thomas, ... 116
   propounded as freeman, ... 125
Coachman, see Cushman.
Coal mine sought for by Plymouth, ... 87
Coale, Robert, ... 159
Cobb, Cob, Henry, ... 65, 104, 140, 143
   one of Barnstable committee, . . 72, 95, 117
   fined for absence from Court, ... 106
   licensed as retailer, ... 73
Coggen, Abigail, administratrix of her husband's
      estate, ... 147
   Henry, ... 65, 71
   takes oath of fidelity, ... 72
   his suit against Waterman, ... 72
   Thomas, ... 75
   Mr., ... 112
Cole, Daniel, ... 42, 52, 124, 134
   propounded a freeman, ... 71
   admitted a freeman, ... 84
   James, 34, 40, 72, 78, 81, 119, 132, 148, 166, 168
   his fine remitted, ... 24
   land granted to, ... 26, 48
   licensed as retailer, ... 79, 80
   his suit against Pope, ... 116
   bound to appear at Court, ... 119, 120
   presented for breach of peace, ... 162

Cole, Job, ... 9, 42, 56, 72, 124
Cole Brook Meadow, ... 30
Collier, Colliare, Colyar, Collyar, Collyare, Colliar,
   Collyer, William, 3, 6—8, 12, 14, 15, 23, 27,
   29, 30, 32, 33, 37—39, 43, 44, 49, 50—52,
   55, 56, 58, 59, 63, 66—68, 71, 74, 79, 80, 85,
   88, 94, 98, 100, 104, 105, 108, 109, 111, 114,
   118, 121, 122, 131, 133, 136, 138, 139, 141
   144—146, 148, 149, 156, 158—161, 164—
   166, 171, 172. 177.
   an Assistant, 8, 15, 33, 40, 52, 56, 71, 83, 115,
                       123, 153, 166
   sent on a mission to Massachusetts, ... 53
   twenty pounds granted to, ... 169
   one of council of war, ... 47, 64
   coroner, ... 101
   Mr., ... 11, 60, 62, 116, 122
Collimore, Collymore, Collymer, Peter, 54, 115, 155,
                       167, 170
Colman, Joseph, ... 124, 134
Combe, Comb, John, . . . 25, 37, 66, 131, 133
   land granted to, ... 29
   assigns servant to William Thomas, . . . 38
   admitted a freeman, ... 71
   Mr., ... 95
   Mrs., her children placed out, ... 131
Committees of each town, 16, 40, 45, 57, 59, 63, 68,
   72, 74, 75, 94, 95, 117, 123, 144, 154, 167,
   168.
Commissioners of the United Colonies, 71, 83, 88, 100,
               115, 123, 139, 153, 166
   their propositions, ... 93
Confederation of the colonies, ... 53, 56
Constables, 9, 15, 34, 40, 41, 53, 72, 83, 101, 102,
              115, 123, 124, 153, 167
Cooke, Cook, Francis, 7, 34, 40, 53, 56, 84, 132, 160,
                      177
   his lands, ... 49, 149, 164
   Hester, married, ... 79
   Jacob, ... 116, 124, 155, 163
   propounded a freeman, ... 114
   admitted a freeman, ... 123
   John, ... 7, 16, 42, 44, 75, 111, 132, 149
   deputy from Plymouth, ... 45
   one of Plymouth committee, . . . 40, 59, 74
   land granted to, ... 29
   his lands, ... 149, 164
   assigns his servant to Samson, ... 6
   John, Jun., ... 48, 59, 78, 110
   one of Plymouth committee, 31, 57, 63, 68, 72,
                     94, 123
   his lands, ... 49
   Josiah, . . . 5, 7, 9, 15, 25, 26, 124, 140, 141
   one of Nawsett, or Eastham, committee, 117, 168
   allowed to sell wine, ... 125
   Mary, married, ... 94

VOL. II.   24

Cooke, Roger, ... 90
   Thomas, inquest upon him, ... 151
  Cooper, Ann, married, ... 79
   John, one of Barnstable committee, . . 46, 57
   Thomas, . . . 102, 116, 150, 155, 162, 163, 167
    propounded as freeman, ... 84, 154
Coroner chosen, ... 101
Council of war chosen, and powers, . . 47, 64, 100
Court of Assistants, when holden, ... 18
Courts for different towns, ... 73, 118
Cowessett, ... 159
Coy Pond, ... 129
Crabtree, John, suit against Edmund West, executor, ... 141
Crackstone, John, ... 177
Crampton, Henry, ... 14
Crimes. Adultery, ... 28
  assault, ... 24
  breach of peace, . . . 42, 73, 96, 147, 162, 165
  dancing, ... 239
  defamation, 12, 17, 18, 24, 45, 54, 87, 98, 140, 148, 165
  disorderly living, ... 36
  drinking or smoking tobacco, ... 4, 12
  drunkenness, ... 66, 111, 138, 156
  extortion, ... 4, 5, 12, 60
  fornication, ... 37, 85, 109, 112, 135, 138
  hiring land of Indians, ... 173
  lewdness, 35, 36, 54, 96, 112, 137, 163, 165, 170, 172, 174
  millers' frauds, ... 112, 135, 138, 140
  murder, ... 132—134
  neglecting public worship, ... 174
  nuisance, ... 18
  receiving stolen goods, ... 137
  reviling religion, ... 36
  Sabbath breach, ... 4, 140, 156, 165, 239
  seditious speeches, ... 70
  selling guns and powder to Indians, 8, 36, 137, 140, 147, 165, 170
  servants running away, ... 30, 36, 59
  stealing, . . 18, 24, 73, 127, 137, 149, 160, 162
  swearing, ... 9, 12, 37
  tailors' frauds, ... 5, 12
  towns not providing arms, ... 135
  towns not exercising militia, . . . 70, 117, 140
  towns not choosing officers, ... 135
  towns not having pounds, ... 36, 42, 163
  towns not repairing ways, . 60, 135, 137, 139, 140
  vagrancy, ... 36
Crocker, Crooker, Croker, Francis, ... 90
  petitions for leave to marry, ... 112
  John, ... 107, 112, 155, 162, 163
   propounded a freeman, ... 141
   admitted a freeman, ... 154
   his suit against Thomas Shawe, ... 111

Crocker, John, licensed to keep an ordinary, . . 141
   William, ... 72
    propounded as a freeman, ... 71
Crispe, George, prosecuted, ... 81
  prosecuted and fined, ... 87
Crow, Crowe, John, one of Yarmouth committee, 16, 40
  magistrate at Yarmouth, ... 73
  Mr., ... 24
  land granted to, ... 128—130
  John, Sen., one of Yarmouth committee, . . 57
   presented for receiving stolen goods, . . . 137
  Yelverton, ... 102
Cudworth, James, . . 30, 141, 144, 158—160, 173
  committee from Barnstable, ... 40
  committee from Scituate, . . . 144, 154, 167
Curtis, Richard, ... 155
Cushman, Coachman, Thomas, . . 5, 7, 25, 111, 177
  time allowed to recover his debts, ... 95
  his claim against Mrs. Combe, . . . 131, 132
  his assignment from Mr. Allerton, ... 133
  Elder, ... 145
Cutbert, Samuel, ... 90, 148, 161
  prosecutions against him, . . . 81, 87, 170, 172
  his suits against Edward Dotey, ... 120
  his suits against Bryant and King, ... 176
Cutbertson, see Godbertson.
Daman, Damman, John, ... 116, 143
  propounded as freeman, ... 125, 167
  prosecuted for smoking tobacco, ... 4
  heir to William Gilson, ... 140—143
Darby, Darbie, John, ... 115
  land granted to him, ... 129
  See Derbey.
Davenport, Lieutenant, of Salem, ... 36
Davis, Dolor, ... 14, 84
  propounded a freeman, ... 84
  admitted a freeman, ... 101
  Philip, a servant of John Cook, ... 6
Dean, Deane, Elizabeth, ... 141
  John, ... 124, 151, 175
  Stephen, ... 177
  Walter, ... 41, 151, 175
Delano, Delanoy, Dellanoy, Philip, 37, 77, 102, 122, 126, 127, 136, 140, 147, 163, 177
Delaware, a plantation settled there by New Haven, ... 169
Dennis, Robert, ... 18, 41, 84, 130, 151
  bound to prosecute Edward Morrell, . . . 9
  propounded as freeman, ... 154
  land granted to, ... 128, 129
Deputies, sent to the General Court from the several towns, ... 45, 46
  See Committees.
Deputy Governor to be appointed by the Governor, 169
Derby, Richard, ... 50
  his claim against Willis, ... 50

GENERAL INDEX.   187

Derby's Ponds, ... 30
   See Darby.
Dexter, Thomas, ... 124, 155
   prosecuted, ... 96
   evidence concerning his bark, ... 142
   Thomas, Sen., ... 173
   Thomas, Jun., ... 115
      prosecuted, ... 135
   Mr., ... 137
      prosecuted, ... 137
Deuell, Deuile, Devile, Devell, Walter, . . 35, 43, 52
   prosecuted by Massatumpaine, ... 20
   William, and wife, and others, prosecuted for
      meeting from house to house on Lord's
      day, ... 162
Didcutt, John, ... 31
Dillingham, Edward, ... 9, 24, 35
   one of Sandwich committee, ... 46, 63
   Oseah, ... 112
   Mr., ... 137
Dimmock, Dimmack, Dimack, Dimake, Thomas, 20,
      35, 65, 72, 147, 158—160
   one of the council of war, ... 47
   one of Barnstable committee, 16, 40, 63, 123, 144,
      154
   magistrate at Barnstable, ... 73
   lieutenant of Barnstable company, . . . 63, 105
   presented for not exercising soldiers, . . 97
Dingley, John, ... 72, 84, 102, 116, 155, 165
   propounded as freeman, ... 69
   admitted a freeman, ... 71
Doggett, Dogged, John, ... 125, 127
   one of Rehoboth committee, ... 123
   propounded as freeman, ... 125
Doane, Done, John, ... 7, 24, 72, 79, 82
   one of Plymouth committee, 31, 40, 45, 57, 59,
      63, 68
   one of Nawsett, or Eastham, committee, 144, 154,
      168
   his agreement with Mary Brown, ... 76
   Lydia, married, ... 88
   Mr., ... 11, 48, 60, 75
Dotey, Doten, Edward, 32, 33, 39, 44, 52, 69, 81, 120,
      161, 177
   his suit against William Almey, ... 18
   grant of land to, ... 26
   his suit against Thurston Clarke, . . . 30, 32
   to indemnify Thomas Symons, ... 33
   his suit against George Clarke, ... 33
   indebted to Manasseh Kempton, ... 67
   his suit against James Shaw, ... 149
   claim of Gray and Cutbert against, . . . 161
Doughty, Francis, ... 9, 17, 135
   presented for selling powder to Indians, . . 8
Duglas, Jane, ... 119
Dunham, Dunhame, Abigail, married, ... 79

Dunham, John, ... 7, 16, 53, 56, 82
   one of Plymouth committee, 45, 63, 72, 74, 117
   land granted to, ... 30
   the elder, ... 32
   land granted to, ... 20
   John, Sen., ... 34, 104, 124, 134, 145
   one of Plymouth committee, . . 94, 144, 154
   fined for absence as committee, ... 106
   John, Jun., ... 107
   propounded a freeman, ... 24
   admitted a freeman, ... 33
   land granted to, ... 26
   bound for his good behavior, ... 108
   his suit against Samuel Edie and others, . 110
   Samuel, propounded as freeman, ... 114
   admitted a freeman, ... 123
   Thomas, ... 73, 125
   forbidden to visit Martha Knott, ... 136
   fined for breach of peace, ... 73
   propounded as freeman, ... 114
Duxbury, Duxbery, Duxborrow, ... 105, 161
   town officers, 9, 15, 34, 40, 53, 62, 72, 83, 84, 101,
      115, 116, 123, 125, 139, 153, 155, 167, 168
   committees, 16, 40, 46, 57, 60, 63, 68, 72, 75, 94,
      95, 104, 117, 123, 144, 154, 167
   rates, ... 18, 64, 92, 109
   soldiers from, ... 90
   bounds of the town, ... 8, 9, 34
   military regulations, ... 60—62
   military officers, ... 88, 105
   claim of John Rowe against, ... 41
   to be enlarged, ... 54
   land desired by, to be viewed, ... 76
   ordinary, ... 104
   claim of Hall against the town, ... 110
   town presented for want of pound, . 36, 42, 163
   surveyors of highways presented, . . 135, 165
   plantation at Saughtuckquett, ... 88
Eastern Swan Pond Meadow, ... 129
Eastham, committees, ... 168
   town officers, ... 167, 168
Eaton, Benjamin, complaints against, . . 59, 138, 172
   Francis, ... 117, 177
   Rachel, married, ... 94
   Samuel, ... 122, 135
   his grant to Love Brewster, ... 79
   presented for dancing, ... 174
   his land measured, ... 147
Eddenden, Eddingden, Edmund, excused from
   serving on the grand jury, ... 84
   propounded a freeman, ... 3
   admitted a freeman, ... 15
   one of Scituate committee, . . . 16, 40, 57
   licensed as retailer, ... 73
   Edward, ... 50, 51, 75, 85
Eddy, Edeth, Elizabeth, ... 112

GENERAL INDEX.

Eddy, Edeth, Edie, Elizabeth, Sen., presented for
    breach of Sabbath, ... 173
    John, apprentice to Francis Goulder, . . . 82
    Samuel, ... 82, 110, 112
    land granted to, ... 26
    suit against John Dunham, Jun., ... 107
    Zachary, apprentice to John Browne, . . . 113
Eel River, ... 23, 75
    inhabitants claim against Barnstable, Yarmouth, and Sandwich, . . . 127, 136, 147
Elcock, [Alcock,] Ann, married, ... 80
Eldredge, Eldred, Ann, ... 97
    William, ... 97
Elections, 8, 9, 33, 34, 52, 53, 71, 83, 115, 123, 153,
    166, 167
    none in 1649, ... 139
Eliot, John, ... 157
Ellis, Elizabeth, ... 85
    John, ... 75, 168
    punished for fornication, ... 85
Elmes, Rodulphus, propounded as freeman, . . 167
England, William, drowned, inquest on him, . . 175
Ensigne, Thomas, ... 34, 41, 84
    propounded as freeman, ... 3, 167
Equeduett, ... 151
Evans, William, ... 12
Excise, receivers appointed, . . . 105, 116, 125, 155
    rates of, ... 103
Excommunicated person forbidden to officiate as
    minister, ... 53
Ewell, Henry, ... 34, 41
    propounded as freeman, ... 17
Falland, Thomas, ... 20, 155, 162, 163
    one of Yarmouth committee, ... 60
    admitted a freeman, ... 23
Fallowell, Followay, Gabriel, 16, 26, 56, 84, 111, 112,
    134
    William, propounded as freeman, ... 23
    land granted to, ... 26
Farniseed, Farnyseede, Farneseede, Farnisside,
    Elizabeth, ... 97
    John, ... 97, 107, 108, 116
Faunce, John, ... 146, 177
Feake, Henry, ... 41
    one of Sandwich committee, ... 57, 60
    John, admitted a freeman, ... 40
Ferry at North River regulated, ... 18, 54
Finney, Fenney, John, 14, 53, 71, 102, 105, 111, 112,
    116, 117, 125, 140
    propounded a freeman, ... 71
    admitted as freeman, ... 75
    land granted to, ... 25
    Robert, ... 83, 102, 111, 124, 134
    married, ... 23
    land granted to, ... 25
    propounded a freeman, ... 114

Finney, Robert, admitted a freeman, ... 123
First Herring Brook, ... 130, 131
Fish, Jonathan, ... 75, 84, 168
    Mary, ... 75
    Nathaniel, ... 75, 167
Fishe, John, ... 124
Fitzrandall, Edward, ... 116
Flawne, Thomas, ... 128
    land granted to, ... 171
Floyde, John, his complaint against Jane Douglas, 119
Forbes, Vorbes, John, ... 167
    propounded as freeman, ... 95
Ford, John, controversy with Jonathan Brewster, . 6
Forde, Foarde, William, presented for fraud as
    miller, ... 112
    propounded as freeman, ... 167
Foster, Forster, Edward, ... 24
    one of Scituate committee, ... 16
    his will proved, ... 73, 75
    Richard, ... 90
Fowling Pond, ... 174
Foxwell, John, ... 90
Freeman, Edmund, 8, 15, 19, 27, 33, 38, 39, 43—45,
    49, 52, 63, 68, 71, 74, 89, 94, 98, 116, 153
    an Assistant, . . 8, 15, 33, 40, 52, 56, 63, 71, 83
    to try a person for stealing, ... 24
    presented for lending a gun to an Indian, . . 36
    one of the council of war, ... 47
    to hold Courts in several towns, ... 73
    one of Sandwich committee, ... 104
    fined for absence from Court, ... 106
    Edmund, Sen., and wife, presented for absence from public worship, ... 173
    Edmund, Jun., ... 102
    propounded as freeman, ... 3
    married, ... 98
    John, ... 168
    propounded as freeman, ... 167
    Mr., ... 22, 35, 42, 86, 95
Freemen propounded, 3, 8, 17, 24, 34, 45, 52, 69, 71,
    84, 101, 114, 125, 141, 154, 167
    admitted, 8, 15, 23, 52, 71, 80, 84, 101, 114, 122,
    123, 154
    of Taunton, land granted to them, ... 18
French request aid in their war against the Mohawks, ... 169
Fresh Lake, ... 25, 48
Fuller, Bridget, agreement with Nehemiah Smith, 13
    married, ... 23
    land granted to her, ... 26
    her suit against Josias Winslow, ... 50
    Matthew, ... 37, 50, 87
    propounded as freeman, ... 45
    land granted to, ... 48
    chosen sergeant, ... 61
    prosecuted and fined, ... 87

GENERAL INDEX. 189

Fuller, Samuel, ... 6, 9, 15, 177
    Mrs., ... 25, 101
Furnell, Furnill, Strong, ... 152, 153
    his acknowledgment to Mr. Prence, ... 152
Gallop, John, ... 168
Gannett, Goodwife, presented for lewdness, . 170, 172
    Thomas, ... 135, 168
Garrett, Richard, ... 150
Gates erected on highways, ... 41
Gaunt, Gant, Mary, ... 112
    Peter, ... 101, 105, 116, 124, 125
    and wife, presented for absence from public worship, ... 173
Gibbens, Major, ... 95, 142
Gifford, William, ... 155
Gilbert, John, Sen., Henry Andrews against, . . 67
    land granted to, ... 98
    John, Jun., ... 87
        complaint against, for felony, ... 82, 83
    Thomas, ... 56, 116, 124
        propounded a freeman, ... 57, 141
        admitted a freeman, ... 167
        presented, ... 140
Gilson, William, ... 89
    his estate, ... 140—143
Glasse, James, married, ... 88
    propounded a freeman, ... 114
    admitted a freeman, ... 123
Godbertson, Godberson, Cutbertson, Cutbert, 119, 132, 177
    Sarah, her estate settled, ... 119
Golope, John, ... 12
Goodman, Thomas, ... 12
Goodspeed, Roger, ... 168
    admitted a freeman, ... 167
Goole, Francis, prosecuted, ... 87
    his surrender to William Hanbury, ... 78
    his suit against John Shaw, Jun., ... 79
Goose Point, ... 18
Gorham, Goarome, Gorome, Gorum, Groome, Ralph, 37
    his claims against Clarke and Combe, . . . 37
    John, ... 124, 168
        propounded a freeman, ... 125
        admitted a freeman, ... 154
        married, ... 79
Goulder, Francis, ... 29, 82, 125
    propounded as freeman, ... 71, 114, 153
    admitted a freeman, ... 154
    Katherne, ... 82
Governor, elected and qualified, 8, 15, 33, 40, 52, 56, 71, 83, 115, 123, 153, 166
    none elected in 1649, ... 139
Grand jurors, 16, 34, 41, 53, 56, 71, 84, 102, 116, 124, 155, 168
    inquire respecting Providence plantation, . . 37
    fined for absence, ... 171, 172

Granger, Graunger, Thomas, tried and executed, . 44
    administration of his estate, ... 50
Gray, Edward, ... 161
    John, presented, &c., ... 97
    Mr., ... 128
    presented, ... 37
    committed to prison, ... 42
Great Basse Pond, ... 129
Greenfield, Thomas, ... 90
Green's Harbor, ... 8
    bounds, ... 9
Groome, Groomes, Gromes, John, ... 67, 76
    land granted to, ... 29
    propounded as freeman, ... 75
    sworn, ... 76
    land granted to, ... 26, 48
    bound to appear at Court, &c., ... 120
    his suit against Thomas Clark, ... 122
Growse, William, ... 95
Haddon, Ferman, ... 165
Hailstone, Hailston, William, . . 71, 168, 175, 176
    propounded a freeman, ... 52, 69
    admitted a freeman, ... 71
Hall, Edward, ... 90, 115
    punished for swearing, ... 9, 12
    suit against Miles Standish and others, . . . 110
    presented for selling timber for exportation, . 174
    George, ... 83, 175
        propounded a freeman, ... 52, 69
        admitted a freeman, ... 84
    John, ... 115
Halle, Goodwife, presented, ... 174
Hallett, Hallot, Hellot, Andrew, . . . 21, 155, 167
    claim of Massatumpaine against, ... 20
    suit against John Alden and others, ... 58
    land granted to, ... 128
    Andrew, Sen., gives a cow to poor of Yarmouth, 70
    Andrew, Jun., ... 53
    Samuel, administration of his estate, . . . 156
    Mr., ... 128, 130
    land formerly granted to, to be laid out, . 20
    land granted to, ... 128
Halloway, Holloway, Joseph, ... 115
    fined for breach of peace, ... 42
    William, ... 84
    propounded a freeman, ... 52, 69
    admitted a freeman, ... 71
    bound to appear at Court, ... 58
    his claim against Taunton, ... 103
    presented for fighting, ... 147
Hamlen, James, ... 53
    propounded as freeman, ... 34
Hammon, Mary, ... 163
    presented for lewdness, ... 137
Hanbery, Handbury, Hambrow, Peter, ... 42
    fined for stealing, ... 73

GENERAL INDEX.

Hanbery, Peter, bound to appear, &c., . . 121, 122
   William, ... 31, 34, 39, 40, 51, 105
      married, ... 23
      propounded a freeman, ... 45
      admitted a freeman, ... 52
      land granted to, ... 48, 49
      his agreement with Francis Goole, . . . 78
      his suit against Francis Billington, . . . 119
      his suit against Abraham Peirce, ... 44
   Mr., ... 52, 105, 169
Harding, Captain, ... 126
Harris, Arthur, ... 135
Harman, John, ... 90
Harvey, Samuel, ... 108
Harvy, William, ... 176
Hassell, John, ... 49, 87
   See Hazell.
Hathawey, John, presented for lending gun to Indian, ... 147
Hatch, Ann, married, ... 66
   Jonathan, ... 4, 90
      punished as a vagrant, ... 36
      to live with Stephen Hopkins, ... 38
      presented for hiring land of Indians, . . 173
   Lydia, punished for lewdness, ... 35
   Thomas, ... 130
      propounded as freeman, ... 17
   William, bound to appear, &c., ... 25
      prosecuted for seditious speeches, . . 24, 25
      lieutenant of Scituate company, ... 63
      his suit against his servant, ... 69
      one of Scituate committee, ... 46, 94
Hatherly, Hatherley, Hatherlee, Hatherle, Timothy, 3,
   6, 8, 14, 15, 23, 27, 33, 39, 42—45, 50, 52,
   56, 59, 68, 69, 71, 73—77, 89, 94, 98, 100,
   104, 106—108, 110, 111, 114, 118, 122, 134,
   136, 138, 139, 141, 143—146, 149, 153, 156,
   160, 161, 164—166, 171, 172.
   an Assistant, 8, 15, 33, 40, 52, 56, 71, 83, 115,
                                      123, 166
   sent on mission to Massachusetts, . . . 46
   one of council of war, ... 47, 100
   commissioner of United Colonies, . 88, 100, 166
   allowed to set up an iron mill, . . . 127, 156
   with others, purchases Indian lands, . . . 157
   Mr., ... 135, 169, 170, 177
Hayward, see Heyward.
Hawes, Haws, Edmund, 34, 40, 71, 101, 104, 105, 116,
                                        125, 126
   one of Yarmouth committee, 94, 95, 117, 123,
                                        144, 168
   propounded as freeman, ... 71
   admitted a freeman, ... 80
   fined for absence from Court, ... 106
   Mr., ... 128, 130
   land granted to, ... 128

Hayle, William, ... 90
Haystack Pond, ... 26
Hazell, Hassell, John, ... 170
   prosecuted, ... 43, 44
   bound to take oath of fidelity, ... 50
   land granted to, ... 141
   presented for meeting with others from house
      to house on Lord's day, ... 162
Hearker, John, vs. Josiah Checkett, ... 66
Hedge, Hedges, Hedggis, William, . 151, 153, 167
   presented, ... 137
   prosecuted by James Walker, ... 135
   presented for letting gun to Indian, ... 137
   propounded a freeman, ... 141
   admitted a freeman, ... 167
   Mr., ... 62
Hesbone, ——, ... 58
Heward, Thomas, Sen., ... 160
   See Heyward.
Hewes, John, ... 160
Heyward, Hayward, Heward, Elizabeth, married, . 88
   John, land granted to, ... 48
   Martha, fined for lewdness, ... 170, 172
   Thomas, ... 80, 102, 123, 139
      prosecuted by an Indian, ... 89
      propounded as freeman, ... 101
      admitted a freeman, ... 114
   See Heward.
Hicks, Hickes, Heckes, Ephraim, ... 124, 134
   propounded a freeman, ... 114
   admitted a freeman, ... 123
   administration of his estate, ... 148
   Margaret, ... 148
   Robert, ... 177
   Samuel, ... 31, 102, 168
      propounded as freeman, ... 24
      admitted a freeman, ... 33
      land granted to, ... 48
      married, ... 88
      one of Nausett committee, ... 123, 144
   Zacharie, presented, ... 165
Higgins, Richard, ... 71, 117, 168
Higginson, Richard, one of Nausett committee, ... 117
Highways, ... 75
   surveyors of, presented by grand jury, . . . 2, 5
   gates made on them, ... 41
   See Ways.
Hiland, Hyland, Thomas, ... 102, 124
   fined for absence as juror, ... 110
Hill, Hercules, ... 90
Hiller, William, ... 43
   to pay John Holmes's charges, ... 6
   purchases Robert Mendame's land, ... 77
Hillier, Hugh, ... 73
Hinckley, Hincley, Samuel, . . 16, 72, 109, 115, 168

GENERAL INDEX.   191

Hinckley, Samuel, *vs.* Joseph Hull, ... 44
    presented for hiring land of Indians, . . . 173
Hinckley, Hincklee, Hinckle, Thomas, 71, 97, 104, 147
    compensation made to, by an Indian, . . . 60
    one of Barnstable committee, . . 95, 123, 144
    propounded as freeman, ... 71
    takes oath of fidelity. 72
    admitted a freeman, ... 84
    fined for absence from Court, ... 106
    authorized to marry persons, ... 155
Hingham inhabitants petition to settle at Seacunck, 43
Hitt, Thomas, propounded as freeman, ... 84
    prosecuted for abusing Ussamequin, ... 99
    fined for abusing Ussamequin, ... 103
Hoble, widow, ... 12
Hodges, Nicholas, ... 90, 117
Hollett, Hollot, John, ... 16, 102
    See Hallett.
Holloway, see Halloway.
Holly, Joseph, ... 16, 72, 75
    takes oath of fidelity, ... 15
    propounded as freeman, ... 75
    Rose, ... 75
Holman, Holeman, Edward, . . . 29, 31, 117, 177
    his account of goods found, ... 35
Holmes, John, ... 6
    his account as messenger, ... 51
    grant of land to, ... 30
    his suit against Daniel Cole, ... 51
    Obadiah, ... 147, 151
    propounded as freeman, ... 125
    his suit against Mr. Newman, ... 150
    presented for meeting with others from
      house to house on Lord's day, 147, 156, 162
    William, ... 6, 38
    his deposition, ... 24
    Lieutenant, his suit against James Luxford, . 22
Honywell, William, land granted to, ... 16
Hook, Mr., ... 58
Hopkins, Caleb, ... 75
    mortgage from Billington, ... 78
    Deborah, married, ... 98
    Giles, ... 53, 155
    Stephen, ... 78, 177
    to have the care of Jonathan Hatch, . . 38
    his will proved, ... 75
    Mr., ... 31
Hore, Hoare, Elder, ... 81
    Hezekiah, ... 168
    John, ... 102, 141, 157
    fined for absence as juror, ... 110
    bound for his good behavior, ... 141
    propounded as freeman, ... 167
    Richard, ... 27, 62, 130
    admitted a freeman, ... 23
    land granted to, ... 129

Hore, Richard, one of Yarmouth committee, 16, 40, 154
Hoskine, William, ... 56, 67
    grant of land to, ... 29
    Sarah, apprentice to Thomas Hinckley, . . 67
House, Samuel, ... 105, 125
    vs. Gowen White 125
Howe, Thomas, ... 20
Howell, Thomas, ... 141
    settlement of his estate, ... 126, 127
Howes, Thomas, ... 41, 72, 76, 102, 126, 156
    admitted a freeman, ... 114
    Mr., ... 20, 81, 129, 130
    grant of land to, ... 128, 129
Howland, Arthur, ... 57
    propounded as freeman, ... 34
    his suit against Robert Mendame, ... 77
    presented for absence from public worship, . 174
    Desire, married, ... 79
    Henry, . . . 84, 140, 155, 160, 162, 163, 166
    John, 25, 29, 44, 75, 96, 104, 132, 158, 159, 160, 177
    one of Plymouth committee, 16, 94, 117, 123, 144, 154, 167
    grant of land to, ... 49
    bound for Jonathan Walker's apprentice, . 57
    Mr., ... 116, 126, 127, 145, 155
Hubberd, Mr., ... 49
Hucheson, Mr., ... 163
Huckins, Huckens, Thomas, ... 102
    propounded as freeman, ... 101, 167
    bound to appear, &c., ... 107
Hull, Joseph, ... 44
    an excommunicated minister, ... 53
    Tristram, ... 36, 115
    propounded as freeman, ... 167
Hunt, Edmund, ... 84
    Edward, presented and fined for breach of
      Sabbath, ... 156
    Peter, ... 102, 155, 168, 172
    propounded as freeman, ... 84
    admitted a freeman, ... 167
Hurst, James, . . . 6, 29, 48, 81, 111, 132, 140
    one of Plymouth committee, ... 117
    Katherine, ... 18
    William, administration of his estate, . . . 18
Hyde, Nicholas, admitted a freeman, ... 123
    his claim against Thomas Blisse's estate, . . 126
Hyland, see Hiland.
Impressment of soldiers, ... 64
Indian makes compensation to Thomas Hinckley
    for taking his cow in a trap, ... 60
    testimony as to Chickatabut's bounds, . . . 157
Indian Head River, ... 54, 156
Indian names : Ahiumpum, ... 157
    Annawamscoate, ... 49

GENERAL INDEX.

Indian names: Aquetnet, ... 145
   Atquiod, alias Acquiatt, neck of land, . . . 21
   Catscimah, ... 157
   Chickatawbutt, ... 157
   Jumpum, ... 157
   Massatumpaine, ... 23
   Masbanomett, ... 157
   Nahatan, ... 157
   Nepaitom, or Nepoytam, ... 21, 118
   Neipnet, ... 89
   Nishamagoquanett, ... 157
   Nobscussett, ... 128
   Nunckatateesett, ... 157
   Paupmunnuck, ... 130, 131
   Pautuxit, ... 158
   Pecunke, ... 157
   Sachamas, ... 118
   Sagaquash, ... 31
   Saughtuckquett, ... 88
   Shawwamett, ... 158
   Sessewitt, Seshewitt, or Sauset, . . . 81, 128
   Shuckquam, or Bound Brook, ... 21
   Teightaquid, ... 76
   Twacommacus, ... 21
   Wampatuke, ... 157
   Wanamampuke, ... 157
   Wannapooke, ... 89
Indians: trade with Indians permitted, ... 4
   proposols for letting the trade, ... 29
   amount received for the trade, ... 10
   persons presented for selling guns, &c., to Indians, ... 8, 36
   sale of land by Indians to Barnstable, . . 21, 130
   preparations for war against them, 46, 47, 63—65
   their complaints against sundry persons, 89, 99, 103
   names of soldiers sent against the Narragansets, and the expense of the expedition, 90— 93
   required to keep within their bounds, . . . 93
   Richard Sares's complaint against Indians, . 118
   measures of defence taken against, . . 145, 146
   they sell land to Mr. Hatherly and others, . 157
   the French request aid against the Mohawks, . 169
Inhabitants, names of males from sixteen to sixty, to be returned, ... 106
Inns, see Ordinaries.
Inquests on dead persons, ... 151, 174—176
Irish, John, land granted to, ... 12, 69
Iron mill set up by Mr. Hatherley, . . . 127, 156
Jackson, Samuel, ... 16, 116
   propounded as freeman, ... 17
Jenkins, Jenkine, Jenkens, Edward, 115, 139, 148, 155, 162, 163, 165, 170
   licensed to keep an ordinary, ... 105
   propounded as freeman, ... 101

Jenkins, Edward, admitted a freeman, ... 114
   John, ... 7, 90, 102, 116
     fined for absence as grand juror, ... 110
   John, Sen., ... 72
Jenney, Abigail, married, ... 79
   John, . . 3, 6—8, 12, 14, 25, 29, 31, 32, 48, 177
     deputy from Plymouth, ... 45
     one of Plymouth committee, ... 16
     suit against Edward Dotey, ... 30, 32
     suit against Startevaunt and Ramsden, . 38, 57
     land granted to, ... 26
   Samuel, ... 31, 69
     fined for breach of peace, ... 73
   Sarah, married, ... 98
   Mr., ... 37
Jenny, Mrs., presented for not repairing mill, . . 76
Johnson, Thomas, ... 90
Jones, Joanes, River, ... 26
   causeway repaired, ... 127
   Teague, ... 91, 146—148
     his suit against Ralph Wheilden, ... 104
     bound to appear, &c., ... 147
Jordaine, John, ... 52
   presented for fraud, ... 5
Joyce, John, ... 102
   execution against Deuell, ... 43
Keene, John, ... 35
   presented for lewdness, ... 36
Kemp, Elizabeth, ... 27, 37
   William, his estate, ... 27, 37
Kempton, Kemton, Ephraim, 89, 102, 155, 162, 163, 165, 170
   punished for several offences, ... 54
   married, ... 79
   propounded as freeman, ... 154
   Ephraim, Sen., deceased, his estate, . . . 85, 89
   Ephraim, Jun., ... 85
   Manasseh, ... 6, 25, 67, 73, 89, 104, 177
     deputy from Plymouth, ... 45
     one of Plymouth committee, 68, 72, 74, 94, 123, 144, 154, 167
Kenelme's Dingle, ... 30
Kennebeck, Cenebecke, trade account of its expenses, ... 96
   trade let, ... 96, 127, 144
Kenrick, Kennerick, George, ... 111
   one of Scituate committee, ... 40, 59
Kerby, Kerbey, Richard, ... 75, 172
   bound to appear, &c., ... 173
   presented for absence from public worship, . 173
Kersley, William, recognized to answer, . . . 28
King, Kinge, Samuel, ... 176
   Thomas, ... 53, 56
Knap, Aaron, ... 99
Knight, Walter, presented for taking tobacco, . . 4
Knot, Martha, ... 136

GENERAL INDEX. 193

Knott, George, ... 53, 102
  widow, presented for absence from public
    worship, ... 173
Knowles, Richard, ... 48, 174
  presented for stopping cattle in highway, . . 5
  his wife presented for sundry offences, . 173, 174
Ladders, persons presented for not having, . . . 135
Lakenhame, ... 26
Lakenhame Meadow, ... 26
Lambert, Richard, vs. Gowin White, ... 16
  Thomas, propounded as a freeman, ... 24
Lands granted to the inhabitants to be laid out, . 21
  in Plymouth to be disposed of by Assistants
    and Committees, ... 32
  sales to be acknowledged before an Assistant, 93
  transferred by livery and seizin, ... 77
Lapham, Thomas, his will proved, ... 169
  widow, ... 169
Lathrop, see Lothrop.
Launder, Thomas, ... 173
  William, a servant, assigned by his master, 38, 66
Laws revised, ... 62, 85
Lee, Robert, ... 102, 132
Leigh, Mr., ... 84
Lennit, Mr., ... 139
Letters patent, see Patent.
Lettice, John, ... 167
  Thomas, ... 160
Leveridge, Mr., ... 137
Lewis, Lewes, George, . . . 124, 140, 155, 167
  vs. Thomas Roberts, ... 12
  John, ... 5, 104, 105
  one of Scituate committee, ... 95
  apprentice to John Vassall, ... 111
  licensed as retailer, ... 137
Lillye, Luke, ... 90
Linceford, Anne, ... 28
  Francis, ... 28
  vs. Thomas Bray, ... 27
  his wife presented for lewdness, ... 37
Lincolne, Linkon, Thomas, ... 151, 155, 174
Little, Thomas, ... 120
Livery and seizin, land transferred by, ... 77
Lord's day, muskets to be carried to meeting, . . 31
Loring, Lorine, Thomas, petitions to settle at Sea-
  conck, ... 43
Lothrop, Lathrope, Thomas, ... 34, 40
Love, Hezekiah, ... 151
Loute Pond, ... 26
Lumbert, Lumberd, Barnard, 65, 102, 126, 140, 143
Lumbert, Thomas, ... 139
Lumkin, Lumpkin, Lumpkine, William, 29, 31, 35, 53,
            56, 76, 95
  and others, claim of Gabriel Wheilden against, 21
Lumkin, Mr., ... 129
Lusher, Eleazar, ... 158, 159

Luxford, James, ... 23, 39
  several suits against, ... 22, 24
Maacy, Massy, Maassee, George, . 75, 139, 153, 168
Magistrates, table of expenses of, ... 101, 127
Man, James, his wife presented, ... 162
Manson, Tomson, married, ... 66
Manton, Edward, land confirmed to, ... 55
Marchant, John, ... 124
Marriages, by whom solemnized, ... 155
  births, and burials to be recorded, ... 96
Marshal's fees for collecting fines, ... 93
Marshfield, ... 60, 62, 105, 127
  committees, 40, 46, 57, 60, 63, 68, 72, 75, 94, 95,
        104, 117, 123, 144, 154
  town officers, 34, 41, 53, 72, 73, 83, 84, 102, 115,
     116, 124, 125, 139, 153, 155, 167, 168
  soldiers from, ... 90
  rates, ... 92, 109
  bounds, ... 34, 42, 54
  to have two constables, ... 70
  ordinary, ... 105
  military affairs, ... 70, 71, 117
  presented for want of a pound, ... 163
Martine, Abraham, propounded as freeman, . . . 84
  Robert, propounded as freeman, ... 84
Massachusetts Path, ... 8, 53
Massachusetts claims Sicquncke, ... 23
  mission to, about Indian war, ... 46
  appoints commissioners to settle bounds of
    Showamet and Patuxet, ... 158, 159
  offers to surrender Showamet, ... 171
Massatumpaine's claim against Andrew Hellot and
  others, ... 20
Masterson, Nathariel, ... 66
Mathews, Mathewes, James, ... 34, 41
  propounded as freeman, ... 45
  admitted a freeman, ... 52
  fined for not serving as grand juror, ... 57
  one of Yarmouth committee, ... 74
  Marmaduke, admitted a freeman, ... 23
  Mr., ... 20, 129
Mattacheese, ... 81
Mattapoyst plantation, ... 9
Maycomber, Maycumber, John, ... 75
  punished for defamation, ... 87, 88
  William, ... 149, 150
  bound to appear and answer, ... 74, 75
Mayo, Nathaniel, propounded as freeman . . . 167
  Samuel, ... 156
  propounded as freeman, ... 154
  his suit against John Williams, ... 125
  Mr., ... 20
Measures, standard of, ... 60, 70
Mendam, Mendame, Robert, ... 41
  his land sold to William Hiller, ... 77
  Arthur Howland against, ... 77

VOL. II.   25

194   GENERAL INDEX.

Mendlowe, Mark, discharged of presentment, . . 4
Merrick, Merick, Mericke, William, 71, 102, 116, 126,
  127, 134
 propounded as freeman, ... 167
Meritt, Merriott, Henry, ... 42, 53, 72
 Henry, Sen., ... 155
 William, ... 115
Messenger's account, ... 51
Military affairs, Captain Standish's authority, . . 146
 officers, 63, 70, 71, 86, 88, 105, 117, 121, 127, 169,
  173
 regulations established, ... 60—62
Mill River, ... 175
Miller, John, ... 124, 165
 Mr., ... 130
 land granted to, ... 130
 propounded a freeman, ... 154
Mills, Mary, prosecuted for leaving her husband, . 149
Mitchell, Michell, Mechell, Edward, punished for
 lewdness, ... 35
 Experience, ... 87, 117, 126, 140, 177
 Elizabeth, married, ... 94
Moate, Nathaniel, ... 90
Mohawks, see Indians.
More, George, attachments against, ... 81
Morrell, Edward, ... 9
Morrey, George, ... 6
Morrill, Edward, indicted for stealing, ... 18
Morris, Robert, land confirmed to him, ... 55
 Thomas, ... 149
 William, ... 149
Morton, Ephraim, ... 123
 married, ... 79
 propounded as freeman, ... 114
 admitted a freeman, ... 123
 John, ... 66, 112, 116
  propounded as freeman, ... 114
  admitted a freeman, ... 123
  licensed as retailer, ... 137
 Nathaniel, ... 3, 102
  land granted to, ... 49
 Sarah, married, ... 79
  her land laid out, ... 7
 Thomas, ... 177
 Mr., ... 95
Mount's Hill Path, ... 26
Mount's Hill Plain, ... 48
Mowers to be presented for extortion, ... 60
Mynard, Maynard, John, ... 42, 84, 85
 paid for work on prison, ... 24
Naemskeckett, ... 4
Namassacuset, ... 54
Namassakeeset, ... 156
Narragansett Indians, see Indians, ... 90—93
Narragansett Hill, ... 26
Nash, Nashe, Samuel, 9, 16, 41, 75, 90, 113, 117, 126

Nash, Samuel, chosen sergeant, ... 61
 lieutenant of militia at Duxbury, ... 88
 Lieutenant, ... 127
 bound for Captain Wright, ... 121
Nauset, Nausett, Nawsett, Nossett, 105, 116, 119, 161
 town officers, . . 102, 124, 125, 139, 153, 155
 committees, ... 117, 123, 144, 154
 made a township, ... 81, 102
 military officers, ... 117
 proportion of rates, ... 127
 presented for want of a pound, ... 163
Nelson, William, ... 50, 132
Nepaiton, ... 22
 agreement with Barnstable, ... 21
New Bridge, ... 5
New Haven requests aid for the plantation at Delaware, ... 169
Newland, Rose, presented for absence from public
 worship, ... 173
Newman, Samuel, propounded as freeman, . . . 84
 admitted a freeman, ... 101
 prosecuted for defamation, ... 140, 150
Newland, William, ... 16, 18, 71, 104, 139
 one of Sandwich committee, ... 63, 94
 licensed as retailer, ... 73, 75
 takes the oath of fidelity, ... 15
 propounded as freeman, ... 17
 admitted a freeman, ... 23
 execution against Applegate, ... 24
 one of Sandwich committee, 40, 57, 60, 68, 117,
  144
 to train townsmen of Sandwich, ... 88
 lieutenant at Sandwich, ... 117
 suit against William Thomas, ... 55, 60
Nicholls, Thomas, presented for breach of peace, . 96
Nickerson, Nickersone, Nickarson, William, 16, 36, 82,
  130
 propounded as freeman, ... 3, 17, 154
 takes oath of fidelity, ... 15
 recognized for good behavior, ... 41
 Mr., land granted to, ... 129
Nickatay, ... 5
Nobscusset Meadows, ... 82
Nobscussett Neck granted to Yarmouth, . . . 128
Norman, Hugh, ... 137, 148
 his wife presented for lewdness, . . . 137, 163
 Sarah, ... 148
North, Captain, prosecuted for sedition, ... 70
North Meadow, ... 26
North River, ... 6, 8, 18
Northcote, William, ... 91
Nowell, Increase, ... 157
Oath of fidelity taken by several persons, 15, 72, 76, 80
Offley, David, vs. Thomas Payne, ... 57
Old comers, or purchasers, list of their names, . . 177
 See Purchasers.

GENERAL INDEX. 195

Ordinary at Barnstable, ... 141
   at Scituate and Duxbury, ... 104, 105
   at Yarmouth and Marshfield, ... 105
Otway, alias Parker, William, ... 176
Paddock, Padduk, Robert, ... 101
   grant of land to, ... 30
   fined for drunkenness, ... 138
   his claim against William Palmer's estate, . . 109
Paddy, Paddie, Pady, William, 6, 7, 24—26, 29, 32,
              35, 44, 48, 85, 110, 145, 163
   one of Plymouth committee, 16, 31, 40, 45, 57, 59,
              63, 68, 72, 74, 94, 117, 123, 144
   grant of land to, ... 23, 25, 26, 161
   licensed to set up a fishing stage, ... 31
   one of lessees of Kennebeck trade, ... 145
   Mr., ... 23, 42, 83, 117, 139, 154, 155
Palmer, John, presented for lending gun to In-
     dian, ... 165
   Walter, ... 155, 172
   one of Rehoboth committee, ... 94, 117
   propounded as freeman, ... 84
   admitted a freeman, ... 89
   William, . . 20, 41, 65, 72, 109, 130, 168, 177
   one of Yarmouth committee, . 46, 60, 63, 68
   lieutenant of troops raised for war, . . . 47
   to exercise townmen of Yarmouth, . . . 86
   lieutenant of Yarmouth company, . . . 63
   fined for contempt, ... 136
   his claim against Winchester's estate, . . 136
   Lieutenant, one of Yarmouth committee, 123, 144, 154
   Mr., ... 95
Parker, John, propounded as freeman, ... 17
   admitted a freeman, ... 23
   one of Taunton committee, ... 40
   William, . . 9, 15, 40, 53, 88, 151, 155, 175
   one of Taunton committee, ... 94
   propounded as freeman, ... 3
   admitted a freeman, ... 8
   licensed as retailer at Taunton, ... 73
   of Yarmouth, ... 34
   of Taunton, ... 34
   Mr., ... 22
Partridge, Partrich, George, . . . 101, 116, 117, 160
   propounded as freeman, ... 95
   admitted a freeman, ... 101
Patent of the colony surrendered by Governor
     Bradford, ... 4, 5, 10
   intrusted to him, ... 11
Patuckquett River, ... 5
Paul, Paule, Paull, Richard, . . . 99, 125, 175, 176
   propounded as freeman, ... 114
Paupmunnuck's sale to Barnstable, ... 130
Paybody, John, ... 87
   William, ... 124, 148, 155, 160
   married, ... 79

Paybody, William, propounded as freeman, . . . 154
   admitted a freeman, ... 167
Payne, Paine, Stephen, . . . 83, 85, 101, 150, 170
   admitted a freeman, ... 84
   petitions to settle at Sickuncke, ... 43
   one of Rehoboth committee, . 117, 144, 154, 168
   Thomas, ... 20, 70
   vs. David Offley, ... 57
   land granted to, ... 128
Pearse, Perse, Abraham, ... 44, 177
Peck, Joseph, propounded as freeman, ... 84
   licensed to marry persons, ... 164
Pellum, John, ... 124
Perry, Susanna, ... 80
   William, bound for his wife's appearance, &c., 80
Phillips, William, ... 125
Pidcock, Pidcocke, Petcock, George, ... 167
   presented for fraud, ... 12
   presented for perjury, ... 174
   exempt from training, ... 67
   presented for not having arms, ... 135
Pinchon, Thomas, ... 168
   and wife, ... 5
Pitney, Pittney, James, propounded as freeman, . 69
   Sarah, ... 165
Plain Dealing, ... 7, 28
Plantation at Mattapoyst, ... 9
Plantations chosen by the old comers, ... 4
Plymouth, ... 7, 23, 60, 105, 122, 161
   town officers, 9, 15, 34, 40, 53, 62, 71, 72, 83, 84,
      101, 102, 115, 116, 123—125, 139, 153, 155,
      167, 168.
   committees, 16, 40, 45, 57, 59, 63, 68, 72, 74, 94,
      104, 117, 123, 144, 154, 167
   rates, ... 18, 64, 92, 109, 169
   soldiers from, ... 90
   bounds of the town, ... 8
   lands reserved for flax and hemp, ... 23
   lands reserved for minister, ... 25
   a bark built by the inhabitants, ... 31
   inhabitants to bring arms to meeting, . . . 31
   committee for granting lands, ... 32
   presented for want of a pound, . . . 36, 163
   lands granted to the church, ... 49, 81
   military officers, ... 61, 121
   grant made to, for searching for a delf of
     coals, ... 87
   presented for not repairing ways, ... 140
   petition for lands at Aquetnet Island, . . . 145
   Sepecan granted to the town, . . . 141, 170
Pockanockett, ... 23
Point Peril, ... 5
Pollerd, George, ... 41
Pontus, Hannah, married, ... 71
   Mary, married, ... 84
   William, ... 7

196   GENERAL INDEX.

Pontus, William, land granted to, ... 29
Poole, William, one of Taunton committee, 16, 46, 74
   one of council of war, ... 100
Poor's stock of cattle disposed of, ... 32
Pope, Thomas, ... 83, 116, 132, 168
   married, ... 98
Porter, John, petitions to settle at Sickuncke, . . 43
Powder of the country, place provided for, . . . 142
Powell, William, ... 73
Pratt, Phineas, ... 78, 177
Pratt, Prat, Prate, Joshua, 7, 16, 25, 26, 29, 32, 48,
   111, 112, 117, 126, 128, 134, 140, 160, 177
   grant of land to, ... 27
Prence, Rebecca, married, ... 98
   Thomas, 3, 6—8, 12, 14, 15, 23, 25—27, 29—
     33, 37—39, 42—45, 48—52, 55, 56, 62, 64,
     66—68, 71, 74, 77, 79, 80, 82, 89, 92, 95,
     100, 106, 109, 114, 118, 121, 122, 134, 139,
     156, 158—162, 166, 170, 172, 177.
   grants of land to, ... 26, 49, 161
   an Assistant, 8, 15, 33, 40, 52, 56, 71, 83, 115,
                     123, 153, 166
   one of lessees of Kennebeck trade, . . . 144
   one of council of war, . . . 47, 64, 100
   his suit against Holman and others, . . . 117
   commissioner of United Colonies, . . 83, 153
   against Strong Furnell, ... 152
Presbury, John, ... 73
Presentments, 4, 5, 11, 36, 42, 96, 97, 112, 135, 137—
       140, 147, 155, 162, 165, 170, 173
Preston, Edward, punished for lewdness, . . . 35
Prichard, Richard, ... 71
   propounded as freeman, ... 52
   admitted a freeman, ... 71
   Goodman, ... 129
   See Prychard.
Prison to be erected, ... 23, 24
Prisoners' allowance, ... 93
Providence plantation reputed to belong to Plym-
   outh, ... 37
Prychard, Hugh, propounded as freeman, . . . 8
   See Prichard.
Pryor, Daniel, ... 77
   presented for smoking in highway, ... 12
   Joseph, his suit against Daniel Pryor and
     wife, ... 77
   his choice of guardian, ... 77
   presented for disturbing church, ... 174
   Mary, ... 77
Pumham, ... 159
Purchase, Purchis, Oliver, ... 102, 115, 176
   propounded as freeman, ... 24
   admitted a freeman, ... 101
   ensign of Taunton company, ... 169
   one of Taunton committee, . . . 154, 168
Purchasers, or old comers, their lands, ... 4

Purchasers, or old comers, their names, ... 177
Rabbit's Ruine, ... 129
Ramsden, Joseph, ... 38, 57, 132
   married, ... 94
   Goodwife, presented for lewdness, ... 174
Randall, William, presented for lending gun to Indian, ... 170
Rates apportioned, 18, 47, 64, 92, 109, 119, 127, 169
   to be paid in corn, ... 45
Raulins, Rawline, Thomas, . 24, 34, 41, 53, 72, 102
   one of Scituate committee, ... 46, 63
   fined for not serving as juror, ... 57
   suit against John Dammon, ... 143
   ———, married to Ephraim Kempton, . . . 79
Read, John, ... 153, 168
   retailer of spirits at Rehoboth, ... 141
   propounded as freeman, ... 154
Reade, William, ... 72
Redstone Hill, ... 49
Rehoboth, ... 91, 105, 116, 120
   town officers, 83, 102, 115, 116, 124, 125, 139,
                153, 155, 167, 168
   committees, . . . 94, 117, 123, 144, 154, 168
   rates, ... 109, 169
   exempted from charges for Indian war, . . 92
   freemen to vote at general election by proxy, 118
   Court there established, ... 118
   licensed to use lands at Sowames River, . . 120
   bounds to be settled, ... 141
   inhabitants presented for meeting from house
     to house on Lord's day, ... 162
Rew, Edward, ... 114
Rexhame, Rexame, constable of, ... 9, 15
   committees, ... 16
   rates, ... 18
Reynor, Elizabeth, married, ... 23
   John, land granted to, ... 25
Richmans Island, ... 149
Rickard, Rickett, Giles, 16, 34, 40, 84, 108, 111, 112,
            116, 132, 134, 155, 163
   admitted a freeman, ... 23
   grants of land to, ... 48, 29
   Thomas, and others, attachment against George
     More, ... 81
Riddings, Thomas, his child bound to Gowen
   White, ... 86
Rider, Ryder, Samuel, ... 65, 139
Ridway, James, ... 141
Ring, Ringe, Andrew, 114, 137, 138, 155, 162, 163
   land granted to, ... 25, 48
   propounded as freeman, ... 84
   married, ... ? 98
   admitted a freeman, ... 101
Ripley, Phebe, married, ... 23
Roades, Zachary, propounded as freeman, . . . 84
Robbins, Nicholas, ... 135

GENERAL INDEX. 197

Roberts, Thomas, ... 12
  not to visit Giles Morey, ... 6
Robinson, Robenson, Isaac, . 105, 116, 124, 125, 143
  one of Barnstable committee, ... 94, 168
  John, ... 90, 126, 127
  Thomas, . . . 71, 85, 155, 162, 163, 165, 170
  one of Scituate committee, ... 63
  fined for not serving as juror, ... 76
  takes oath of fidelity, ... 80
  his execution against Stedman, ... 161
  propounded as freeman, ... 154
Rock, Furland, ... 129
Rogers, Roggers, John, 72, 75, 77, 81, 126, 127, 135,
                         157, 160, 164
  admitted a freeman, ... 33
  propounded as freeman, ... 24
  his land laid out, ... 149, 150
  bound to be of good behavior, ... 166
  Joseph, ... 75, 88, 111, 112, 146, 177
  land granted to, ... 53
  lieutenant of Nauset company, ... 117
Rowe, John, his claim against Duxbury for over-
  flowing his land, ... 41
Rowley, Henry, ... 9, 15, 28, 102, 114, 143
  one of Barnstable committee, ... 59
Rowse, John, ... 12, 42, 83
Russell, George, ... 90, 116, 138, 158
  prosecuted for beating Katherine Winter, . . 172
  presented for other trespasses, . 139, 170, 172
  John, ... 53, 90, 124
  propounded as freeman, ... 69
  admitted a freeman, ... 71
Sabin, Sabine, William, ... 150
  propounded as freeman, ... 84
  presented for fraud, ... 138, 140
Sadler, John, propounded as freeman, . . . 8
Sagaquash, fishing stage set up there, ... 31
Sampson, Abram, ... 124
  presented for drunkenness, ... 111
  Henry, 6, 16, 119, 122, 136, 140, 147, 155, 160,
                        162, 163, 177
Sandwich, ... 19, 105
  town officers, 9, 15, 34, 40, 53, 72, 83, 84, 101,
    102, 115, 116, 124, 125, 139, 153, 155, 167,
                                168
  committees, 16, 40, 46, 57, 60, 63, 68, 72, 75, 94,
          104, 117, 123, 144, 154, 168
  rates, ... 18, 64, 92, 109
  soldiers from, ... 90
  Courts held at, ... 73
  inhabitants presented for neglecting public
    worship, ... 173
  licensed to make military regulations, . . . 62
  lands to be surrendered to, ... 106
  military officers, ... 117
  presented for not training, ... 140

Sandwich Plains, ... 76
Sasuet Neck, ... 128
Saughtuckett lands granted to inhabitants of Dux-
  bury, ... 88
Saunders, Edward, ... 90
Savory, Thomas, ... 27
Schadingmore Meadows, ... 100
Scituate, Seshewit, Setuatt, ... 8, 81, 95, 105
  soldiers from, ... 90
  rates, ... 18, 64, 92, 109
  town officers, 9, 15, 34, 40, 42, 53, 72, 83, 84, 94,
    102, 115, 116, 124, 125, 139, 153, 155, 167,
                                  163
  committee, 16, 40, 46, 57, 59, 63, 68, 72, 74, 104,
                    117, 123, 154, 167
  bounds of the town, ... 54
  military officers, ... 63
  ordinary, ... 105
  constables called to account, ... 114
  inhabitants to have their lands measured, 143, 171
  presented for not training, ... 70
  presented for not choosing militia officers, . . 135
  presented for not having stock of arms, &c., . 135
  presented for not repairing ways, . . 135, 139
  ways to be laid out, ... 106
Sears, Sares, Richard, suit against Sachamus and
  other Indians, ... 118
Second Brook, ... 5, 25
Sicquncke, Sickuncke, Seacunck, claimed by Massachusetts, ... 23
  sold by Ussamequin, ... 49
  persons licensed to settle at, ... 43
Sepecan to be used by Plymouth, ... 141
  granted to Plymouth, ... 170
Sharpe, Sharp, Robert, 124, 139, 150, 155, 162, 163
  propounded as freeman, ... 154
Shaw, Shawe, Shaue, Sawe, James, ... 149
  prosecuted and fined, ... 81, 87, 170, 172
  John, ... 7, 53, 90, 105, 108, 132, 177
  land granted to, ... 49
  suit against John Barnes, ... 50
  prosecuted, &c., ... 170, 172
  John, Jun., ... 79, 149
  prosecuted and punished, . . . 81, 87, 140
  John, Sen., ... 72, 134
  prosecuted and fined, ... 81, 87
  Thomas, ... 102, 107
  punished for trespass, ... 111
Sheep, exportation of, prohibited, ... 17
Shepherd, William, punished for stealing, . . . 149
Shereve, Thomas, ... 163
  presented for pilfering, ... 162
Sherley, Shurley, James, ... 177
  money received for, of Mr. Hatherly, . . . 76
Sherman, William, ... 72
  vs. John Barker, ... 127

GENERAL INDEX.

Shillingsworth, see Chillingsworth.
Shipwreck, persons prosecuted for taking the
 goods, ... 29, 31
Showamet, bounds settled, ... 158, 160
 Massachusetts offers to resign, ... 171
Shuckquam, ... 19
Shurtleff, Shertcliffe, Shirtley, William, ... 162
 fined for breach of peace, ... 73
Sillis, Richard, ... 16, 75
 allowed to sell wine, ... 125
Silvester, Richard, propounded as freeman, . . . 167
Sirkman, Henry, married, ... 23
Skiffe, Skiff, James, ... 53, 56, 102, 124, 126
 one of Sandwich committee, ... 72, 94
 land granted to, ... 16
 propounded as freeman, ... 69
 admitted a freeman, ... 71
 suit against Samuel Jenney, ... 69
Slocom, Slocomb, Slocome, Slocume, Anthony, 151,
   173, 176
 Edward, ... 115
 John, inquest upon, ... 174
Smaley, Smalley, John, ... 115, 139
 propounded as freeman, ... 24
 admitted a freeman, ... 33
 land granted to, ... 30
Smith, Smyth, Edward, and wife, presented for
 meeting with others in private houses
 on Lord's day, ... 162
 Henry and Edward, propounded as freemen, . 84
 John, ... 73, 168
  bound for his good behavior, ... 69
  propounded as freeman, ... 141
  admitted a freeman, ... 167
 Nehemiah, agreement with Bridget Fuller, . 13
  prohibited to carry sheep out of the colony, 17
 Ralph, settlement with Henry Crampton, . . 14
 Richard, married, ... 98
 William, ... 115, 168
  propounded as freeman, ... 84
Smylt Brook, ... 29
Smylt River, ... 5
Snakes Furland, ... 129
Snow, Snowe, Anthony, ... 116, 134, 168
 admitted a freeman, ... 167
 land granted to, ... 30
 Nicholas, ... 5, 7, 115, 125, 177
  one of Nauset committee, . . . 123, 154
 William, presented for lewdness, . . 170, 172
Socanoco, ... 159
Soldiers raised and equipped for war; their arms
 and wages; press warrants issued, . 64, 65
 names of those sent against Narragansett In-
  dians, ... 90, 91
Sone, Elizabeth, married, ... 66
Soule, Sole, George, . 53, 56, 88, 104, 108, 117, 177

Soule, George, one of Duxbury committee, 46, 94, 95,
   154, 167
 Zachariah, required to give up a skiff, . . . 163
South River, ... 70
Souther, Sowther, Hannah, married, ... 23
 Nathaniel, . . 3, 6, 7, 9, 24, 26, 32, 82, 85, 106
 grants of land to, ... 26, 27, 48, 54
 clerk of Plymouth company, ... 61
 his farm laid out, ... 76
 receives surrender of patent from Governor
  Bradford, ... 10, 11
Southworth, Southwood, Constant, 9, 15, 71, 88, 144,
   148, 163
 one of Duxbury committee, . 117, 144, 154, 167
 ensign of Duxbury company, ... 105
 Thomas, ... 53, 71, 72, 145
  married, ... 23
  propounded as freeman, ... 45
  land granted to, ... 49
  admitted a freeman, ... 52
  lieutenant of Plymouth company, . . . 121
  allowed to sell wine, ... 125
 Lieutenant, one of Plymouth committee, . . 167
Sowamsett, Sowames, lands used by Rehoboth, . 120
Sowamsett River, ... 5
Sparrow, Richard, 7, 53, 56, 84, 112, 116, 117, 124,
   126, 132, 134, 155
 lands granted to, ... 25, 29, 48
 presented, ... 162
Spooner, William, to pay Mr. Combe's debt, . . 51
 to have the care of Mr. Combe's children, . 131
Sprague, Sprage, Francis, . . 43, 124, 153, 177
 recognized to answer, &c., ... 43
 licensed to keep an ordinary, ... 104
Squerrell, ... 27
Stacy, Richard, ... 124, 151, 176
Standish, Alexander, propounded as freeman, . . 114
 admitted a freeman, ... 123
 Miles, 3, 5—9, 11, 12, 14, 15, 19, 22, 23, 27, 32,
  33, 37—39, 42, 52, 75, 81, 82, 85, 88, 89,
  94, 98—100, 104, 106—111, 114, 118, 121,
  122, 128, 130, 133—136, 138, 139, 141, 142,
  144—146, 148—150, 156, 157, 160, 161,
  163—166, 171, 172, 177.
 an Assistant, ... 8, 15, 83, 115, 123, 166
 Treasurer, ... 76, 101, 115, 123, 166
 one of Duxbury committee, ... 46, 63
 commissioned to dispose of Yarmouth lands, 21
 his claim against Walter Devell, ... 43
 one of the council of war, ... 47, 64, 100
 appointed commander of forces, . . . 47, 146
 sent on mission to Massachusetts, ... 47
 captain of Plymouth company, ... 61
 his claim against Gilbert Brooks, ... 116
 to exercise Marshfield militia, ... 117
 holds a Court at Yarmouth, . . . 121, 128

GENERAL INDEX.   199

Standish, Miles, holds Court, &c., ... 128
   his bounds settled, ... 117, 122
   his claim against Benjamin Eaton, ... 138
   land granted to, ... 164
   Miles, Sen., ... 149
Starr, Staare, Starre, Stare, Star, Comfort, vs.
   Thomas Clark, ... 50
   one of Duxbury committee, ... 46
   John, ... 139, 155, 165
   Thomas, ... 20
   grants of land to, ... 21, 81
   his suit against Samuel Hinckley, . . . 109
   Mr., ... 42, 95, 130
   complains of being overrated, ... 95
Stasy, see Stacy.
Statuckquett River, ... 19
Stedman, Isaac, ... 124
   admitted a freeman, ... 122
   presented, ... 170, 172
   Isaac, the younger, presented, . . . 160, 237
   Isaac, Sen., ... 161
   Nathaniel, presented for stealing, . . . 161
Stetson, Steedson, Robert, ... 53
Stockbridge, John, ... 16, 53, 84, 102, 124
   bound for his good behavior, ... 38
   fined for reviling the government, ... 45
   propounded as freeman, ... 154
   married, ... 66
Stockman, Isaac, ... 115
Stone, John, ... 161
Street, Mr., ... 58
Strong, Stronge, John, ... 102
   one of Taunton committee, 16, 40, 57, 59, 63, 68
Sturgis, Sturgess, Sturges, Edward, 9, 15, 102, 129,
                  130, 155, 165, 168
   propounded as freeman, ... 52, 154
   admitted a freeman, ... 166
   licensed to keep an ordinary, ... 105, 141
   bound for Richard Berry, ... 146
Sturtivant, Sturdevant, Stertevaunt, Samuel, 38, 57,
                  118, 160, 168
Surrender of territory, ... 4, 9—11
Surveyors of highways, 34, 40, 41, 53, 72, 73, 84, 102,
                124, 139, 155, 168
Sutton, George, ... 68, 115
   Simon, ... 68, 126
Swanholt, ... 30
Swift, Swyft, William, settlement of his estate, 53, 54
   Joane, ... 53, 54, 75
Symons, Thomas, complaint against Edward
   Dotey, ... 33
Symonson, [Simmons,] Moses, ... 177
Sympkins, Symkins, Nicholas, ... 27, 65
   discharged of presentment, ... 4
   vs. William Chase, ... 20
   vs. Walter Devile, ... 35

Sympkins, Nicholas, to save harmless Emanuel
   White, and others, ... 20
   presented for several offences, ... 36
   Mr., presented, ... 97
Tart, Thomas, ... 14, 141
Taunton, ... 91, 105
   town officers, 9, 15, 34, 40, 53, 72, 73, 83, 84, 102,
      115, 116, 124, 125, 139, 153, 155, 167, 168
   committees, 16, 40, 46, 57, 59, 63, 68, 72, 74, 94,
          104, 117, 123, 144, 154, 168
   rates, ... 18, 92, 109
   grant to the town for repairing ways, . . 17, 109
   land granted to the freemen, ... 18, 19
   the town petitions for enlargement, ... 58
   persons prosecuted for making an alarm at, . 75
   charges of Indian war abated, ... 92
   bounds of the town, ... 99
   allowed to purchase land for calves' pasture, . 102
   to take charge of a pauper, ... 103
   surveyors of ways presented, ... 135, 137
   military officers, ... 169, 173
Taylor, Tayler, Richard, ... 110, 124, 168
   Tobias, vs. John Shawe, ... 105, 108
Teghtacutt, ... 157
Templer, Templar, Richard, ... 83, 139, 155
   his claim for expenses in Indian war, . . . 95
   land granted to, ... 129
Thacher, Anthony, 20, 27, 41, 65, 72, 73, 76, 85, 104,
               105, 108, 120
   one of the council of war, ... 47
   licensed to draw wine at Yarmouth, . . . 73
   one of Yarmouth committee, 57, 63, 68, 72, 74,
               94, 95, 117, 168
   register keeper at Yarmouth, ... 112
   Mr., ... 105, 129, 130, 137
   land granted to, ... 128, 130
   fined for absence from Court, . . . 106
Thomas, Nathaniel, ... 46
   one of Marshfield committee, ... 46
   lieutenant of Plymouth company, . . . 61
   captain of Marshfield company, . . . 70, 71
   propounded as freeman, ... 69
   admitted a freeman, ... 71
   William, 29, 36, 38, 39, 43—45, 52, 55, 56, 58,
      59, 63, 66—68, 70, 71, 74, 77, 80, 96, 100,
      104, 107—111, 114, 118, 121, 122, 133, 134,
      136, 138, 139, 141, 144—146, 149, 156, 157,
      160, 161, 164—166, 177.
   one of the council of war, ... 47
   one of Marshfield committee, ... 16, 94
   suit of Thomas Broughton against, . . . 86
   his suit against William Newland, . . 55, 60
   an Assistant, 33, 40, 52, 56, 71, 115, 123, 153
   Mr., ... 62
Thurston, Thurstone, Charles, ... 81
   prosecuted, ... 73, 81

GENERAL INDEX.

Thurston, Charles, fined, ... 87
   his agreement with William Hanbury, . . . 105
Tibbott, Walter, propounded as freeman, . . . 8
Tilden, Tylden, Joseph, ... 68, 71, 168
   Thomas, ... 115, 124, 149, 150
   presented for suffering prisoners to escape, . 155
Till, James, bound for his good behavior, ... 68
   apprentice to Timothy Hatherly, ... 69
Tilley, Tilly, Hugh, ... 36, 41
Tilson, Tillson, Tylson, Edmund, ... 111
   his settlement with Crampton, ... 14
   propounded as freeman, ... 24
   admitted a freeman, ... 33
   Edward, ... 116, 168
Timber, destruction of, prohibited, ... 145
Tinckhame, Ephraim, land granted to, . . . 43, 48
Tisdall, Tisdale, John, 71, 83, 116, 151, 155, 162, 163
   admitted a freeman, ... 52
   propounded as freeman, ... 45
Titus, Tytus, Robert, ... 115
   propounded as freeman, ... 84
   admitted a freeman, ... 122
   one of Rehoboth committee, . . 123, 144, 154
Tobacco, law against drinking, ... 108
   retailing, regulated, ... 127
Tompkins, Tomkins, Samuel, ... 116
   propounded as freeman, ... 114
   admitted a freeman, ... 123
Tomson, Tompson, Thomson, John, . 81, 90, 126, 153
   prosecuted, ... 81
   fined, ... 87
   married, ... 94
   punished for fornication, ... 109
Torrey, Torey, Tory, James, ... 80
   married, ... 66
   Joseph, ... 112, 124, 134
   admitted a freeman, ... 123
   bound to appear, &c., . . . 111, 147, 156
   prosecuted for meeting with others in private
     houses on Lord's day, ... 162
Toute, Richard, ... 90
Town clerks, to keep registers of marriages,
   births, &c., ... 96
Towne, Charles, ... 14
Towns, to be supplied with arms, ... 96
   to send in names of male inhabitants, . . . 106
Tracy, Stephen, ... 41, 44, 146, 177
Trade with Indians permitted, ... 4, 29
   with other governments proposed, ... 82
Treasurer chosen, . . . 34, 76, 101, 115, 123, 166
Treasurer's accounts, ... 82, 92, 117, 148
Truant, Morris, ... 95, 102, 149, 150, 153
Tupper, Thomas, ... 84, 85, 101, 116
   one of Sandwich committee, 72, 117, 123, 154,
       168
   presented for lewdness, ... 36

Tupper, Thomas, licensed to marry persons, . . 155
Trustee process, ... 132
Turner, John, ... 90
   married, ... 94
   John, Sen., ... 168
   Goodwife, presented for absence from public
     worship, ... 173
   Humphrey, 41, 53, 56, 68, 104, 115, 124, 143, 173
   one of Scituate committee, 16, 40, 72, 74, 94,
        95, 117, 154, 167
   Michael, ... 34, 40, 75, 102, 155
Twacommacus, ... 22
   his agreement with Barnstable, ... 21
Twining, Twincing, Twincy, Isabel, married, . . 19
   William, ... 91
   propounded as freeman, ... 167
   William, Jun., ... 167
Twisden, John, ... 17
   bound to answer, &c., ... 14
United Colonies, see Commissioners' confederation.
Ussamequin, Ussamequine, ... 58
   evidence of his sale of Secunck, ... 49
   his complaint against Cheesborrow and Hitt, 99,
        103
Vassall, Varssell, Francis, married, ... 108
   John, ... 170
   his complaint against John Lewis, . . . 111
   William, ... 52, 54
   one of Scituate committee, ... 46
   one of the council of war, ... 47
   ferriage allowed to, ... 54
   Mr., ... 18
Victualling houses at Plymouth at Court times, . 169
Vincent, Vencent, John, one of Sandwich committee, ... 144, 154, 168
Vixon, Wixon, Wickson, Robert, 81, 102, 112, 115,
       117, 155, 162, 163
   propounded as freeman, ... 154
   admitted a freeman, ... 166
Vobes, see Forbes.
Waddesworth, Waddsworth, Christopher, 41, 126, 135
   one of Duxbury committee, ... 46
Walker, James, ... 124, 134, 135, 175, 176
   propounded as freeman, ... 141
   admitted a freeman, ... 154
   bound to appear, &c., ... 57
   Sarah, married, ... 94
Wallen, Ralph, ... 7, 177
   Thomas, ... 149
Wallis, Henry, ... 12, 13
War with Indians, preparations for, . 45—48, 63—65
   See Indians.
Warner, Katherine, prosecuted for leaving hus-
   band, ... 149
Warren, Elizabeth, ... 177
   Joseph, ... 168

GENERAL INDEX.

Warren, Nathaniel, married, ... 94
Warren's Wells, ... 48
Warwick, Earl of, ... 10
Washburn, Washborn , Washbourne, John, 84, 90, 117,
   126, 139
   admitted a freem n, ... 101
   land granted to, ... 12
   his bounds settle , ... 39, 52
   married, ... 94
   John, Sen., ... 122, 160, 165
   John, Jun., ... 155
Watchymoquett, ... 55
Waterman, Robert, . . . 53, 56, 72, 104, 105, 144
   one of Marshfiel committee, 60, 68, 72, 75, 95,
      117, 123, 144, 154
   propounded as fr eman, ... 45
   admitted a freem n, ... 52
   presented for lew lness, ... 165
Watson, George, ... 7, 25, 69, 111, 112
Way, George, ... 149
Way from Mr. Bradf rd's farm to the bay, . . . 75
   from Jones Rive to Massachusetts, or Matta-
      chuset, Patl 116, 127, 157, 160
   laid out for Cons int Southworth, ... 163
Ways laid out, ... 7, 18
   presented for bei g out of repair, ... 60
   in Scituate laid o t, ... 106
Weights at Yarmouth 126
Wellingsley, ... 7, 27
Wells, Weels, Isaac, ... 53, 56, 124, 134
West, Edmund, ... 141
   Francis, ... 34, 41
   Twiford, ... 90
Weston, Edmund, ... 127
Wetherell, William, c ie of Duxbury committee, . 46
Wheilden, Whelding Wheildin, Wheildon, Ga-
   briel, ... 34, 41, 110, 115, 129
   his claim against umpkine and Tilly, . . . 21
   Henry, ... 91
   Ralph, ... 104
   Ruth, ... 110
Whetston, John, ... 29, 31
Whetcomb, John, pro jounded as freeman, . . 167
White, Emanuel, . . 9, 20, 34, 41, 53, 84, 102, 147
   propounded as fr eman, ... 34
   admitted a freem n, ... 40
   presented for def mation, ... 165
   bound for Teague Jones, ... 147
   Gowen, ... 16, 72, 86, 125
      fined, ... 24
      propounded as freeman, ... 71
      his suit against Samuel House, ... 125
      presented for b cach of Sabbath, ... 165
   Resolved, land gr nted to, ... 54
   Peregrine, ... 168
      Lieutenant, pro pounded as freeman, . . . 167

White, Peregrine, presented, ... 138, 147
   "auncient bearer" in Indian war, ... 47
   Sarah, ... 138
Whitney, Thomas, ... 67, 100
   Winefride, ... 67
Wilbor, Joseph, ... 175
Willard, George, complaint for defamation, . . 14, 17
Willes, Wills, William, propounded as freeman, 101,
   114
   admitted a freeman, ... 167
Willet, Willit, Willett, Thomas, 7, 31, 32, 35, 81, 101,
   105, 119, 133, 139, 148
   one of Plymouth committee, ... 104
   captain of Plymouth company, ... 121
   one of lessees of Kennebeck trade, ... 144
   an Assistant, ... 166
   Captain, ... 145, 155
Willis, John, 34, 41, 98, 105, 107, 108, 116, 125, 134,
   135, 168
   propounded as freeman, ... 167
   Lawrence, ... 90
   Nathaniel, ... 9, 15
   Richard, ... 50
Williams, Alexander, a runaway servant, . . . 36
   John, ... 9, 115
   one of Scituate committee, 59, 68, 72, 74, 117,
      123
   John, Sen., ... 125, 153
   John, Jun., propounded as freeman, . . . 167
   Richard, ... 88, 104, 151
   one of Taunton committee, 63, 94, 123, 154,
      168
   propounded as freeman, ... 52, 69
   admitted a freeman, ... 71
   fined for absence from Court, ... 109
   Thomas, ... 139
   his claim against Thomas Tart, ... 14
   Mr., ... 49
Wilmoth, Thomas, ... 150
Wilson, Jacob, ... 75
Winchester, Alexander, propounded as freeman, . 84
   deceased, his estate, ... 126, 136
   his children disposed of, ... 169
   Mr., ... 170
Wing, Daniel, ... 53
   John, ... 41
   presented for lending gun to an Indian, . . 36
   Stephen, fined for fornication, ... 112
Winnetuckquett, ... 88
Winslow, Edward, 9, 15, 19, 23, 27, 30, 32, 33, 37—
   39, 42, 45, 49—53, 55, 56, 58, 59, 63, 66, 68,
   71, 74, 77, 79, 80, 89, 94, 98, 100, 104, 107,
   108, 118, 122, 177.
   one of the council of war, . . . 47, 64, 100
   an Assistant, 8, 15, 33, 40, 52, 56, 83, 115, 123,
      153

VOL. II.   26

GENERAL INDEX.

Winslow, Edward, Governor, ... 71
   a commissioner of the United Colonies, . . 71
   sent to Massachusetts to treat about confederation, ... 53
   sent to Massachusetts to treat about Indian war, ... 46
   one of lessees of Kennebeck trade, ... 144
   Helene, ... 118
   John, . . . 6, 26, 34, 41, 43, 48, 55, 60, 177
     land granted to, ... 49
   Josiah, 9, 15, 41, 50, 58, 75, 85, 96, 104, 105, 108, 121, 134, 139, 140, 158, 159
     one of Marshfield committee, 57, 63, 68, 95, 117, 168
   Josiah, Jun., ensign of Marshfield company, . 127
     propounded as freeman, ... 154
     admitted a freeman, ... 166
   Kenelme, ... 7, 16, 34, 44, 74, 75, 115
     punished for several offences, . . . 4, 85, 98
     one of Marshfield committee, 40, 46, 60, 63, 72, 144, 154, 168
     his wife assents to his sale of lands, . . . 118
     his discharge from James Adams, . . 176
   Mr., ... 22, 29, 60, 62
   Goodwife, ... 132
Winter, Christopher, ... 24, 148
   presented for fornication, ... 135
   bound to keep the peace, ... 119
   John, ... 170
Winter Harbor, ... 149
Wives to acknowledge sale of lands, ... 93
Wickson, see Vixon.
Wood, Henry, ... 124, 134
   land granted to, ... 26, 29
   propounded as freeman, ... 114
   admitted a freeman, ... 123
   married, ... 79
   Jane, ... 75
   John, ... 4, 5, 160, 163, 168
     land granted to, ... 26
   Stephen, ... 134, 155
     Stephen, land granted to, ... 26, 29
     married, ... 79
     propounded as freeman, ... 114
   William, ... 75, 117

Wood Island, ... 25
Woodfield, John, propounded as freeman, . . . 167
Woodward, Nathaniel, ... 151, 175
   Walter, ... 84, 85, 102, 170
     propounded as freeman, ... 3
     admitted a freeman, ... 8
Woolsey, George, ... 133
Worden, Peter, ... 128, 168
Wright, Anthony, ... 84
   George, ... 111—113, 121, 127
   Nicholas, ... 168
   Peter, ... 139, 168
   Richard, ... 89, 112, 117
     propounded as freeman, ... 71
     admitted a freeman, ... 84
     married, ... 79
   William, ... 177
Wyatt, Wyat, Wiat, Wiate, Wyate, James, 72, 73, 105, 116, 124, 125, 134, 139, 175, 176
   propounded as freeman, ... 101
   admitted a freeman, ... 123
   lieutenant of Taunton company, ... 173
Yarmouth, ... 19, 21, 86, 105, 112
   town officers, 9, 15, 34, 41, 46, 53, 73, 83, 84, 102, 115, 116, 124, 125, 139, 153, 155, 167, 168
   committees, 16, 40, 57, 60, 63, 68, 72, 74, 94, 95, 104, 117, 123, 144, 154, 168
   rates, ... 18, 92, 109
   soldiers from, ... 91
   allowed to make military regulations, . . . 62
   bounds, ... 19, 21
   committee to dispose of lands, . . . 20, 130
   Courts held at, ... 73, 128
   fortification, ... 65
   gift by Andrew Hellot to the town's poor, . 70
   land confirmed to the church, ... 62
   lands granted to the town, ... 128, 129
   military officers, ... 63
   ordinary, or inn, ... 105
   presented for want of a pound, ... 42
   presented for not repairing ways, ... 60
   required to make a rate, ... 20
   standard of weights, ... 126
Yates, John, administration of his estate, . . . 170
   Mary, ... 170

www.ingramcontent.com/pod-product-compliance
Lightning Source LLC
Chambersburg PA
CBHW050147170426
43197CB00011B/1996